RACHAEL MADDOX

ReBloom

ARCHETYPAL TRAUMA RESOLUTION
FOR PERSONAL & COLLECTIVE HEALING

First Edition

ISBN: 978-1-7344118-1-2

Cover design & layout: Heather Dakota | www.heatherdakota.com
Cover flower art: watercolornomads.com
Cover bee art: Lisa Nagel | www.wildsensitivesouls.com
All interior art: Rachael Maddox

This book is a prayer to Life itself.
A dedication to our potential as a human family
to relate to ourselves and each other
from a place of love and courage.
And to all the souls in the ReBloom garden.

Invocation

We are gathered here together to remember our wholeness.
To sense, feel, and awaken the hidden Blueprints of health at the centers
of our souls, bodies, and culture.
To grow into powerful facilitators for an emergence of regenerative aliveness,
love, and care on Planet Earth.
May every moment be a homecoming of embodied wisdom.
May trust rebloom where trauma once shrouded us in fear.
May we know deeply and fully just how much we are in this together.
And may our knowing move us to act in ways that honor, celebrate,
and uplift the power and preciousness of all living things—ourselves
and each other included.

This invocation is read at the beginning of every lesson and gathering for the ReBloom
Coach Training to anchor us into our shared reason for being together.

Table of Contents

Dear Beloved Reader...

January 11, 2021

I'm writing this love note nine months into the pandemic, on the heels of an attempted coup at the U.S. Capitol building by white supremacists. Times are troubling. I, like many of us, am both exhausted and spirited. Uncertain and determined. I know the road ahead doesn't come with guarantees that things will get easier or simpler. Instead, it asks us to become more resourced, connected, adaptive and resilient. More devoted to love than ever before.

Over the last decade of living into questions about post-traumatic growth, the insight I continue coming back to is this: *Together, we've got this. Alone, we're toast.*

This book is an ode to togetherness.

ReBloom begins with a myth—an allegory that tells a story of our togetherness before we were interrupted by capitalism, patriarchy, colonization and white supremacy. A myth that reveals our fracturing—how it happened and why—at both individual and cultural levels. A myth that invites you to live your own questions of post-traumatic growth so that you can step forward into the soil of our uncertain world and plant gardens of possibility rooted in the remembrance of what you most wish to rebloom.

As you read the ReBloom Allegory, I invite you to notice what you experience inside. What parts of the story pull at your heart strings, tug at your soul? Which characters feel most resonant, familiar or foreign? What from the tale inspires, arouses, bothers, or soothes you?

Be gentle with your body as you take in these sacred clues. Your embodied and emotional experience of the allegory can act as an oracle about your current place in our collective story. And if you listen closely, it may reveal your next best step in your personal ReBloom journey.

I'm so grateful and honored to be living in these times with you, brave soul. May your path be blessed with many friends to grow gardens of possibility alongside.

All my love,
Rachael

PS – A note about gender and sexual orientation in the ReBloom Allegory: we are much more magical than the binary boxes we're put inside. I'm very grateful to Varvara Erochina and Tanya Neumeyer for helping me break down the gender binaries and bring real-life magic into this allegory. Please know that all of the ReBloom archetypes are 100% interchangeable in terms of gender and sexual orientation. Anyone can identify with any of the archetypes, as you'll see described plenty throughout the book. As you read the allegory, feel free to play with the pronouns of each archetype to see what delights your soul.

PPS – I want to acknowledge my positionality in writing this allegory as a white Jewish settler on Turtle Island, specifically, Kumeyaay land. I offer this allegory as a collective myth, rather than personal memoir. I honor the original peoples of this land deeply, as well as each indigenous person's right to tell their story as their own.

Last PS! – Throughout this book, I share stories from both my personal and professional life. In every instance where someone else's story is told, I've either changed their name and the details of the story to protect their anonymity, or gotten explicit permission to share their identity and story with you.

The ReBloom ALLeGoRy

Once upon a time, there was a garden. And in this garden, there was a cast of characters. Sort of like a family…but more like a village.

There was the baby, so pure and innocent. He loved to cry and giggle and poop and sleep. He always let the whoooole village know what he needed with cooing or screaming or darling eye gazing. He didn't have fancy ideas or complex emotional experiences. But he did have a superpower (besides being so dang cute): his internal barometer of neediness. He had a scale that scanned his body and energy for whatever felt slightly off, then communicated accordingly in the simplest way possible. His name was Soul Seed. He was a love-nugget of receptivity.

Soul Seed was adored by all, but most especially, the grandmother of the garden—Groundsmama. Groundsmama took great pride and joy in caring for all of Soul Seed's needs. Not only did she love rocking Soul Seed into sweet slumber or bubbling laughter, she also took great pride in knowing that when she cared for Soul Seed, everyone else in the village could do their important tasks. Groundsmama reveled in having this kind of effect on the village—so much that her hands were almost always full and her feet almost always in motion, as she cleaned, weeded and watered the garden—all with chipper consistency and a radiant zest for life.

While Groundsmama joyously kept peace and order inside the garden, she wasn't exactly the sassy young spitfire that was Gatekeeper.

Gatekeeper—well, she was overflowing with burgeoning hormones. She had an instinctual sense of power that was prideful and protective, and because of this, her elders spent time initiating her confidence into discerning guardianship over the whole village territory. With ancient, sacred love rituals, Gatekeeper was shown the most holy and erotic, gorgeous and glorious gifts of the garden. It was known in the tradition of the village that the more enchanted Gatekeeper was by the garden—the wiser and more devoted she would be to keeping those holy grounds safe. So her elders had her pray every day to the sunrise dew and the flowers in bloom…and spend plenty of time listening to foreboding stories of villages without discerning Gatekeepers.

Of course, there would be times when Gatekeeper would accidentally let something unsafe through the garden doors. So her elders trained her for the moments when she would need grief- and shame-resilience, rituals for rupture, and repair.

Mostly, she was the stud of the village—proud and powerful on the outside, but pure mushy-gushy in the middle. She was guided to grow both sides of her nature—strength and softness—and this made her sovereignty sturdy, centered and caring.

When things went terribly wrong or terribly well, Gatekeeper would go to Sage, the queen rose of the garden, and Sage would offer her guidance or praise. Sage was the rose who'd been made fine and rare through time and experience. She'd lived through all the ages and stages of the village. Eras of neglect, exploitation, shame, and repression, violence, and colonization. She knew what could go wrong in the muscle memory of her roots. She couldn't be fooled by connivers or cons.

She was clear-sighted, potent, and aligned.

But time had not made her hard or brittle. After all, she was still a rose. Her stories of the dark were equally matched by those of rapturous romance and cinematic soulmates. She'd grown into a sensual, soft, sensible advisor. Her love language was being listened to. Her heartbreak was being ignored. Good thing Sacred Gardener considered her their most Beloved.

Sacred Gardener—SAG for short—had an ever-present energy in the village, as if they could hear you and see you even when they weren't near. Sometimes, right in your moment of struggle, doubt, or despair, they'd suddenly appear next to you with the most attentive listening ear. It often felt like they could fix anything without any action needed. But then, after a long time listening, they'd get up and rearrange something—and the whole village would come into greater order. They were the King, but always made it known that the Queen runs the show. "I just listen and respond," they'd say with soft and cheerful humility. "Put my Beloved Queen's wishes into effect." The truth was, they needed each other—form and formlessness, spirit and matter. Co-creators of a divine equality.

SAG often struggled with how big their vision was. How much they could see about what was misaligned or out of integrity. How vast they could dream— for regeneration, for peace. How much distance there was between foresight and reality. How little they could do, but also, how they had to keep showing up and listening, creatively responding, because that was their call, their unbreakable impulse. When SAG would get really depressed or hyper-wound with impetus to take on the weight of the world, they'd roll out a mat under the stars next to Sage, and she'd sing them her salvation songs. Something about that let their eyes rest quelled for a while.

SAG's favorite part of the village (besides the fountain where they visited Sage) was the interplay between Expressionista and Pollinator. To SAG, the erotic dance of loved and lover was a sign that all was well in the village. That everyone was safe enough, nourished enough, protected enough, and expressed enough to open up, let others in. Trusting enough to give their gifts without worry that they were being taken from. Fed enough to not have to pillage or grasp. The sweet song and dance of the bees buzzing past, the honey collecting in the hive, the pollen mixing and mingling across flowers: these were all SAG's way of knowing a lineage of intimate belonging was living on.

Expressionista, the young bloom of heart-felt radiance, was full of fragrant enchantment. She loved to be in the center of attention, and the truth was, she was meant for it. After all, her plump, plush magenta petals had just come out of the protection of her bud for the very first time. She was in her prime and stunningly attractive.

There were many flowers like her, young and romantic, full of heart and shameless flair. They each had their own color palette and petal shapes, attractions, genders and opinions to say. There was nothing quite like a new season of spring babes blossoming—finding themselves, letting themselves be found, for the very first time. It was a bit loud, their raucous teenage exploration, but full of erotic potential.

Speaking of erotic potential, Pollinator knew without words when Expressionista was finally ready for his nuzzling dance to romance her nectar-filled petals. He never went too soon. Always waited for her to open in full bloom, nearly beg for his entrance. And while Pollinator loooooved stroking and slurping the sweetness of Expressionista's medicine, he also didn't discriminate. After all, Pollinator was quite polyamorous. He loved to taste all the garden flowers. The old and the young. The tulip and the azalea. The lily and the buttercup. He was like a litmus test for the health of the grounds, buzzing about to see who needed more attention and how, all the while collecting a delicious, nutritious, bountiful reward.

While the rhythms of the village lived on, Pollinator carried a quiet grief inside. For year-after-year, fewer medicinal flowers were being born. The heaps of beautiful bounty that Pollinator and his fellow bees used to collect were dwindling in size and potency. In effect, his bees were starving—their song and dance disappearing, and the signs of a sweet life going with them.

Why was it that the medicinal flowers were disappearing? Why was it that so many bees were dying?

We can't blame any of the villagers by themselves, for everyone was under great pressure when the corporate colonizers came.

SAG was first to sense the threat—their 360-degree vision locating the colonizers, even from faraway. Sage also had a sense deep in her roots that left her curling inward and up just a tad bit, just a hair. When SAG whispered their great fear, Sage nodded in resonant recognition. Then, wordlessly, together, they began planning their defense.

SAG called Gatekeeper and all her brazen young friends. Told them, they better be ready to protect and defend. SAG didn't like preparing for battle; they preferred to prepare for weddings. But they wouldn't be known as the King who let their village be taken by corporate greed, domination, or genetically modified toxicity.

Sage consoled with Groundsmama, who held Soul Seed to her chest. They whispered about the initiations. Would the young be able to do them? Would the village be strong enough to ward off colonial threat? They decided all village members needed daily training and daily ceremony to grow their spiritual strength with unwavering consistency. The disciplinary sides of the matriarchy emerged to train the young.

Expressionista, unimpressed by the rules put on her wildness, started opening her petals with haste, trying to quickly give her sweet taste to all the bustling bees. Meanwhile, many of her friends pulled their petals back, sensing the foreboding attack, the growing hunger of the buzzing swarm.

Pollinator began to go against his reverential nature and intrude with force into the flowers whose petals had once been more open and trusting, tender and lusting.

But the village was doing its best to prepare for what was coming.

The story from here is one of what happens when we live in conditions of systemic threat, violence, and fear.

SAG, sadly selling parts of their soul to the chief intruders—making a deal with the devil they thought might protect their people, all the while becoming the embodiment of both that devil, and its defeat all in one.

Sage, with her wisdom unheeded, growing hypervigilant and manipulative, trying to convince anyone who would listen to follow her all-knowing advice. Sometimes, so disoriented by being ignored, she'd fall face forward into the arms of a narcissistic colonizer. He wouldn't quite listen to her, but he would at least extract from her, and that felt better than getting no attention at all.

Groundsmama, desperately trying to maintain order in a land of chaos and confusion, becoming inordinately strict with all the young kids who added to the noise of her once-serene garden. At night, unable to manage the stress, she'd tend the fire and throw back the flask. When the sweet ones came wildly giggling past, she'd pull one off to the side, yell straight into its eyes, and then slap it in the face in a fit of frustration.

Gatekeeper, with no guardians guiding her, began harassing Expressionista and all her friends—picking at them for their sensitivities, shaming them for their authenticities. Underneath all that, a lost young soul with no sense of knowing where to direct her feral power.

And Soul Seed, sweet little Soul Seed, at the whims of everyone else's inconsistent attention, starting to cry a whole lot more with no response. His cry, so loud, the whole village tuned him out—unable to cope with their broken-down hope, their feelings of helplessness about the crumbling garden.

In the village now, there's an ever-present neglect born from a stress too great for response. A defeated denial that's somewhat invisible, the mechanisms of outside control living even inside their own minds.

They lost their battles to the weaponized and digitized, the sparkly and advertised.

Tired of so much fighting, one time, they even flocked together—moved the whole village somewhere safer, more secluded, until the Colonizers found them there, too.

They tried to grow their tribe with whole seasons of extra fornication. But all their attempts hadn't quite strengthened their collective medicine enough to reign victorious over the incessant will of greed that insisted on controlling every square inch of mystery.

At this point, they were faced with a choice:

Surrender their souls to the ever-pressing system of extraction. Dissociate to save energy. Defense through contraction. Buy in so as not to feel bought out from the village, no matter that the village lost its soul long ago to the Man.

Or—re-embody their medicines from head-to-toe, full-fold, come hell or high water. Betray their narcissistic savior who now ruled as fascist dictator. Re-gather their Blueprints for listening, cooperating, loving, protecting, needing, and receiving…

Decide to honor their lineage, re-member their village, reawaken those peaceful times, reconnect with the laws of nature and the miracles of the divine.

They would have to reteach what was once intrinsically lived.

They would have to recover from and release the deep wounds of their traumatized bodies.

They would have to find—somehow find—pockets of space and time that were kept truly safe, where they could practice restoring their faith and well-being.

They would have to grow those spaces stronger, more potent with that original medicine of wisdom and hope, so others could come taste their own remembrance and go back out to the world, to their own struggling villages, and revive their local medicine as well.

They would have to innovate, create, make art, magic, and miraculous evolutionary leaps. Adapt new capacities in the tender places where old wounds might never fully heal.

They would have to tell the story—of what happened and how, of what could happen next and how the future depended on them.

They would have to change the systems—re-imagine and re-invent them in ways that honor and uplift all living things.

They would have to taste their ancient honey—the song and dance of their dear lineages. The spells of a sweet life incanting hope in their resilient hearts.

They would have to say, "We are willing. We are ready."

They would have to listen.

Listen to the seeds of their dreams still buried deep in their souls.

Listen to the cries of the child, the physical and spiritual body that knows.

Listen to the magic of the garden.

Listen.

They would have to get very quiet and listen.

Introduction

Your Secret Call & Mine

The ReBloom Allegory came to me like mythology fallen from the stars. Like science, observable right in plain sight. Like poetry dripping into me in cadence and color. Until finally, it came like characters in a movie, scenes of humanity you could touch, feel and see.

By definition, an allegory is a story, poem or picture that can be interpreted to reveal a hidden meaning, typically a moral or political one. Author Michael Meade teaches that stories—living myths—are full of secret messages and codes, sacred opportunities for revelation. Each scene in a myth can be teased out and lived inside, animated with deeper significance for the specific listener's life.

Take a moment to pause and consider: what part of the allegory jumped out at you? Was there a character? A specific moment? A symbol or phrase? A feeling or pace? Where did your heart tug? Where did your soul sigh? What part of the allegory grabbed you in the gut or awakened something in your spirit?

When I first wrote the ReBloom Allegory, my heart cracked open for the experience of the Sacred Gardener. The way they could sense what was coming with 360-degree vision. Their grave depression about how much they could see, but how little they could do. The deals they made with the devil while trying to protect their people, all the while accidentally selling them out.

Our emotional responses to stories, myths and allegories can act as oracles or symbols for the current moment in our lives. Based on the part of the story that stirred something deep inside, you can land on a question—a question that connects the allegory to your life.

For example, my affinity for the Sacred Gardener's struggle reveals my own struggle as a visionary wrestling with how to co-create sane responses to the insanity of our times. It leaves me asking myself, *How might I sit in a deeper listening space, attuning to Sacred Gardener's capacity to wordlessly sense and respond? How might I become a living prayer for the sake of our shared thriving in a culture that's collapsing under unjust systems and structures?*

The beautiful thing about stories is that they're meant to be shared in community, not kept for one person only. By making meaning of mythology together, we can find ourselves in the shared story of our time. We can discover the role we're each meant to play in our collective healing.

When I read the allegory to Chela—my coach and mentor of many years—she noticed that the pace and rhythm of the story seemed to speed up as emergency set in, until the very end, when the disaster was too great, and we were all left standing at a quiet, critical choice point.

For Chela, her relationship to the allegory might be showing her that the world isn't what it once was—the pace has changed, and she's at an important choice point. *How to proceed now that there's no turning back—only new ways to meet the new realities of our world?*

When I read the allegory at a ReBloom workshop, Denise, one of the participants, shared that the Gatekeeper stood out to her as strange and foreign.

"I couldn't understand her," she whispered solemnly. "I understood all the other roles, but the Gatekeeper...protecting, honoring, growing strong in her reverence and boundaries…I just kept thinking, *huh*? That one went over my head."

Denise, living inside questions about sovereignty—what it is, what it means—ended up experimenting with her confusion the whole weekend. By the end of the workshop, she felt more connected to her sense of personal space and reawakened her right to say *yes* or *no* according to the truth of her body and heart.

Another workshop participant, Vanessa, felt drawn to the Expressionista. "It appeals to me to be flirty, expressing in the garden as a big, beautiful flower. But I'm not embodying that, and it sucks. I cover up, hide out, pull back. I think because my Gatekeeper has been offline for so long, I don't feel safe showing my magic."

All weekend, Vanessa carried the question, *How can I grow a safety that empowers me to shine more fully?* Partway through the workshop, she declared to the group that she wouldn't be doing anything inauthentic to please or pamper others. She stood with a fierce commitment to her own self-consent. By the end of the workshop, something wild and self-trusting opened up in her, and feeling safer than ever, she danced erotically for the whole group to see.

When Angela, one of the developmental editors for this book, heard the allegory, she was struck by the sadness of the Pollinator, then flooded with her own hopelessness.

"When the Pollinator asked, where are all the medicinal flowers? my heart sank into a grief too big to even feel," she told me, looking up with a tender pause. "Then my mind quickly chimed in. It's all too hard. The world is too big to save. Screw it. Let's just give in to reckless hedonism. I'll fuck all the flowers in sight, even if they're not medicinal!" I nodded in compassionate understanding.

She went on. "Then I got clobbered by a feeling of depression, and a fast desire to hide in the closet with a hedonism hangover. The truth is, all the feelings feel too big—joy, intimacy, presence, pain. Who can feel that fully in a world like this?"

For Angela, her relationship to the allegory illuminates her dissociated grief around the desecration of connection. Angela's a woman who lives for art, romance and creativity, but at the same time, she's terrified of the heart-shattering disappointment she senses will come if she lets herself fully embrace this uncontrollable world.

Is it worth it? To be so alive? To feel both the pleasure and the pain of the world today? Those are the questions Angela's living inside.

Within any allegory, we can find an oracle. Oracles aren't the end-all-be-all prediction of your life. They're the moment's divine clue in response to your heart's most true and current question. When you live the question, as Ranier Marie Rilke says, as opposed to trying to know the answer, there's a magical efficiency that can take hold—a portal that opens only in the surrendered space of not knowing.

You came to this book, in this moment of your life, with a particular question in your heart. Three years from now, if you read the allegory again, the question in your heart will be different. The oracle you'll see, the meaning you'll make, and the mythical medicine of the moment will all be different as well.

But right now, there's a holy hint pointing you toward the question you're in currently. And if you can let yourself feel your question, if you can stay longer in the not-knowing instead of rushing to the answers, then true answers, genuine deep epiphanies of understanding, can find you in the open space.

WHAT'S YOUR ReBloom ORACLE?

The part of the allegory that stood out to me the most was:

What this might be telling me about my life is:

The question I'm living inside is:

My personal ReBloom oracle

Before we dive into the heart of this book, it feels important for you to know why I'm writing it. My affinity for the Sacred Gardener is a major clue.

Over the last ten years, I've been working with humans in very personal ways. Helping them heal from what hurt them the most, live their individual callings and dreams, and come to embody deep pleasure, power and purpose, despite their life experiences, traumas, challenges or upbringings.

In the last five years, as my career has narrowed in on trauma resolution, I've worked with hundreds of people recovering from sexual, developmental, complex or systemic trauma. I've learned and practiced the ins-and-outs of nervous system dynamics, timeline travel, boundary repairs, basic attachment resolution , increasing capacity for intensity, and the necessity of orienting toward health and vitality even (and especially) in the dark.

My clients most often thank me for creating a space of impeccable safety within which they can develop the essential skills of self-trust, self-consent, voice, choice and sovereignty. With these deep foundations of self-regard in place, the things they used to struggle with—from sexual to relational to financial difficulties—get shored up, and they open to more capacity for pleasure, joy, and aliveness.

While facilitating a personalized approach to healing has been tremendously meaningful, and while my clients have gotten significant results, a few years ago, I began to feel frustrated with the limitations of personal development.

A client would work with me and experience major transformation around her embodied fear in intimacy. Her life would change forever. Never again would she find herself in bed without access to her voice, her choice or her truth. Her nature would go from slightly dissociative and people-pleasing to fully embodied and empowered around her desires. In fact, she'd become more embodied and empowered across the board in her life. At work, she'd ask for a raise and get one. With her kids, she'd create more healthy limits. She'd devote with greater ease to the movement routines that added a serious pep in her step.

Of course, this kind of transformation would have an undeniable ripple effect on the world. Her children, her co-workers, her lover…they would all benefit from a woman tapped into her medicine—and in turn, they, too, would experience a level of healing through osmosis.

But there was a hang-up, a limitation, a thing I couldn't help this woman with using the lens of personal development, alone: diverging from a culture she didn't believe in that often oppressed and repressed her. Because this woman wasn't aligned to the predefined script of success. Single family home, nuclear family, get rich on your own, save money for retirement—that vision alone wasn't inspiring to her, didn't scratch the itch of her soul's deeper calling to be of coherent service in this world. This woman saw the things that her self-care alone could never change: systemic racism, wealth inequity, environmental destruction and loss of community. This woman longed for a different, more ancient, circular way of growing and dying together, of winning, losing, and loving together. She wanted to leave the world of isolation and competition for the world of cooperation and togetherness, and her personal development, while important—necessary, even—would never, by itself, be enough.

It was clear to me that what we do to ourselves, we do to the whole, and what we do to the whole, we do to ourselves. But just because I felt an obvious correlation between the personal and the collective, didn't mean I had a way of effectively helping them intersect.

That became my soul's mission. I could sense the spiritual technology waiting in the dark. I didn't know the answer in my mind, or even my heart. I just knew my questions:

How can we heal ourselves and the world simultaneously?

How can everything I've learned about individual physiology and soul-ecology be put to use in sacred service to the shared liberation of all living things?

How can our shared liberation truly free us, not leave us enslaved to the struggle?

How can we rebloom together, the whole damn garden, not just some in tiny patches of privilege?

How might we become a resonant field of medicinal embodiment, together? A powerful energetic acupuncture point on the planet?

If the infinite all-aloneness of our culture is part of the secret trap, how do we break free of that?

When I came to know these questions, my deepest wish and intention was revealed—to make it so us humans can fulfill the bigness of who we really are: erotic, creative, mystical, sensitive, humanitarian, collaborative, caring, courageous souls come to Earth in these days, in these times, to rewrite the future of our planet. To remember right-relationship, interbeing and cooperation. To grow regenerative abundance for all.

Day after day, I carried my questions to the altar of my heart. I walked, prayed, danced, and sang with them. I lived inside the dark, sublime mystery of them. I felt the pain—the dramatic, intense difficulty of them.

Until the questions began prying me open to greater creativity.

I started taking the medicine of ReBloom religiously. Every day, I'd do a Coherence Practice to awaken the seven Blueprints of Health that correlated to the seven ReBloom archetypes. I'd ask a question, then let the medicine illuminate a super-aligned way forward.

This way forward wasn't just based on the whims of my emotions, personal goals or individual desires. It wasn't just a reaction to traumatic fear or panic. It was based in congruence with the essential energies that cultivate a regenerative human family on Planet Earth.

The Seven Natural Blueprints of Humanity

Worthiness & Receptivity

Sovereignty

Whole Self Expression

Clarity & Choice

Vitality & Empowered Safety

Intimate Belonging

Co-Creation

As this book goes on, you'll learn that each of these Blueprints didn't emerge out of thin air. They correlate to specific body parts, as well as developmental cycles—of both human life and the growth of a healthy garden.

They each also have a traumatic imprint to which they're vulnerable—a challenge, difficulty or violation that's the opposite energy of the Blueprint.

The Seven Traumatic Imprints of Humanity

Neglect

Exploitation

Shame & Repression

Manipulation & Control

Violence & Chaos
Isolation & Alienation
Colonization

Through connecting to the Blueprints of each archetype using the ReBloom Coherence Practice, I've grown more potent in my own medicine, my own capacity to meet the intensity of not just my one-on-one clients, but the world at large that's mirrored inside their individual stories.

My coaching students and clients have experienced the same from this medicine. A sense of deep, powerful rootedness that's in true integrity with the health of humanity. And you can, too.

Who this book is for

I've written this book as an invitation to mystics and alchemists who are ready to be on a cosmic dream team of planetary awakening. People who want to be able to work confidently with trauma, meet the nervous system with skill and grace, safety and wizardry. People who want their clients to be forever changed, without feeling like they need to saved. If that's you, wonderful. I'm going to do my best in this book to teach you everything I know about facilitating safe and profound post-traumatic miracles with your clients, students and loved ones.

I've also written this book for people who want to facilitate and experience more than *personal* post-traumatic growth. For people who secretly know that the solo approach to personal development falls short: there is no total transformation of self inside a toxic garden of isolation or oppression. This book is for you if deep in your heart you want to grow into a collective medicine so potent that the momentum of our shared aliveness births a new portal of possibility for our whole human family.

While it can be scary to lean into these radical edges, the truth is, I'm not settling for the humanity I was born into. I'm calling in co-conspirators of a more seductive, romantic mission. I'm going for cinema. This book is for you if you're going for cinema, too. If you want the personal healing you facilitate to be directly tied to the rebirth of our human family. Systemically. Ceremonially. Intentionally, not just accidentally. If you want the rebirth of our human family to go beyond a revolution of who wins the next fight and into an evolution of win-for-all solutions.

I know the fear of stepping up to this kind of call. The way it requires leaving behind the outdated illusions of our conscious and subconscious minds. The way culture wants to keep us caged. The way our families gawk and our reptilian brains object. The way we're given so little space to even see or feel just how off-center our systems and structures have guided us, too busy trying to survive inside of them.

I know the resistance to the bigger dream—the way its failure would mean bigger heartbreak. But I also know the dissatisfaction of pretending my calling is small and can fit neatly inside a conventional box.

I know the disillusionment, dissociation, shame and regret we're all too susceptible to when we sit idly by, letting the world of hyper-individualism and toxic competition be the train we never get off.

I know how easy it is to be soothed or numbed into apathy by the neon glow of social media dopamine hits, Netflix addiction, or another toke of the bowl. I know the dance between numb and panic when another disaster hits or shooting strikes, and we feel so flooded with heartache that we never put our stake in the ground for the more beautiful world our hearts know is possible, as Charles Eisenstein calls it.

I know the tendency to think that if we're gonna go all in it's gotta be fast, furious and final. I also know the truth is that change happens little by little, day by day, in deep devotion to cultivating a new way. Planetary awakening isn't about grand gestures of saviorism, but small doable steps of nurturance, coherence, courage and care.

I know that if the blaze in your belly is ready to start small, but with big love for the sake of our personal and collective reblooming, this book can be your medicine.

I've written this book specifically for coaches, therapists and guides who want to learn how to work with trauma in a soulful, safe, powerful way. Throughout the book, I'll be sharing insights, practices and direction for the professional application of the ReBloom medicine.

If you're not a coach, therapist or guide, but you've come to this book seeking personal revelation, healing or hope, fear not: there will be much medicine for you here, as well. You can apply the practices, insights and inquiries directly to your own life. Or, you can perhaps hire a ReBloom Coach to work through the material with you.[1]

My mentorships, trainings, and very human approach

I have been enormously blessed with phenomenal mentorship, without which, this book and body of work would never be possible.

My first real guide was Jen Lemen, a mentor, activist, and incredible map-maker. For over a decade, Jen encouraged me to go all the way to the edges of my curiosity, rebellion, creativity and healing. She taught me how to slow down, how to dream big, how to be a good neighbor, how to say yes to magic, how to let my heart break for the world, how to get up and do something with my pain, but only after staying with the trouble long enough to act from a place of true care. She was the first person to ever tell me the traumas I experienced were not okay. Jen taught me so much about how to share, how to be there for others, how to show up for your beloveds. Jen's words, thinking and vision are forever laced into mine.

Brigit Viksnins was and still is my trauma resolution teacher and personal guide. She created a training called Alchemical Alignment: Trauma Resolution and Embodiment of Spirit that's origins are rooted in Somatic Experiencing, Craniosacral Therapy, Pre and Perinatal trauma resolution, Biodynamics and more. I've studied and worked closely with Brigit for more than five years and learn new things from her in every interaction we have. She is a master of physiology, the nervous system and health like no one I've ever met. I am deeply grateful for her life changing influence and guidance.

For five years, Master Integral Coach Chela Davison has mentored and

---

[1] *You can head to rebloomtogether.com/coaches to find a list of trained and certified ReBloom Coaches.*

coached me into the leader I've needed to become to carry and birth this body of work. I've learned so much about how to effectively guide people into their next evolutionary edges by working with Chela, and her wise and brilliant approach has influenced mine for the better.

In addition to being trained as an Alchemical Alignment practitioner, I am a professionally certified Co-Active Coach through the Coaches Training Institute. I've trained in mindfulness facilitation with the Awakened Leadership Academy and I've done 100+ hours of in-person experiential group work on privilege, oppression, race, class and identity dynamics at the University of Maryland. I am committed to continually unlearning my implicit biases and redistributing unearned privilege.

Over the last 10 years I've worked with hundreds of humans on developmental or sexual trauma—in one-on-one, group, retreat, workshop and intimate immersive settings. I am devoted to the art and craft of deep, safe and effective transformation. In every session, I learn more about the human experience from my clients. They are also my teachers.

However, be warned: I will be very human with you in the pages of this book. Because I am not just a professional. I am an artist. I am a survivor. I am a one-day-wanna-be-Rabbi raised by a Jewish mom and a Baptist dad. I am a poet. I am a sensual seductress. I am a radical visionary. I am a playful, non-monogamous, devotional, queer, hetero-leaning, cis-gendered, sometimes selectively slutty lover of love, romance and lust. I am 100% witch. Cackle, cackle. I am whole. I love the edges. I am incredibly grounded. I am sometimes visited by non-human beings. I am happiest with my phone off and fingers dirty in the soil, mud or dust.

I bet you've got your own laundry list of identities, too.

My professional identity is an important one. Within it, I am committed to safety, excellence, integrity, ethics, continued education, and top-quality care. I lean into my professional self to help maintain role clarity with clients and students, and healthy boundaries during sensitive healing journeys. However, my professional identity is nestled within my bigger human—and my bigger human is an essential informant of my professional self.

In this book, I am sharing with you from both my professional self and my bigger human. It is my hope and intention that through sharing in this holistic way, you'll come into contact with the many facets of your identity, as well—your big human self, your professional self, your still-healing heart...all of you.

Last, I want to acknowledge that my identity as a white, cis-gendered, pretty, able-bodied, upper middle class, hetero-presenting woman limits my perspective and biases my work. While researching and writing this book, I've hired a diversity of people to help deepen it to meet a wider range of identities and experiences. You'll hear me cite and credit my teachers throughout. That said, this is a living, growing, imperfect and evolving body of work. If there's something you notice that you'd like to offer feedback around, I one hundred percent welcome your perspective and wisdom. Please share with me at hive@rachaelmaddox.com.

Reading this book in a trauma-informed way

Beloved human, I encourage you to be mindful about your internal state as you're reading this book. If, at any moment, you feel overwhelmed to the point of anxiety, fogginess or disembodiment, let yourself pause, ground, shake, or exhale real big. You matter here. You don't have to force feed yourself this book. You can receive it bite by bite, digest it at a doable pace. While I intentionally tell stories of both health and difficulty in this book, some pieces may be challenging to read. You're always welcome to skip parts that feel like too much to take in.

Also, if you notice yourself spinning in a downward spiral, see if you can catch yourself and look for something stable, beautiful, safe or sturdy around you or within you. Perhaps flowers, a beautiful tree outside, the solid ground beneath you, a sweet animal friend, or the tenderness of your precious, resilient heart. Allowing yourself to pause and synch up with something a bit more stable or nourishing can help soothe potential triggers and reawaken your capacity to choose your next best step.

Those who have histories of trauma may sometimes be prone to embodying a negativity bias, resonating with pain, while having less access to pleasure, joy or hope. If that's the case for you, I'll recommend to you the same practice I'd recommend to my clients or students:

As you read this book, see if you can look for what's working in your body, life, heart, soul, or spirit. What feels good, hopeful or inspiring to connect with from the text? In what ways are you embodying resilience? What feels doable for you to digest in the material? What tools are empowering you, or what tools are you already using? In other words, can you identify the places where your Blueprint is already alive in you as a way of noticing that you've got some powerful foundation you're working with?

I'm not encouraging you to bypass difficult feelings. If you need to weep, by all means, weep! If there are parts of this book that bring up challenging things for you, that's okay and really normal. But perhaps through blurry eyes if need be, you can look for signs of what's working inside you: your devotion to growth, your ability to pause if it feels like too much, your courage to show up in the first place, your awareness that you feel sad or mad, and your willingness to reach out, let someone witness and care for you in your pain. Noticing what's working even as things are challenging can help you receive the medicine you came for with more ease, gentleness and grace.

This book is packed with experiential invitations, practices and opportunities to embody the words on the page. Some of these practices are for the human you—because your growth and healing are essential to your professional capacities. Other practices are tools you can use with your clients.

It's your call whether you'd like to read the book through and then perhaps go back to some of the practices or pause when you come across an invitation that speaks to you. There's no right or wrong way. What's most important is honoring your capacity and following your curiosity.

Our bodies and souls have unique timelines for healing and growth. What if, just for fun, you experimented with trusting your impulses to lean in or lean out from a certain practice? What if, instead of making it mean you're too resistant or afraid, you played with the possibility that by listening to your hunches, you'll get just what you need?

Chapter 1

The Roadmap to ReBlooming

The meaning behind the word "ReBloom"

I have orchids on my kitchen windowsill. Every fall, I witness the bright magenta and pearly white flowers wither and decay, dropping to the soil in surrender. A whole winter passes with no blooms in sight, but still, I water the roots weekly. I tend to the unseen possibility of vibrant new life reemerging from the dark.

Sometimes, during this long, slow winter, I wonder if it's worth it, all this caring for a hungry spirit. But when the spring comes and I see the first hint of that new stem growing, when I watch day after day as it rises upward like a strong spine until a small baby bud of majesty cocks its chin and smiles, opening brightly, wildly unfurling, as if announcing to the kitchen—no, the whole house!—that it is here and it is not afraid, then I know nature is a courageous cycle, rebirthing itself over and over. I know it was worth every day of doubt, every day that I showed up anyway, petitioning to the mystery for another chance. All along, the chance was predictable. Secretly expected. All along, this rebloom was designed to happen.

Unless the soil is riddled with toxicity too lethal to bear. Unless the magic medicine of each flower is kept hidden in the shadows, denied necessary sunlight or shamed for its radiant colors. Unless no hands extend water, pruning, or repotting to the eager life that's ready to burst forth.

Like orchids, our lives have their own natural cycles of birth, life, death and renewal. But here's the thing: the first time I ever had an orchid, I thought it was dead when winter came.

Sometimes, us humans are like this, too. We think our bloom is gone forever. We throw ourselves out to the curb too soon, not knowing we've got regrowing to do. This is the spell of trauma: a dissociation of awareness, embodiment and relationship to our natural lifecycle, our ever-regenerating lifeforce. I refer to trauma as a spell, because we often don't realize we're living under its veil. We're eclipsed by it as it's running the show in unconscious, energetic ways.

To invoke the prayer of reblooming is to devote to reviving our natural lifecycles, our imminent lifeforce. Reviving our bodies, our relationships, our land and our ancestors. Reviving and deciding, with gentle trust and a friendly attitude, to tend to the not-yet-dead bloom in you and me and all the damn flowers in the garden. So we can rebloom again, more beautiful than before.

Orchids can live a lot longer than we may expect. As long as there's the tiniest bit of green life still left in the leaves at the bottom of their stem, you can bring them to bloom again.

Us humans are the same. As long as the smallest bit of life still lives in the secret pockets of our hopeful hearts, we can rebloom. We just need a map that shows us where we are so we can find ourselves through the foggy haze and begin, day by day, our long exploration home.

You can be that explorer. This book can be your map.

While post-traumatic growth is nuanced, there are three main sections of this map—this ReBloom journey—that makes the exploration safer and doable:

1. Discovering your current ReBloom oracle.
2. Growing embodied coherence.
3. Cultivating relational coherence.

In the last chapter, you explored your ReBloom oracle and the current questions on your heart in regard to your post-traumatic growth.

Growing embodied coherence is the practice of completing incomplete physiological trauma responses, regulating the nervous system, and nurturing resilient aliveness in the body. In other words, breaking the somatic trauma spell.

Cultivating relational coherence is the art of inhabiting the seven Natural Blueprints of Humanity in ways that bring you into regenerative relationships with yourself, others, your vocation, and our world.

The confluence of these three processes is the bird's eye view to reblooming. First, letting your ache, longing and hunches guide your curiosity, path and process. Second, healing your physiology and nervous system. Third, coming into life-giving relationships with all that is.

Defining Coherence and Incoherence

I first got into the idea of coherence when I took a class with a business alchemist named Fabeku Fatunmise. He used coherence to describe the quality of having all your parts aligned in the same intentional direction: the direction of your Bigness. I like to think of coherence as alignment that regenerates lifeforce.

The natural world around us, left to its own devices, is the epitome of coherence. Somehow, miraculously, the mycelial network nourishes the soil and feeds the roots of trees, the trees oxygenate the air and provide shelter for animals and humans alike, the inhale of oxygen into the human body enlivens the bloodstream, and the exhale of carbon dioxide back to the atmosphere eventually gets reabsorbed by the earth and digested again by the mycelial network.[2] All of this happens in symphonic resonance. While the individual contribution of each component differs, they each add their separate voices to the shared choir, the anthem of organic regeneration.

Incoherence is whatever blocks that sacred song from being sung. Old traumatic imprints stored deep in the body that hinder lifeforce, that keep you small or withdrawn from your role in the family of things. Structural oppression, systemic violence, inequities, and collective toxicity that prevent us from receiving the nourishment we need to grow and thrive. Environmental degradation we can feel in our flesh and bones, because of course, we are nature—our bodies know. Whether incoherence is rooted in our personal muscle memories or our shared soil, the call remains the same: to come back into alignment with the symphonic beauty of our natural design on both personal and collective levels…to reawaken and regenerate lifeforce.

When we're feeling lost or afraid, exhausted or uncertain, we can consult with nature as a resource and a guide. As a reminder of the roots from which we've grown and to which we'll return home. As a felt-sense experience of the abundant Blueprint that we miss when we're too stuck under the trauma spells of man-made matrixes.

The Natural Blueprint of Health and Blueprint Essence

Below the nervous system, there lives in each of us a Natural Blueprint of Health.[3] A design for physiological wellness with divine intelligence. An organic wisdom that's untouchable, unbreakable and infinitely available to you. It's always there, but sometimes it gets buried beneath traumatic imprints or difficulties that strike the body, soul, or lineage.

---

[2] *The mycelial network is a worldwide underground web of the roots of mushrooms. It's a key communication and nourishment source for plants and trees. I highly recommend the movie Fantastic Fungi (watch.fantasticfungi. com) to learn more.*

[3] *The concept of a Natural Blueprint of Health was taught to me by Brigit Viksnins, and taught to her by Anna Chitty, founder of the Colorado School of Energy Studies.*

Your Natural Blueprint of Health is the part of your being that knows to bleed when it gets cut, then scab and heal. It's the part of you that recognizes pangs in your stomach as signs of hunger, then knows how to feed yourself or cry to be fed. It's the part of you that effortlessly develops and grows from baby to child to teen to adult to elder. It's even the part of you that eventually passes on, making space for future generations. It's your lungs that oxygenate your brain, your blood that warms your body, your lips that smile or frown to express emotion. Yes, there are more intricate brain and nervous system centers that control these operations, but your Blueprint is the miraculous divine underlying design.

We as humans also have a Collective Natural Blueprint of Health—the original web of togetherness that's designed to keep us vital and well. After all, our individual health is not possible in isolation. Personal wellness is predicated on togetherness, despite individualized models of therapeutic care. We can't help but seek and need connection.

We witness our Collective Natural Blueprint of Health in the new mother who knows she needs a team of women around her in the period just after giving birth. The children who wish to run free in nature together, following their curiosities, expressing their innocent wildness. The grandparents who wish to counsel their grandchildren, providing relief to their children during the pressures of parenting. The community farmer who offers vegetables to his neighbor in return for tutoring his son in reading. The way the whole human family pours money, hands and care to other parts of the world when natural disaster strikes.

In life, experiences may happen—physical, emotional or systemic—that leave imprints of difficulty or trauma upon your personal Blueprint, and our collective one, too. But the Blueprint itself—the original design of wellness, functionality, harmony and flow—is unbreakable.

Additionally, each person's Natural Blueprint of Health has its own unique Blueprint Essence. An individual scent, or medicine, that's unique to the soul of your being. This mysterious backdrop of your heart's loves and longings, gifts and talents, has perhaps been with you all along. It's why career coaches will have you revisit your childhood passions when you're feeling lost about what to do with your life. Blueprint Essence. The spirit of your unique you-ness. Identifiable from the very beginning.

As a coach or guide, when you work with the idea that all humans have a Natural Blueprint of Health and a Blueprint Essence, you cultivate solid, supportive grounds for working with the nervous system. Bringing awareness to Blueprint can create a foundation of stability, capacity and hope, especially in tricky or tender territory.

Growing Embodied Coherence

When I first began coming into conscious contact with my nervous system, I remember feeling like I was becoming aware of a secret sixth sense. I was reintroduced to the language of my subtle body that had been there all along but had also become desensitized. I've since learned that there's a sensual science to diving below the mind and emotions, and into physiology. It's a somatic approach to healing that cultivates the most deep and embodied miracles. And it's the heart of embodied coherence.

Can we heal our traumatic triggers through mental understanding or perspective shifting alone? Most trauma-informed practitioners would say a clear and resounding no.

Many therapeutic models will work only with the story of a trigger, or perhaps the emotional experience that happens in tandem with that story. These approaches, while helpful to many, leave out the underlying experience that's happening in the non-cognitive, non-verbal, instinctual parts of the body—the parts of us that are operating with much greater speed and automation than our higher-level meaning-making minds.

When we learn the moves of embodied coherence—coming into greater physiological stabilization and regulation, correcting false perceptions of threat, responding to real danger, discharging outdated emergency energy from our bodies, and activating our capacity to synchronize with our instincts in a conscious, intentional way—we can shift the inner-layer of our stuckness, opening us up to incredible levels of creativity, empowerment, intimacy and self-trust. Then, our emotions and mindset follow suit with the transformation of our nervous systems, not the other way around.

When you learn how to work with a client to help them cultivate this kind of fundamental embodied coherence, the efficiency, velocity and alignment of their life-force becomes super-charged. The once incoherent energy that was spiraling them into emergencies of anxiety, depression, chronic illness, chronic pain and more, can now feed and protect their aliveness, fueling a positive feedback loop of new capacity.

Chapter 11, Trauma-Informed Coaching Skills, focuses in depth on the practitioner moves that most support the facilitation of embodied coherence.

Cultivating Relational Coherence

In a healthy garden, everything relates to the spiral of coherent abundance. Everything, in its own unique way, shows up to do its part, giving to the whole. Needing, protecting, providing, blooming, nourishing, feeding, releasing, tending, luxuriating, guardianing, plotting, sharing. Sometimes, even blight or beetles come along destroying what wasn't built with enough coherence. Like a village with a cast of characters, in every garden there's a team of various roles, baring diverse gifts, challenges, and medicines.

We as humans are no different than a garden. Each of us, in our own personal ecologies, has the chance to bring alive the various roles of the ReBloom archetypes, archetypes that follow a developmental maturation process from seed all the way to gardener—from neediness and receptivity, to protector and provider, lush expressive bloom, wise medicinal fruit, daily devoted rhythm-keeper, singing and dancing ritual-tender, and finally, architect of a thriving community.

We are ripe with potential to bring forth the gifts of the earth and share them in ways that help all humans thrive. Embodied coherence alone won't get us there. Regulated nervous systems are an important foundation, but they don't guarantee relational integrity. With nature as our guide, we can witness and watch, observe and learn from the ways the wild is not so arbitrary after all. There is order. There is hierarchy. There is death and ruthlessness, yes. There is also honor. Mostly, there are unavoidable relationships, and these relationships have the chance to be coherent or incoherent. Coherence regenerates Life. Incoherence exterminates it.

I've used the word regeneration a few times, so I want to pause and share its precise meaning. In the world of permaculture, regeneration is referred to as a step beyond sustainability. While sustainability is the process of keeping something going as it is, regeneration is the process of cultivating a positive feedback loop, where health begets more health and the whole ecosystem spirals into greater abundance.

With relational coherence, we come to remember how to relate powerfully to ourselves, each other and Life itself. We learn to heal the traumatic imprints of neglect, exploitation, shame and repression, manipulation and control, violence, isolation and alienation and colonization. We devote ourselves to becoming good ground, ground where healthy things can grow and thrive. We relate to ourselves, others and the earth as if it matters that we wake up and tend to what needs our attention, because we understand that it does, because we can feel in our hearts the truth: together is how we get hurt, and together is how we heal. And the time is now for healing.

We were born to weave generous creations and consensual negotiations. Born for feeling worthy of and receptive to our mother's milk, our guardian's protection. We were born to be held and tended to, then taught how to stand on our own two feet, still needy, but sturdier, too. We were born to bloom with hearts forward toward the sun. Born to hear and trust our own intuition. We were born to gather and born to belong. Born to dance and sing our true songs. We were born to co-create with the magic or mud all around us. We were born to sense when we've taken too much. We were born to heal our broken bones then give them back to the earth when they've finished their run. We were born to find out what it really means to be alive in relationship to this mysterious, sublime planet.

We're not above or beyond right-relating. We're designed for it. We've just forgotten how to embody it. But we're ready to remember. Relational coherence is a path and a portal. And the ReBloom Coherence Practice is a clear process of remembrance.

Chapter 2

The ReBloom Coherence Practice

Origins

It was the day Dr. Christine Blasey Ford testified against Brett Kavanaugh, the then-nominee for Supreme Court Justice who sexually assaulted her in high school. The country was on high alert. Women were watching their greatest fear play out before their eyes: state-sanctioned sexual abuse by those with systemic power. Gaslighting. Denial. Grievous injustice. Adrenals were shot. Hearts were broken. Nervous systems were screaming, and then slowly, gently freezing.

My neighbor at the time, an alcoholic and pot addict, was on a bender. Knowing my line of work, he had once revealed to me that his ex-wife took him to court for molesting his daughter. He was found innocent, and now had full custody over her. In a seeming-panic that day, he came banging at my front door. Thinking maybe something was wrong, I opened the door, only to be met with shouting fits of rage in my direction.

Immediately, I closed the door and panicked. Should I call the cops? If they went over there and talked to him, would it make things worse? *I still have to be neighbors with this guy.*

I decided to pause with it. I called my boyfriend, told him what happened, and asked if he'd come over. Then, frazzled, jumped in the shower.

The ironic thing was all week I'd been studying the effects of physical and emotional abuse on the nervous system. I was in a research rabbit hole about manipulation, control, narcissism and addiction. And everywhere I looked, those very things were running rampant.

Now, I don't believe that we call in all of our traumas or create our reality with our thinking. I do believe, however, that the momentum of our physiology—in the direction of either health or emergency—can sometimes magnify the way we experience the realities of the world. Often, when we're spinning in emergency, more emergency finds us, and we find more of it. Conversely, when we're rooted in capacity, we tend to have more access to seeing and amplifying capacity around us, even in difficult situations.

In this moment, life was mirroring the dark side of my work back to me, and I couldn't stop thinking, "I need to amplify my capacity. I need to amplify my capacity." Because it wasn't just a one-time thing. Each time I wrote another archetype chapter, the energetics of that archetype's wound began showing up all around me.

In the shower, shaky with fear, I dropped my hands to my belly, an umbilicus of worthiness, and asked, this time with greater intention, "How can I amplify my capacity…? Is there a quick and simple way I can connect to my Blueprints so the imprints have less access to my system?" I waited for an answer, but it didn't come in words. Not at first. At first, it came in sways.

Swaying my hips left to right, rubbing my belly, I anchored a feeling of gravity and soothed myself with attention and care. Soon enough, I heard a deep presence arise from the recesses of my inner-self:

"I am here.
I am now.
I matter."

I began to whisper these words—words of my soul, my humanness, my assertion of aliveness—over and over again.

"I am here.
I am now.
I matter."

My hands were rubbing my belly button, my umbilicus. The part of the body that's home to the Soul Seed, the first archetype in the developmental ReBloom model. The one most connected to fundamental physical needs and our youngest, most vulnerable selves.

"I am worthy of feeding my needs.
I am designed to grow and thrive."

I began to cry, sensing just how much violence my system was fighting against, just how suppressed my lifeforce felt. What do I need? I wondered. Then I whispered aloud…

"I need to feel safe in my home.
I need my neighbor to never talk to me again.
I need the violence to subside.
I need space to breathe and cry.
I need to be held.
I need to connect to my Blueprints daily, grow them bigger and more robust, so the energy of the imprints have less access to my field."

Then I whispered a final affirmation of possibility.

"I am receiving.

I am receiving.

I am receiving."

I imagined all of my needs coming to fruition with divine support, with cosmic care. A warmth and steadiness came into the shaky parts of me, and my body began to settle. A small sense of trust was growing within. The world's dangers hadn't changed, but in that moment, I did—just a bit. Just enough to feel like maybe I wasn't totally powerless in the face of the assholery and danger around me.

I was still scared, but I also felt more empowered. More connected to my own safety, worthiness and receptivity, less frozen in fear or denial. Then I realized, whoa—I'd just begun to answer my prayer for amplified capacity in a simple, powerful way.

Realizing I'd been working with the first archetype—Soul Seed—I wondered, what if there's a movement and affirmation that can awaken each archetype's Blueprint?

I brought my attention down to my hips, home of the Gatekeeper—the sovereign decider, the proud protector. I began to sway in passionate pendulations a sensual dance of power.

"I get to decide what comes in and what stays out!"

I was nearly shouting, with tears streaming down my face.

"I get to decide what comes in and what stays out!"

I motioned my hands in concert with my words, inviting new life-force energy in and then pushing old toxic energy out.

"I get to decide what comes in and what stays out!"

A fierce fire of love began to grow in me, a roarous might, and I wondered, *what exactly do I want and need to say "yes" to? And what needs my righteous "no?"*

I began to sing my insides.

"I say yes to feeling safe in my space!" I cried, drawing in an energy of aliveness.

"I say no to being intruded upon!" I declared, pushing out unwanted energy.

"I say yes to physical and energetic protection!"

"I say no to feeling powerless amidst the whims of our unpredictable world."

"I say yes to having space to feel my tenderness."

"I say no to holding that space all alone."

I went on and on until I could feel my system shoring up even more. Until my body began to grow vitality and my heart renewed a feeling of resiliency.

Whoa… this is working, I thought.

I went through every archetype until the shower got cold, experimenting with different movements and affirmations for each. As the process went on, my inner-alignment began to grow, giving me a powerful sense of cohesion and strength. I was amazed at the way the archetypal Blueprints were coming to life in my cells. And—I was also noticing my body growing tired from expanding into so much aliveness. Attuning to myself with care, I got out of the shower, tucked myself under my covers and napped until my boyfriend arrived.

"How are you doing, babe?" he asked upon arrival, gently soothing me awake.

"I'm exhausted," I told him. "But I think I figured out a key practice for ReBloom."

"Babe, can this just be about you right now, not your work?" he asked, knowing a bit of my tendency for non-stop creativity.

"It *is* about me. It's about how I can grow resiliency and capacity inside my work. Otherwise, I'm gonna need to quit everything I'm doing."

He chuckled with love, "You're something else." Then he pulled me into the safety of his strong, caring arms. We closed our eyes and fell into slumber together.

This was the birth of the ReBloom Coherence Practice. Me. In the shower. Terrified and exhausted. Desperate for a quick and simple way to access more of my embodied and relational coherence, my Natural Blueprints of Health.

By the way, one morning two months after creating the Coherence Practice and engaging it regularly, I woke up to a moving truck parked in front of my house. It was for my neighbor. He was moving out. When I realized what was going on, I squealed with miraculous joy, then thought… Maybe this is a coincidence, or maybe the energetic momentum of my own coherence created a field of health too vibrant for him to be near. Maybe the vortex of my wellness pushed him away. We'll never know for sure, but my spidey senses tell me it was more than coincidence.

The ReBloom Coherence Practice for Post-Traumatic Growth

The ReBloom Coherence Practice is a movement and affirmation process that helps you connect to and awaken the Blueprints, wisdom and vitality of the ReBloom Archetypes in your life, body and soul in a streamlined and deep way. Through slow felt-sense awareness, optional subtle movements and evocative affirmations, the Coherence Practice calls on and synthesizes all three parts of your brain—reptilian, limbic, and neocortex—to revive an experience of integrated wholeness, clarity and health. It works at all four layers of your humanness: Blueprint, nervous system, emotions and mind.

When you access each Archetype's Blueprint in a sequenced series that can be done in as little as thirty minutes, coherence grows within. This coherence connects you to levels of self-regulation, inner trust, clarity, confidence and super-aligned guidance where things may have previously felt wobbly, uncertain, challenging or even dangerous.

Since each Archetype not only has a Blueprint of health, but also an imprint of trauma and a hyper and hypo way that the traumatic imprint expresses itself, it's easy to get lost in dysregulation when we're triggered, overwhelmed or trying to change old patterns. For instance, when we're healing our Soul Seeds—returning to the Blueprint of worthiness and receptivity from the traumatic imprint of neglect—it's easy to slip into the hyper-response of extreme self-sufficiency, or the hypo-response of self-denial of needs. Doing the Coherence Practice for the Soul Seed can re-root your body, nervous system and cognitive awareness into the groundedness of the Blueprint. It's a pathway back to regulation that retrains your neural networks for receptive worthiness and self-regard.

Amber's Soul Seed was once dissociated and malnourished. She was unable to feel and ask for her needs and carried a constant feeling of resentment that her boyfriend was never "meeting" her. She didn't realize that her own developmental neglect was impacting her capacity to sense, speak into and receive her needs. By engaging the Coherence Practice regularly, she grew a powerful feeling of worthiness, rooted in an awakened receptivity, that then trickled out into her relationship with her boyfriend. By meeting herself in the truth of her needs, attuning to what they were and imagining herself receiving them, she opened a coherent channel for them to get met. And whaddaya know—her boyfriend began meeting her in that place.

This is just one tiny example of how the Coherence Practice has helped one person heal, grow, and thrive. Since creating the ReBloom Coherence Practice, I've taught it to hundreds of people—one-on-one clients, students, and groups—both virtually and in-person. It continues to be one of the most impactful and supportive pieces of the ReBloom model. People tell me over and over again that it's changed their relationship to their body, sexuality, business, friendships, communities, families—everything.

The same can be true for you and your clients.

The Coherence Practice is a self-healing method. It's a pathway to internal truth, wisdom, sensations, visions, and capacities. It is a process of liberatory self-connection and listening.

Personal and collective post-traumatic growth is not a small task. It's a big deal to pursue for yourself, it's a big deal to help others experience it, and it's a big deal to work toward it in our communities, families, and culture.

I once heard my teacher Brigit say that the momentum of emergency—in our bodies, psyches, and world—can be fast and contagious. We need something with equal and opposite power to embolden and resource us on our journey. Something that can spiral us into regenerative health and capacity on the regular. The ReBloom Coherence Practice is designed to do just that.

Of course, there are people for whom the ReBloom Coherence Practice is not ideal, and times when it's not quite the medicine needed. Sometimes, saying an affirmation feels inauthentic or too forceful. Sometimes, we need wordless movement or stillness to give the body a chance to reveal its truth, before insisting it adopt a new one. Sometimes, we need safe, body-based, somatic guidance that offers the physiology a chance to feel and heal old imprints of violation, danger or difficulty. Sometimes we just need a trusted beloved to hold us. The Coherence Practice is not a miracle cure-all that works for everyone right off the bat.

That said, because we're always unconsciously running stories and scripts, and because our bodies are always unconsciously living the wirings we inherited or developed when we were young, we're left with a choice. To let the unconscious patterns run our lives—or to bring them into the light, and interrupt them with more helpful, supportive scripts, stories and sensations.

In the coming chapters you'll be learning about all seven ReBloom Archetypes in depth. Before you do, I encourage you to take some time to connect to their natural Blueprints—their original superpowers—through engaging the Coherence Practice.

You can read the practice below, or even be guided through the first archetype for free at rebloomtogether.com/coherence.

This practice is medicine. Sometimes it goes down with ease, other times with a bit of difficulty. Every experience you have is valuable information. If some part of you has been shut down, numb or offline for a while, there might be a sensitive, emotional, painful or agitating reawakening. Know that you can always pause, modify or opt out of any part of the practice. But also know that as you continue to engage it, as you bring more of your Blueprint online, overtime, the "heavy lifting" of healing deeper traumatic imprints will lighten, and your coherence will come with more ease, flow, and joy.

The Coherence Practice is an experiential, developmental, mind-body map to reblooming your sex, love, passions, and business. It is a portal to embodied purpose when you go all the way with it. It is a possible practice for healing our world.

I invite you to try it on. To let it work on you. Slowly. In whatever ways are doable and digestible to your system.

While each archetype invites you into specific movements and affirmations, this practice is not intended to be a pre-designed experience that you follow to a T. It's intended to guide you to your own remembrance of the regenerative health that lives inside you.

This means that if you're working with a certain archetype and the movement feels inaccessible, you don't have to do it. If a particular archetype feels extra rich and juicy, you can stay with the resonance longer. If a specific affirmation doesn't land, you can leave it out. If a specific affirmation is working wonders on you,

you can engage it with more spaciousness, softness and presence—letting it linger inside your lips, lungs, luscious bones. If there are movements or affirmations, I didn't suggest that feel like they might awaken the Blueprint of an archetype—add them in! Let the Coherence Practice work on you by adjusting it to work for you.

You can start small, with one archetype at a time. As each archetype begins to integrate into your being, add another to the practice, until eventually, you feel ready for all seven. Or, if you're eager to dive in, do them all together one time through. See what comes up for you. Which were easy? Which were hard? Take it as a litmus test for which archetypes you can draw on for support (the easy ones are in your corner!) and which archetypes might be desiring some slow, tender attention. You can do the same thing with your clients to help identify their strengths and difficulties in their current post-traumatic growth journey.

With new clients, I often recommend two weeks to two months with the first archetype alone—the Soul Seed. Then, when they feel more integrated with the Soul Seed, they can add in the Gatekeeper. Clients will often feel embarrassed that they need so much time with the Soul Seed, but the truth is, it's our first archetype for a reason. Soul Seed is the foundation of everything. Taking time at the foundation will only strengthen all the other archetypes.

If you follow along with the free video at rebloomtogether.com/coherence, each individual archetype Coherence Practice is under ten minutes. There's also a full ReBloom Coherence Practice with all seven archetypes that's condensed into forty minutes. But you can do the practice at your own pace—shorter or longer, by simply using the following invitations.

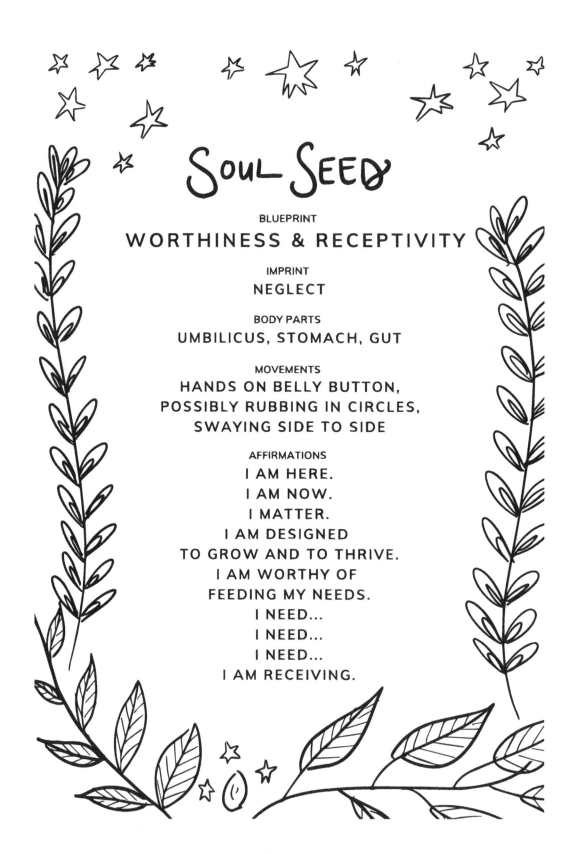

Soul Seed

BLUEPRINT
WORTHINESS & RECEPTIVITY

IMPRINT
NEGLECT

BODY PARTS
UMBILICUS, STOMACH, GUT

MOVEMENTS
HANDS ON BELLY BUTTON, POSSIBLY RUBBING IN CIRCLES, SWAYING SIDE TO SIDE

AFFIRMATIONS
I AM HERE.
I AM NOW.
I MATTER.
I AM DESIGNED
TO GROW AND TO THRIVE.
I AM WORTHY OF
FEEDING MY NEEDS.
I NEED...
I NEED...
I NEED...
I AM RECEIVING.

GATEKEEPER

BLUEPRINT
SOVEREIGNTY

IMPRINT
EXPLOITATION

BODY PARTS
HIPS, PELVIS, GENITALS, WOMB-SPACE

MOVEMENTS
HANDS ON HIPS, SWAYING,
SWEEPING HANDS UP AND IN AS YOU SAY YES,
SWEEPING HANDS DOWN AND OUT AS YOU SAY NO

AFFIRMATIONS
I GET TO DECIDE WHAT COMES IN
AND WHAT STAYS OUT.
I KEEP MY TEMPLE HEALTHY, HAPPY & HOLY.
I FEED MY SEED WHAT IT NEEDS TO THRIVE.
I SAY YES TO...
I SAY YES TO...
I SAY YES TO...
I SAY NO TO...
I SAY NO TO...
I SAY NO TO...

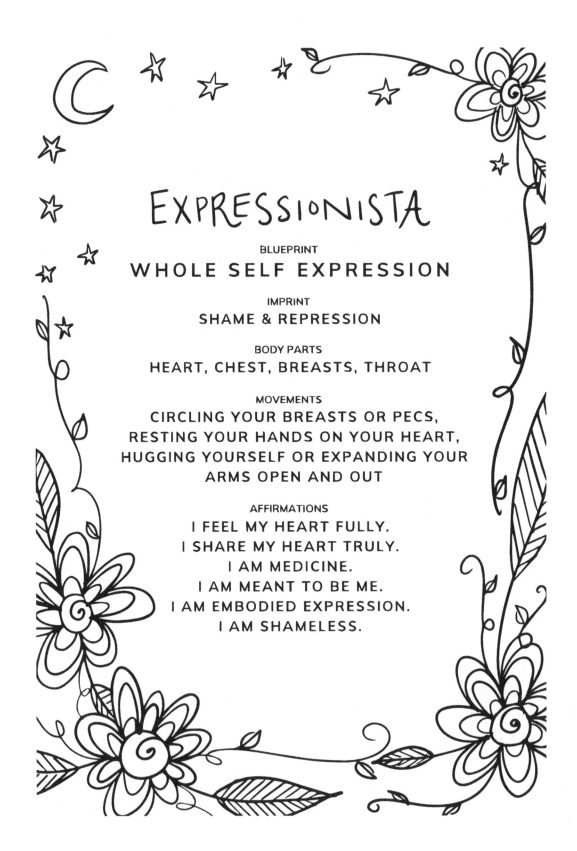

EXPRESSIONISTA

BLUEPRINT
WHOLE SELF EXPRESSION

IMPRINT
SHAME & REPRESSION

BODY PARTS
HEART, CHEST, BREASTS, THROAT

MOVEMENTS
CIRCLING YOUR BREASTS OR PECS, RESTING YOUR HANDS ON YOUR HEART, HUGGING YOURSELF OR EXPANDING YOUR ARMS OPEN AND OUT

AFFIRMATIONS
I FEEL MY HEART FULLY.
I SHARE MY HEART TRULY.
I AM MEDICINE.
I AM MEANT TO BE ME.
I AM EMBODIED EXPRESSION.
I AM SHAMELESS.

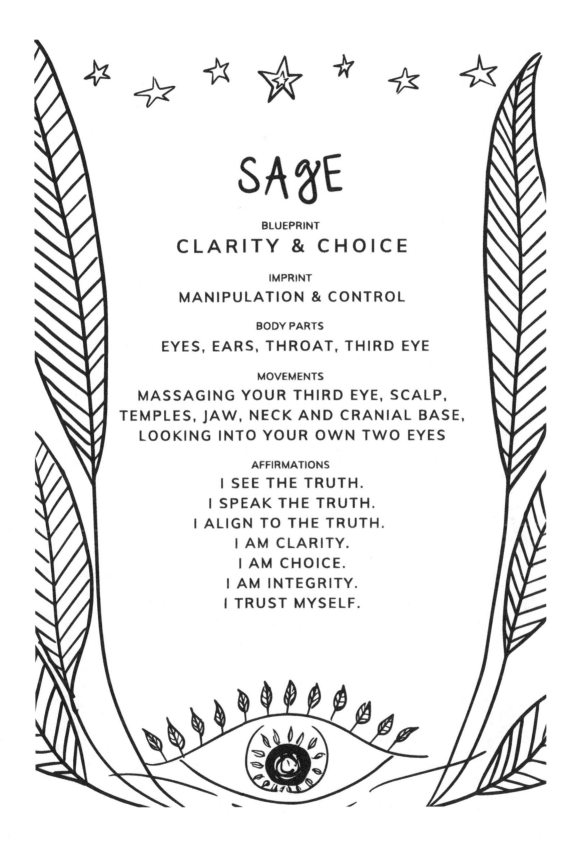

SAGE

BLUEPRINT
CLARITY & CHOICE

IMPRINT
MANIPULATION & CONTROL

BODY PARTS
EYES, EARS, THROAT, THIRD EYE

MOVEMENTS
MASSAGING YOUR THIRD EYE, SCALP, TEMPLES, JAW, NECK AND CRANIAL BASE, LOOKING INTO YOUR OWN TWO EYES

AFFIRMATIONS
I SEE THE TRUTH.
I SPEAK THE TRUTH.
I ALIGN TO THE TRUTH.
I AM CLARITY.
I AM CHOICE.
I AM INTEGRITY.
I TRUST MYSELF.

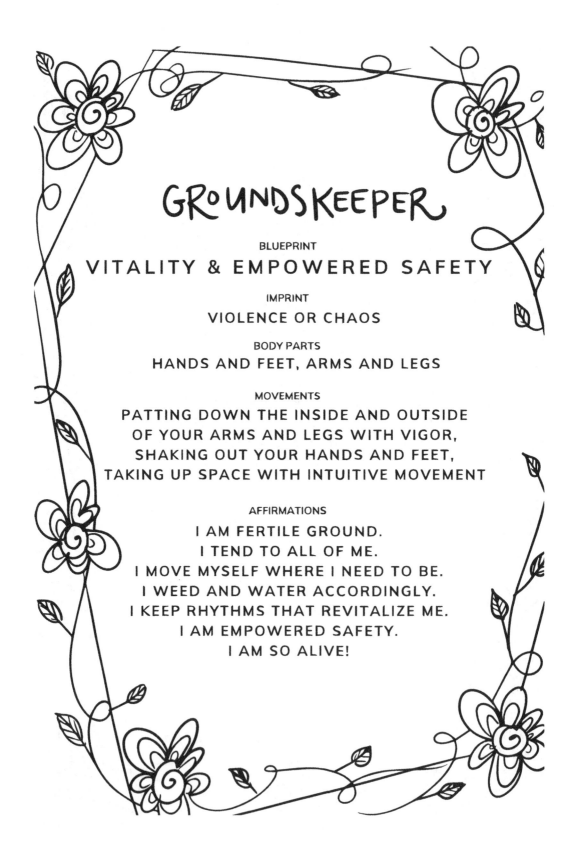

GROUNDSKEEPER

BLUEPRINT
VITALITY & EMPOWERED SAFETY

IMPRINT
VIOLENCE OR CHAOS

BODY PARTS
HANDS AND FEET, ARMS AND LEGS

MOVEMENTS
PATTING DOWN THE INSIDE AND OUTSIDE
OF YOUR ARMS AND LEGS WITH VIGOR,
SHAKING OUT YOUR HANDS AND FEET,
TAKING UP SPACE WITH INTUITIVE MOVEMENT

AFFIRMATIONS
I AM FERTILE GROUND.
I TEND TO ALL OF ME.
I MOVE MYSELF WHERE I NEED TO BE.
I WEED AND WATER ACCORDINGLY.
I KEEP RHYTHMS THAT REVITALIZE ME.
I AM EMPOWERED SAFETY.
I AM SO ALIVE!

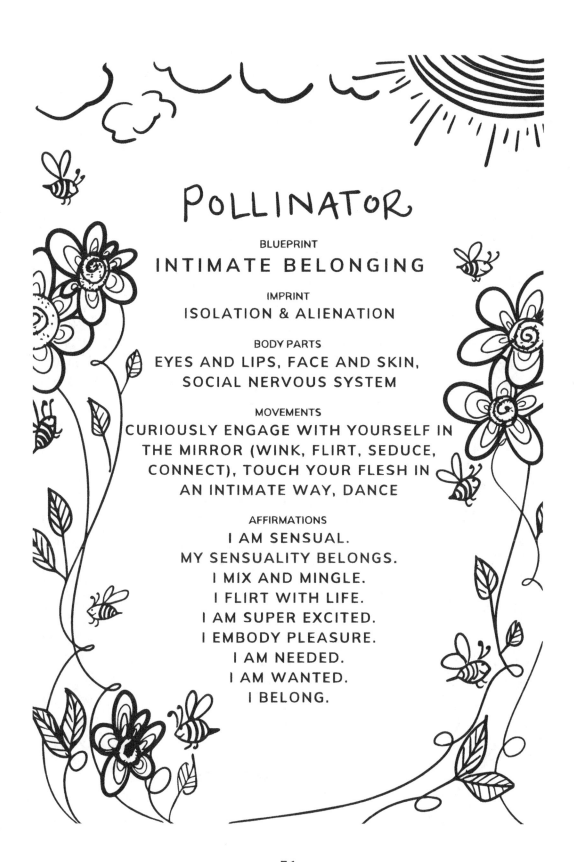

POLLINATOR

BLUEPRINT
INTIMATE BELONGING

IMPRINT
ISOLATION & ALIENATION

BODY PARTS
EYES AND LIPS, FACE AND SKIN, SOCIAL NERVOUS SYSTEM

MOVEMENTS
CURIOUSLY ENGAGE WITH YOURSELF IN THE MIRROR (WINK, FLIRT, SEDUCE, CONNECT), TOUCH YOUR FLESH IN AN INTIMATE WAY, DANCE

AFFIRMATIONS
I AM SENSUAL.
MY SENSUALITY BELONGS.
I MIX AND MINGLE.
I FLIRT WITH LIFE.
I AM SUPER EXCITED.
I EMBODY PLEASURE.
I AM NEEDED.
I AM WANTED.
I BELONG.

SACRED GARDENER

BLUEPRINT
CO-CREATION

IMPRINT
COLONIZATION

BODY PARTS
CROWN, SPINE, BOTTOMS OF FEET

MOVEMENTS
REACH YOUR ARMS UP TO THE SKY, ALLOW YOUR HANDS TO COMB ENERGY DOWN THE FRONT OF YOUR BODY, REPEAT THIS MOTION

AFFIRMATIONS
USE ME MOVE ME
MAKE ME AN INSTRUMENT
FOR THE HIGHEST EXPRESSION OF LOVE,
THE DEEPEST RESONATING TRUTH,
AND THE GREATEST GOOD FOR ALL –
MYSELF INCLUDED
FEED ME, FILL ME,
MAKE ME A VESSEL
FOR THE HIGHEST EXPRESSION OF LOVE,
THE DEEPEST RESONATING TRUTH,
AND THE GREATEST GOOD FOR ALL –
MYSELF INCLUDED
I AM LISTENING
I AM WILLING
I AM DEVOTED
THANK YOU

ReBloom Coherence Practice Digestions

My Soul Seed needs...

It feels so good imagining my Soul Seed receiving...

My Gatekeeper says yes to...

And no to...

My Expressionista feels...

Its true medicine is...

My Sage's truth is...

Integrity would look like...

My Groundskeeper's rhythms include...

It removes, adds, or rearranges...

My Pollinator's most pleasurable excitement is around...

It belongs as...

My Sacred Gardener's guidance is...

Its devotion is...

Remember, you can be guided through the Soul Seed Coherence Practice for free at rebloomtogether.com/coherence.

Chapter 3

Nervous System Essentials

In the coming chapters, you're going to go deeper with the seven ReBloom Archetypes through many personal and professional stories. As you read those anecdotes, you'll be catching references to concepts that relate to the nervous system and physiology, such as "hyper-arousal", "hypo-arousal" or "window of tolerance." These concepts (and many others) are foundational for understanding, working with and healing trauma. Let's ground into these concepts together, now, to set you up for a deeper understanding of post-traumatic growth.

The Many Layers of Humanness

I like to think of humans as akin to the earth. Lusciously layered.

- **The innermost layer:** the Natural Blueprint of Health and Blueprint Essence (most connected to the divine—energy that originates from the core, lineage, and spirit, and permeates someone's entire being)
- **The next layer out:** the nervous system (most connected to the reptilian brain)
- **The layer beyond the nervous system:** the emotional body (most connected to the limbic brain)
- **The outermost layer:** the cognitive mind (most connected to the neocortex)

The outer layers (cognitive mind and emotional body) can influence the inner layers (nervous system and Natural Blueprint of Health), especially the more one develops energetic mind-body awareness through the prefrontal cortex. However, according to neurobiology and leading mind-body therapeutic research, the inner layers more often influence the outer.

The most powerful cognitive healing modalities do not seek to force change from the level of the mind alone. Instead, they utilize the mind as an instrument of co-creation to mediate between what is currently happening and what wishes to happen. Ever try to do an affirmation that feels really out of reach? It's kind of pointless. You just want to vomit. On the other hand, when you can land on a small and doable iterative mindset shift, one that allows for parts of your current mindset to still remain, but also invites more possibility in, an opening happens. Your body relaxes.

I believe in teaching to all four layers of humanness because each client will have layers that are most accessible to them. However, many therapeutic approaches neglect to learn about the inner two layers—the nervous system and the Natural Blueprint of Health—and therefore miss the opportunity to facilitate deeper alchemy with greater safety.

Your Fantastic Nervous System

The nervous system is an intricate part of our human wiring that coordinates sensory information with actions. There are two main branches of the nervous system: central and peripheral. For the purposes of understanding and working with trauma, we want to focus mostly on a subsection of the peripheral nervous system—the autonomic nervous system.

The Autonomic Nervous System is responsible for:

1. **Automatic bodily functions:** digestion, heart rate, respiratory rate, urination, pupil dilation, sexual arousal, hormonal release, metabolism, sleep-wake cycles, tissue repair, and more.
2. **Your embodied trauma responses:** hypersocialization, hypervigilance, fight, flight, freeze, flock, and fornicate.
3. **Social engagement with other people and mammals.**
4. **How your senses perceive and pick up what's around you.**

The autonomic nervous system has three levels: sympathetic, parasympathetic and social. Let's take a glance at all three.

The Sympathetic Nervous System is responsible for:

- Preparing the body for intense physical activity
- Getting up and going!
- Fight or flight
- Increasing blood to the arms and legs
- Increasing heart and breath rate
- Protecting and defending
- Exercise and activity (running, working, etc...)
- Increasing adrenaline

The Parasympathetic Nervous System is responsible for:

- Relaxing the body
- Inhibiting or slowing high-energy functions
- Resting and digesting
- Lowering the heart rate
- Lowering oxygen, lowering metabolism

- Freeze and immobility responses
- Allowing us to go into shock if we're punctured so we don't bleed to death
- Sending us into conservation mode under stress or to renew our physiology

The Social Nervous System is responsible for:

- Self-expression
- Orientation (turning our neck and head to take in the environment)
- Listening
- Speaking
- Calling or asking for help
- Communicating in general
- Love
- The ability to feel empathy and happiness by allowing us to assess another's emotional state and connect with others

All of these functions are part of our miraculous Natural Blueprint of Health, our inherent design that keeps us safe, well, resourced, protected and regulated.

Within our Autonomic Nervous System functions is our capacity to experience and utilize our neuroception—our body's perception of danger and threat. When the body senses a level of danger greater than its capacity to cope, it calls on support from embodied emergency responses (also known as "trauma responses").

Embodied emergency responses are part of the essential health and design of humans. Much like a commercial kitchen is designed to include a fire extinguisher in case an accident happens—humans have a variety of fabulous safety back-ups built into the design of their physiology to be used in the case of both physiological and emotional danger. Let's look at these embodied emergency responses more in-depth, along with their physiological cues, so you can begin to notice when they might be happening for you or your clients.

Embodied Emergency Responses

Hyper-Arousal Responses

Hyper-Arousal, activated via the Sympathetic Nervous System, arises when the body automatically detects that it can win against a real or perceived threat.

Hypersocialization – Acting in a way to appease, over-accommodate, soothe or nurture unsafe behavior in others, in order to mitigate that behavior and therefore, maintain safety.

> *Physiological cues:* hypervigilance, quickened heart rate, over-engaged social nervous system, accommodating voice, anxiety, smiling when upset.

> Think of the act of cooking and cleaning so that your partner has an easier life. Are you cooking from a foundation of love, or a foundation of threat? Can you sense the subtle physiological difference between love and fear motivators?

Hypervigilance – Embodying a state of guarded, heightened alertness, ready to spot and respond to danger in any moment.

> *Physiological cues:* dilated pupils, breathing quickly, restlessness, sleeplessness, high sensitivities to noise, light, or people's expressions or tones of voice, startling easily, overreacting, hostility.

> Think of the act of monitoring a child's every move. Are you doing so perhaps from a foundation of regulated alertness (perhaps in a busy public location), or a foundation of fear (perhaps in a relatively safe environment)?

Fight – Moving *toward* perceived or actual threat with speed, intensity, attack, irritation, frustration, rage, or aggression.

Physiological cues: heat, speed, less mental cognition, trembling, tense muscles, rapid heart rate and breathing, adrenaline, increased strength or immediate awareness of animal instincts.

Flight – Moving *away from* perceived or actual threat with panic, fear, anxiety, worry, or concern.

Physiological cues: heat, speed, less mental cognition, trembling, tense muscles, rapid heart rate and breathing, adrenaline, increased strength, or immediate awareness of animal instincts.

Flock – Banding together in numbers, location and resources, uniting to protect against a common threat.

Physiological cues: longing for connection, urgency to hold others close, quickened instincts to gather (rooted in our limbic instincts to find safety in the pack), hypervigilance about outsiders.

Fornicate – Procreating for the sake of keeping one's specific group alive in the face of threat, extinction, or danger.

Physiological cues: sexual arousal with a strong drive to make babies, grief, quickened heart rate, moving urgently toward others like you.

"The magnolia trees near New Orleans flowered after Katrina. They knew this principle. Death is near, make babies. People called it wacko. However, there's a deep intelligence at work in the wisdom of nature." - Brigit Viksnins

Hypo-Arousal Responses

*Hypo-Arousal, activated via the Parasympathetic Nervous System, arises when the body automatically detects that it **cannot win** against the real or perceived threat.*

Freeze – Experiencing motionlessness, immobility, voicelessness or numbness to what's happening in the body in order to experience less pain (physical or emotional)—otherwise known as dissociation.

Physiological cues: cold, fuzzy vision, cloudy mind, little to no access to words or voice, numbness, decreased heart rate, inability to experience sensation or emotion, heaviness, immobility.

Levels of Freeze:

Deer – A freeze response with a sympathetic (hyper-arousal) tone, in which, beneath apparent stillness, the body is actually ready to bolt. This ready-to-bolt quality can show up to mobilize as thawing from freeze begins.

Owl (camouflage) – Blending in, flying under the radar, making oneself seem invisible, "if you can't see or sense me, you can't hurt me."

Possum (immobility) – "Playing dead," unconsciousness, dissociation, leaving one's body, painlessness, little to no experience of sensations.

Deep Freeze – When hyperarousal and sympathetic nervous system responses are so exhausted due to prolonged exposure to violation or threat, one can enter into a prolonged state of "deep freeze" on one or many levels of being (body, heart, sexuality, drive, immune system, etc.). This can create an experience of some part of you being totally "gone," "offline," "flimsy," "disappeared," "tonically immobile" or "not home," as my teacher Brigit describes it.

Chronic Pain, Fatigue or Illness – Prolonged experiences of pain, fatigue or illness, far past the usual length of such occurrences, with seemingly hard to detect or hard to heal sources.[4]

---

[4] *If you or a client are dealing with chronic pain and sense it may be trauma related, I suggest reading the short, illustrated book* Pain is Really Strange *by Steve Haines. It demystifies chronic pain in a very helpful way.*

Depression – Experiencing a persistently "turned off" mood, loss of interest in activities, feelings of grief, alienation and hopelessness.

Physiological cues: decreased heart rate, blood pressure, temperature, muscle tone, facial expression, sex drive, eye contact, awareness of the human voice, social behavior and immune responses.

Shame – Feelings of embarrassment, remorse or regret that motivate you to stop certain unwanted behaviors.

Physiological cues: feeling bound, frozen, stuck, wordless, pit in the stomach, foggy brain, shrinking, heart racing, sweating, desire to hide.

Window of Tolerance

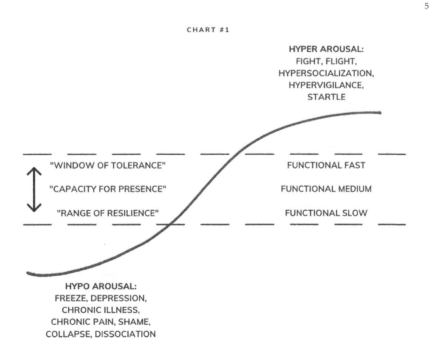

CHART #1

HYPER AROUSAL:
FIGHT, FLIGHT,
HYPERSOCIALIZATION,
HYPERVIGILANCE,
STARTLE

"WINDOW OF TOLERANCE"   FUNCTIONAL FAST

"CAPACITY FOR PRESENCE"   FUNCTIONAL MEDIUM

"RANGE OF RESILIENCE"   FUNCTIONAL SLOW

HYPO AROUSAL:
FREEZE, DEPRESSION,
CHRONIC ILLNESS,
CHRONIC PAIN, SHAME,
COLLAPSE, DISSOCIATION

[5] *Image originally learned from Brigit Viksnins Alchemical Alignment training.*

The Window of Tolerance, a term coined by Dr. Dan Siegel, is the physiological state within which you can be present to the ebbs and flows, ups and downs and intense challenges and joys of human experience—without looping in hyper- or hypo-arousal.

Within the Window of Tolerance (pictured in Chart #1), you still experience hurt, anger, pain, exhaustion, sadness, shut down, difficulty, excitement, love and lust (functional fast, medium and slow versions), but your nervous system is able to stay more-or-less regulated. Your neocortex and limbic brain stay "online." With emotional and cognitive brain functions still working, you're able to be fully present to your feelings, integrate information, make both embodied and higher-level decisions, perceive accurate levels of threat and experience intensity with a level of resourceful capacity. You can embody self-care and relational regard for others simultaneously. I've heard my teacher Brigit also refer to the window as a "range of resilience." which has a bit more ring to it!

The goal of life isn't to always stay within your window or range, but to cultivate greater capacity to bounce back more quickly when you fall out of it. Take Chart #2, for example.

CHART #2

[6]

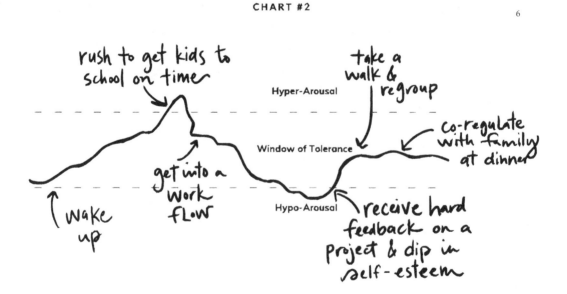

[6] *Image originally learned from Brigit Viksnins Alchemical Alignment training.*

When someone experiences acute or chronic overwhelm, difficulty, violence or trauma, it can hinder their capacity to stay within their Window of Tolerance. They can more easily shoot up into hyper-arousal and loop there—or drop down into hypo-arousal and stall out there. (See Chart #3.) This is one of the key symptoms of being stuck under a trauma spell: difficulty responding to the ups and downs of life with resilience, neutrality, creativity or resourcefulness.

CHART #3

[7]

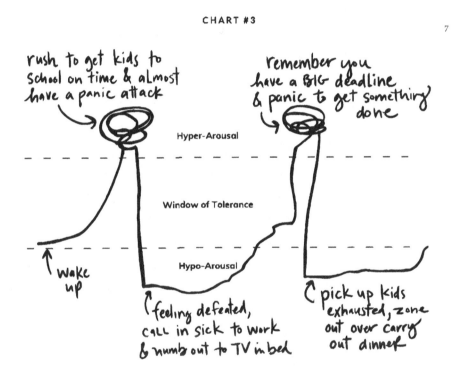

Trauma to Turn On

How do we grow from quick subconscious trauma responses into a regulated sense of creative agency, so that we can choose what feels good more often? In moments when we're experiencing physical or emotional pain or distress—including any of the above-mentioned trauma responses—in essence, our Blueprint is crying to come back online.

[7] *Image originally learned from Brigit Viksnins Alchemical Alignment training.*

The Blueprint is bigger than the brokenness. Always. It's our origins, no matter what we go through. We always eventually return to the Blueprint, even if it takes multiple generations or lifetimes. But that doesn't mean it's always easy to access or amplify.

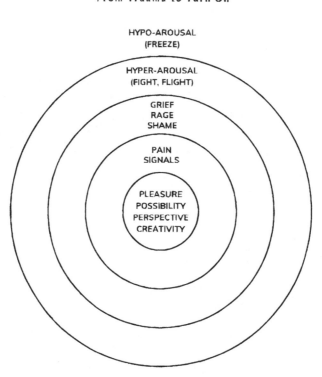

CHART #4
From Trauma to Turn On

HYPO-AROUSAL
(FREEZE)

HYPER-AROUSAL
(FIGHT, FLIGHT)

GRIEF
RAGE
SHAME

PAIN
SIGNALS

PLEASURE
POSSIBILITY
PERSPECTIVE
CREATIVITY

Chart #4, From Trauma to Turn On, shows five concentric circles of experience. In the center, there's your Natural Blueprint of Health—your ability to feel pleasure, gratitude, possibility, hope, wellness. In this place, you are resourced with creativity, care and a glimmering zest for life.

Surrounding the Blueprint, there's pain. Pain both alerts when difficulty is happening and protects from difficulty increasing by sending signals to the brain to call in physical or emotional back-ups. Pain can be emotional, physical, energetic, or mental.

Surrounding the pain, there are the causes of pain—experiences that create emotions of grief, rage or shame. When we have the ability to feel, process and respond to these causes of pain, seeing and sensing our agency to shift reality, perhaps because the cause of pain isn't too big to bear, then our alertness subsides, our pain soothes, our defenses modulate, and access to the experience of our Blueprint comes back online.

However, when the causes of pain are too intense, violent, overwhelming, or ongoing, this is when we move into either hyper- or hypo-arousal. Unfortunately, this is not a cognitive process. It's an automatic, embodied, nervous system response, which is why nervous system healing is so essential. Depending on whether or not our body senses it can win against the threat or violation, our system will first check to see if hyper-responses (fight or flight) could work; if not, it opts for freeze. All of this happens in a split second, without any rational reasoning.

In order to rebloom from trauma to turn on, there's a gentle, sensitive *reverse order of operations* the body tends to go through.

1. Thawing what's frozen (layers of immobilization, depression, toxic shame).
2. Discharging the stored emergency energies of fight, flight, panic, or hypervigilance.
3. Experiencing empowered choice, agency, care, and compassion surrounding the original cause of pain, which allows for a newfound sense of safety, self-trust and trust in others.
4. Giving plenty of time for the pain to release, unwind and renew into a transformed sense of identity, possibility, power, creativity, connection, narrative, self-perception, and perspective on life.

For our clients' bodies and souls to go through a process like this, they must sense that there's enough compassion, consistency, care, presence, patience, and unconditional positive regard in the shared relational space. Otherwise, it might feel like too large a risk with not enough safety to open to the pains of the past. It also helps to have context about what's going on below the surface, so there can be a level of informed consent or mental orientation that facilitates trust.

Most cognitive models of change or healing focus primarily on the fourth and final step of transformation—the perspective shift. But when we work with the nervous system, we don't need to hyper-focus on mindset. Rather, mindset transformation happens as a naturally flowering emergence of health. We forgive, without forcing it, because our bodies and souls feel different. We maybe (not always, but sometimes) feel grateful for the weird, fucked-up journey our lives took us on—not as a bypass, but because a sense of purpose and capacity has grown out of the long and arduous path. We experience a renewed sense of identity— not because we merely said our positive affirmations, but because we also acted differently in moments of intimacy. We feel hopeful—not because the world is free from violence or instability, but because we are radically connected to newfound inner resources and physiological resilience; we've realigned to Life's Blueprint, and we sense we can be part of a grand realignment among all living things.

Embodied Coherence is all about growing from trauma to turn on—below our minds, in the deepest wiring of our cells and souls. As we come back into our Natural Blueprint of Health, our sense of possibility, creativity, resiliency and trust increases. We renew our physiological superpowers to respond to accurate threat and revel in safe and sensual joy.

Chapter 4

Soul Seed

From Neglect to Worthiness & Receptivity

The Blueprint

Soul Seed's journey begins in a womb of unlimited nourishment for the first nine months of their becoming. Then, when they're born, the umbilical cord is cut, and immediately an instinct takes hold: they cry. They cry for the nourishment they still need, even though they've matured past the womb, even though they're now more advanced. They're empowered with a voice to let everyone know when they're hungry for food, attention, nuzzling or rest.

Imagine sweet little Soul Seed immersed in a community of care and family support, with a safe and nourishing home. Imagine their caregivers responding to their calls, meeting their expressions, holding them close. Imagine them embedded in healthy rhythms of feeding and sleeping, stillness and play, nurture and nature, stable loving predictability. Imagine them growing the felt-sense knowing that they matter, *they really matter*.

Like an actual seed, Soul Seed (perhaps fallen from the stars, a cosmos of ancestors) gets planted in a dark, warm womb, and there, they learn the first essential skill of being human: receptivity. In this primal gestation space, there's nothing Soul Seed needs to do—nothing they *can* do—but depend on their biological mother for nourishment.

Soul Seed is a combination of possibility plus need—potentiality plus requirements for sprouting. When Soul Seed's needs get met, they grow, expand and actualize. But their needs don't disappear or diminish as their dreams begin to manifest. In fact, as Soul Seed grows bigger and truer, their needs often shift and increase. Throughout your life, your Soul Seed has one core directive: to receive your deepest needs so that the glorious possibilities gestating within your DNA can blossom, and the whole ecosystem can revel in your gifts.

When we experience developmental or ongoing neglect, our relationship to needing and the vulnerability of asking that's often required for receiving, can feel as dangerous as the actual consequence of not asking—which is starving. Walled off with invulnerable self-sufficiency, we take care of everything we need all alone. Exhausted by the pressure to perform this endeavor, we lower our standards of what we need, dim the wildness of our desires, or seek them from deviant, half-fulfilling sources.

Our human family has a Collective Soul Seed as well—a not-yet-fully formed wild, thriving genius—that has just as many needs as we do individually. If we look at the ways our human family has neglected to care for our Collective Soul Seed's needs, it's no wonder that there's a collective fear keeping us underground and small, walled off and enclosed, silent and timid in the face of systemic neglect, displacement and negligence. Indeed, the world can look bleak on many days in many ways. It's tempting to throw in the towel on needing anything at all.

But the cry of your Soul Seed—our Collective one, too—is stubbornly wise. If we can remember to feel for what we really need in order to thrive…If we can hold on to our capacity to cry—the fundamental physiology of longing…If we can receive the way life meets us…we can know with irreverent hope that the world is not a black hole of hopelessness after all, but a tremendous canvas of opportunities to care.

Soul Seed hungers—unapologetically, instinctually, voraciously, and mercilessly. Because they feel from an instinctual, momentous power that they must LIVE. They must grow. They must become. They must bloom upwards toward that miraculous sun and be a part of something—truly part of something—so sublime and redemptive that it cannot be named, much like the ineffable Source from which they came.

Soul Seed at a Glance

Body Connection: Umbilicus, Stomach, Gut

Your umbilicus is the place through which you first receive all you need from your biological mother's body, inside her womb. It's the part of you that embodies *inherent* receptivity, nourishment and a sense that the world can provide for your hunger.

When you're born and the umbilical cord is cut, you're disconnected from that original source, and are required to call out for your hunger to be fed. At this stage in the game, your caregivers help normalize and regulate your hunger by responding to your needs with attuned recognition and responsiveness. The more you're responded to in infancy and early development—both physically and emotionally—the more you grow agency around speaking and receiving your needs. Feelings of later-in-life worthiness directly relate to experiences of receiving what you need from others developmentally.

Natural Blueprint of Health: Worthiness and Receptivity

You have an inherent sense that your core needs and identity deserve to be met and matched, honored and loved, seen and known, guided and tended to. You know what you need in order to experience health with yourself and others. You trust at your core that you are worthy of love, care, safety and belonging. You have the capacity to sense your needs, speak your needs, and receive your needs— both in relational settings and on your own. When help, support or nourishment arrives, you can let it in, sense it filling you up, truly receive it.

Traumatic Imprint: Neglect

You endure the experience of being ignored, untended to, abandoned, unfed, unseen, unheard, unmet, unguided, stranded, starved, excluded, not given empathy, unloved, untouched or left alone. Your guardians are too busy, distracted, absent, or otherwise out of the picture.

Neglect can be *physical*—not having your needs met for food, shelter, touch, supervision, or presence.

Neglect can be *emotional*—not having your needs met for being seen, known, loved, praised, guided, supported, helped, or acknowledged.

Note: many people have experienced levels of developmental *emotional* neglect, but don't identify with having experienced neglect because they had all their *physical* needs cared for. *Emotional* neglect is real and valid and can create big Soul Seed imprints.

Hyper-Response to Neglect: Deviance

- Going outside the bounds of the "safe family unit" to get your core needs met, even if the way they get met is unhealthy
- Fear of aloneness or abandonment that moves someone into dysregulated action
- Escaping into anything that will "meet" them:
  - Taboo relationships or affairs
  - Food addiction
  - Sex, porn or love addiction
  - Substance addictions
  - Video game addictions
  - Workaholism

When someone's embodying Deviance, it can often feel threatening to their system to go without their needs getting met so they take it upon themselves to get them met via unsafe, unhealthy or degenerative outlets. Strong reasoning, excusing, hiding or lying often accompanies Deviance as a way of preserving the temporary relief from the deep pain of neglect and disconnection.

Common fears and inner dialogues include:

- "I know he's married, but he loves me like no one ever has before."
- "I know it's not the healthiest coping mechanism, but I really need it."
- "There's actually nothing wrong in this situation…"
- "I'm just really into _____." (whatever the escape is)
- "No one can know about my secret escape."
- "No, I didn't drink anything tonight! What are you talking about?"

Hyper-Response to Neglect: Rigid Self-Reliance

- Meeting all your needs yourself
- Not trusting others capacity to show up for you
- Fear of abandonment, disappointment, being hurt or being let down
- Taking on more than your share—in your own life and in relationships (hyper-care-taking)
- Not reaching out for support or depending on others
- Fear of needing others—even in healthy ways
- Fear of vulnerability
- Over-holding

When someone's embodying Rigid Self-Reliance, it can often feel threatening to their system to trust others. They will find ways to feel like they have everything they need, so long as they don't have to withstand the vulnerability of needing others.

Common fears and inner-dialogues include:
- "People always let me down anyway."
- "No one can do it as well as I do."
- "Why should I extend trust to someone else, if I can just do it myself?"
- "I'm always the one people come to when they need something."

- "Who can I trust to take care of ME?"
- "I'm so exhausted from taking care of everything, but there's no one else who can or will."

Hypo-Response to Neglect: Self-Denial

- Neglecting the very parts of yourself that've been neglected by others
- Not knowing your needs or your core self/identity
- Having a secret sense that you don't really matter
- Feeling afraid of yourself or your individuality
- Feeling like your needs are too much and too big to care for
- Feeling afraid of centering your needs and experiences
- Staying in dissatisfying relationships with self, others and work

When someone's embodying Self-Denial, it can often feel threatening to their system to even *imagine* tuning into their own needs. Often, they have difficulties *sensing* their needs at all, let alone asking for and receiving them.

Common fears and inner dialogues include:

- "People will think I'm selfish if I put myself first."
- "I'm not designed to feel, ask for and receive my needs! It feels way more comfortable to center other people's needs, care-take, or dim my life-force and need nothing at all."
- "I'll lose the relationships I love if I start having needs."
- "I just don't know what I need! I'm too numb to do this. And I feel really ashamed about that."
- "Am I really worthy of having my needs met? I doubt anyone would care enough to meet me."
- "I'll be way too much."
- "If I don't play the role everyone knows me as, how will I belong?"

The very root of mattering

I was sitting on the couch with my good friend Leo, in terrible back pain. I'd neglected to do anything—anything at all—about my immobilizing pain for six whole months. As if it were an invisible, impenetrable burden I just had to live with for the rest of time, I'd been soldiering on, both hyper self-sufficient and denying my need to feel better. But on this sunny afternoon, I hit an all-time low.

Leo was a mischievous mystic of sorts, full of care and curiosity.

"Rach, I'm worried about you. Can we do an exercise?" he asked with loving concern.

"Sure," I said in desperate surrender.

He took the lead.

"Open up your journal, and without talking, write the answer to this question at the top of your page: If this pattern you're in—if it were the title of a chapter, what would it be?"

Instantly, the words came to me, but frozen, I could barely write them down. Until I did.

I don't matter, I wrote.

When my pen stopped, he gently asked if I wanted to read it aloud to him.

"Not really," I replied, a haze coming over me. "But I'll let you read it," I whispered, handing him the journal.

"Mmmm. *I don't matter.*" He paused, nodding with loving compassion, then started to ask a follow-up question. I stopped him with a gentle hand to his wrist, curled into a ball on the couch, and cried.

Still this? I thought, ashamed and silent, knowing just how many times I'd found worthlessness at the bottom of my barrel of wounds. *Still this,* I sighed.

I sat up and looked at Leo with dread.

"Is this showing up in other places of your life?" he asked.

"Of course," I replied, a bit smug, but soft.

Of course, indeed. I'd been ignoring so many important things in my life under the premise that I didn't matter. It was a very familiar pattern to me.

One thing I see in so many of my clients is this same imprint of not mattering. An imprint that forms at a very young age and places itself in the most reptilian part of the brain. An imprint that's cooked into the foundation of our culture and becomes the subconscious message we eat for GMO breakfast. An imprint that now asks the most earnest, innocent question: *If I mattered, why would they have used me, abused me, ignored me, hurt me, contorted me, forced me, left me, shamed me?*

And sometimes, these imprints of not mattering can sink into the very way we do…almost everything. Without us even realizing it.[8]

I don't matter, so I'll ignore the pain in my back until it's so bad that I can't move. I don't matter, so I'll force myself to stay in a job that sucks my soul. I don't matter, so I won't eat lunch. I'll just work straight through, even though I know I'll be cranky later from skipping a meal. I don't matter, so I won't prioritize spending time with friends or in nature. I don't matter, so I'll put others' needs above my own. I don't matter, so I'll have no boundaries. I don't matter, so I won't receive help. I mean, really, I could keep going for pages.

I don't matter, so I'll have sex or relationships with people who don't really turn me on or feed my heart. I don't matter, so I'll check my phone while driving. I don't matter, so I'll never get tested for STDs, nor insist on safe sex practices.

I don't matter, so I'll settle. I don't matter, so I'll have no hope for my life or my future. I don't matter, so I'll hide from my song, my dance, my writing, my passion. You see where this is going.

There's a quiet, subconscious whisper that can run our lives if we have developmental histories of not mattering, when our parents or caregivers didn't give us what we needed, when our cries were ignored, our hunger unfed. *Who*

---

[8] *For more on developmental trauma, check out Nurturing Resilience by Katy Kain and Steve Turrell.*

cares that it hurts, that I'm suffering, that this isn't good for me in the long run? I'm not what matters most.

I know how deep this feeling of not mattering can run, and how it can control and direct our lives in an invisible way. I know how long it can take to transform the pattern. And I know the way the unreasonable difficulty of it can feel so shameful and embarrassing.

*Why do I suck so hardcore at this? I should be further along by now. I feel worthless and stupid that I can't do this. I know I matter **intellectually**. Why don't my choices reflect that outwardly? I'm pathetic.*

Here's the thing: sometimes when we have developmental histories of neglect, big or small, dramatic or unintentional, we can develop faulty "safety meters" in our bodies. As tiny humans, we rely on co-regulation with our caregivers to let us know when we're in danger and when we're not, when to sleep and when to stay awake, when to eat and when to rest. This consistent co-regulation allows us to grow our capacity for self-regulation—for sensing and discerning on our own the difference between what's safe and what's dangerous, what's healthy, and what's not.

If we don't get as much co-regulation as we need developmentally, then later in life we might have difficulty caring for ourselves, and struggle with going hypo around our needs. We might also become *obsessive* about caring for ourselves, not trusting anyone to care for us at all (hyper self-reliance). Or, we might become deviant, getting our needs "met" but in unhealthy places like affairs, unsafe sex, or food addictions.

As adults, we still seek what we never got as children. And we seek these things at the level of the body—the primal place that still craves the most basic care. I've found that for adults, the drive to compensate for neglect shows up most in sex and food. When we subconsciously sense we can receive meaningful worthiness from others, we often turn to sex. When we subconsciously fear there's no one who can give us the physical love, care, sensuality, or touch that we need, we often turn to food.

Many people feel a bit overwhelmed upon seeing these things spelled out in plain language. Remember that these later-life habits are often non-cognitive. Developmental attachment histories rear and steer so much of our adult lives from the background. The good news is, with support and intention, care and courage, we can relearn co-regulation and self-regulation.

Back on the couch with Leo, my shame was beginning to settle, and I felt ready to see what was possible.

"Rach, I'm curious if you can remember a time when you felt like your body mattered, not just intellectually, but viscerally."

In that moment I drew a bit of a blank. I looked up at him, shy and sad.

"Come here," he said, and he pulled me into his arms. He didn't say anything at all, just held me there for a good long while.

"I don't think I can let it in," I whispered with a bit of tender honesty.

"Let what in?" he asked.

"The care," I said back.

"What do you think it would take?" he wondered out loud.

"I don't know exactly, but I can feel in my chest like I'm holding something in."

"Maybe whatever you're holding doesn't want to come out. And maybe that's okay?"

I didn't say anything. We didn't push or strain. We just sat there in the sad, beautiful truth, until warm tears started to stream down my face, the ache in my chest started to soften, and I began to remember things—sweet things, not scary things. The scent of my grandmother's skin. The smell of autumn in Maryland, my body laid atop a huge pile of fallen leaves. The softness of my mother's breasts.

"I don't know if this is what it feels like to matter," I whispered, "but I think I can let it in..."

The Cycle of Regulation

When Tina came to me, she was unable to let anyone know when she was struggling or needing support—not even her closest friends or family. She was also putting tremendous pressure on herself to perform perfectly around matters of work and money. I had a hunch we were dealing with a Soul Seed difficulty.

Tina grew up with abject levels of parental neglect and violence from her alcoholic father. So used to people not being safe, she walled herself off from intimacy, and took care of her every last need on her own. It didn't dawn on her how much she was missing a wide base of community care, intimate friends or partnership even, until she found herself alone in a hospital bed on Christmas with a ruptured spleen and no one she felt comfortable calling, afraid to disturb everyone else's holiday.

She found me after that Christmas, thinking she needed healing around a singular incident of sexual trauma she'd experienced in college. Maybe that was the reason she was so afraid of men, she thought. While that experience *did* impact her, we discovered together that her challenge went much deeper.

Many of your clients may present in similar ways, coming to you for support around something acute, when the full picture of their path is more complex. Tina was embodying both the hyper and hypo expressions of neglect; denying her needs for intimate care and connection, while simultaneously soldiering through her whole heavy load all alone.

The both/and of hyper and hypo responses to complex challenges is common and often keeps our clients from seeing the trap they're running. They may be thinking, "I don't need anyone—I'm awesome at taking care of myself," while internalizing all their anxiety as an unrelated problem.

Like Tina, my clients who are struggling with feeding the needs of their Soul Seeds rarely know it, and usually don't like to face it. When I share with them the archetypes, they want to go straight to the Expressionista or Pollinator, feeling almost embarrassed or ashamed that a space needs to be made for their youngest selves—for their most basic, primary neediness.

The truth is, it's tender to go straight to the core—the place where our patterns are most calcified, quiet with rigidity, secretly holding on for dear life. Your Soul Seed is the most vulnerable, dependent archetype of them all, and when you work with it, you're coming into intimate contact with the oldest patterns of body, psyche and energy system. Attachment wounds, the formation of a narrative around our lovability and even our relationship to money, food and substances all connect to the Soul Seed. To bring these close-in patterns into the light, even with gentle compassionate care, can feel like a tremendous undressing of the private ways we feed or starve our feral hungers.

This is why as guides, when we're working with the Soul Seed, it's important to move with extra care, extra titration of pace, as well as extra trust in your client's Natural Blueprint of worthiness and receptivity. Remember—the Soul Seed is also connected to infinite cosmic potential, wisdom and creativity. If you forget your client's wholeness, the great mysterious power of both their spirit and their flesh, you'll short-circuit their opportunity to reawaken it.

When working with someone like Tina who experienced levels of developmental neglect, co-regulation is often a necessary step toward cultivating capacity for self-regulation, healing and thriving. Beyond co-regulation, community-regulation and nature-regulation are also tremendously helpful.

Co-Regulation is a term originally fostered in attachment parenting, and refers to the process by which the child or dependent learns how to regulate emotional states due to the parent or caregiver meeting their stress with care, compassion, and consistency. The caregiver also helps the child accurately perceive danger, threat, need, and risk by reinforcing actual threat, (*Yes, it's dangerous when the dog tries to bite you and your fear is warranted*) and assuaging non-threat (*Yes, the dog is big, but*

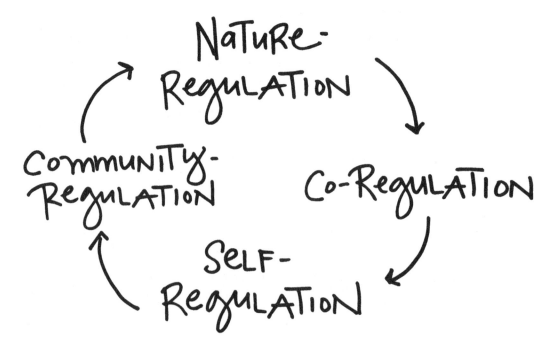

it's kind, calm, sweet and elderly—you don't need to be scared. It's okay. I'm right here).[9] When someone's Soul Seed was not tended to developmentally—particularly in their first six weeks of life, but even up until three or four years old—the need for a steady outside source with whom they can practice co-regulation may be higher.

As coaches, it's helpful to know when your client is bringing early childhood trauma into your relationship. It's also helpful to discern for yourself if attachment repair work is something you have capacity, qualification, or passion around serving. The need for predictable, consistent care is often higher when a client has a history of developmental neglect.

Self-Regulation describes the capacity to come down from high stress emotional states, self-soothe in fear, and awaken rational thinking around perceived danger or threat. It's the ability to return to a window of presence even amidst the intensities of life. As your client comes to expect that difficulty can be soothed due to the positive imprints of co-regulation, their capacity to self-regulate after challenge or amidst stress often increases. They trust that others will be there for them if they're in need, and this, in turn, empowers greater independent resiliency.

Nature-Regulation is when we go to the wilderness (in reality or in our imaginations) to orient, synchronize, and attune with the organic rhythms and abundance of Earth. When we're overwhelmed with difficulty or the unpredictability or unrelenting pain of relationships or systems, we might connect with all that's stable, solid, slow or steady in nature. We might witness the river flow and find the parts of us that have been brittle or harsh softening around the edges of our lives. We might feel the fertile ground of fallen leaves beneath our bare feet and sense all the ways life grows in and from us, even as some things die or shed, even as seasons, relationships, and realities change, even as challenge persists.

We might watch the sun dip below the ocean and the stars rise in the sky and remember just how predictable and ancient, powerful and steady the constellations, solar system, galaxies, and stardust are.

---

[9] *Concept developed from Nurturing Resilience by Steve Terrell and Kathy Kain.*

Community-Regulation is when we lean into sustained social networks for support, celebration and sense of self inside the whole. Maybe you fall madly in love and then a year later experience the worst break up of your life, but through it all, your new moon and full moon sister circle is there: witnessing, celebrating, grieving with, consoling, and believing in you. Maybe no matter what you're going through—highs or lows—you always show up to Sunday ecstatic dance, meeting yourself in movement, letting community meet you exactly where you are. Maybe you host Shabbat dinners. Maybe you sing praise in a community choir. Maybe you look forward to your weekly martial arts class. Whatever it is—community regulation is when you have a people and place who know you and care about you, who you can lean on through difficulty, share great successes with, be seen and known, and formed through the fire together.

Co-Regulation is not Codependency

When we're working with clients who are struggling in big ways, the impulse to care-take rather than empower can be a slippery slope. Let's look at some terms to help anchor into a clear distinction between healthy and less healthy professional boundaries.

Codependency is when one person takes responsibility for another's difficulties or emotional experiences, in ways that block the other from the opportunity to rise into their own growth, resiliency or resourcefulness—and does so in a chronically disempowering way. Codependency is a means of subconsciously controlling uncomfortable realities. As coaches, codependency might look like trying to fix your clients' challenges for them or taking responsibility for being their primary emotional support, thus preventing them from cultivating the relationships or community they need in their life.

Often, codependency is an adaptive attempt to not abandon each other in our places of need, when the systems or structures of our world are less often built for ongoing community care. The hyper- and hypo-responses to personal and cultural neglect are not inherently bad or wrong. They are wise unconscious defense mechanisms that often work and serve in short term ways. But when utilized for too long, they can become syndromal.

As quality coaches and guides, our job isn't to save our clients. It's to help remind them of the abundant opportunities for entry into regulation and coherent relationships.

Empowered care is when you can empathize with your clients' challenges, while also anchoring into their wholeness. It's when you can help them problem-solve without taking on their problems as your own. It's when you can be present with them in their difficulty, without merging to their difficulty. It's when you can contextualize the ways they don't have enough structural support (because our systems strip so many of us of the kind of care we need) and help them imagine or commit to creative forward motion.

Can you offer radical care without taking on the position of savior?

I believe the more coaches can look critically at the ways culture has failed so many of us, the more we can include culture-making in our healing modality, encouraging our clients to view their difficulties not just as personal problems with personal solutions, but community problems with community solutions. This is why offering groups, encouraging non-monetary community care within our healing offerings, as well as encouraging our clients to join local community groups is critical to deep, sustained healing of attachment needs.

How to know when your client needs Soul Seed support

The Soul Seed is the archetype where everything begins and the foundation upon which everything else is built.

- Can your clients feel the needs of their body and soul—in sex, love, work, relationships, or negotiations?
- Can they open to their needs, with clear requests and receptivity, trusting that asking or reaching out will lead to eventual fulfillment?
- Can they let others meet them, let love and care all the way in?
- Can they do these things—feel their needs, ask for their needs to be met, and receive what they need—in the most tender and intimate territories of their lives?

These are the muscles of a healthy Soul Seed. No matter how clever your clients are, when they have histories of developmental neglect—parents ignoring their spiritual, emotional, sensitive, intuitive, or creative gifts, going without food, supervision or some level of consistent care—their ability to feel, share, and receive their needs can freeze over or twist into deviance or hyper self-sufficient perfectionism.

The good and bad news is this: when your clients are having trouble attuning to and meeting their needs, Soul Seed will often find secret ways to cry out by presenting sneaky circumstances that require a more specific type of attention. A pinpointed illness, a recurrent emergency, an infuriating creative block, a relationship disaster, a financial collapse—something will occur in their life that will require them to meet themselves more fully, with more attention and care. Like Tina, they may end up in the hospital on Christmas with no one to call and finally realize they can't hold it all. Like me, they may end up at the end of their rope on the couch with a friend, praying they can let themselves receive love, care and tenderness.

When a state of holy, harrowing neediness is reached (in your clients' lives or your own), it's a good time to get curious about the age or identity that's crying out. Usually, the ages of self that we're most afraid to look at, listen to or commune with, are the ages of self that have been most deeply hurt, abandoned, or neglected. We often feel shame, avoidance, anger, or grief in relationship to these ages. And these ages of self that we tend avoid are usually the ones running our lives from the shadows.

When working with women or femme-identifying folks, I call this part of ourselves our Secret Bad Girl,[10] but the concept applies to all genders. Central to resolving the trauma of neglect is calling this abandoned part of ourselves home to the fertile soil where she can rediscover her innocent, fragrant nature, her gorgeous worthwhile needs, her inherent goodness—without shame or abuse.

We call home the hungry, tired, sexual, sensual, emotional, sensitive, brilliant, grieving, or wildly creative parts. We make sure she knows she belongs. She can

---

[10] You can find my first book, Secret Bad Girl, at rebloomtogether.com/secretbadgirl

root here. She's allowed to grow and blossom and thrive. We'll tend to her, care for her, weed, and water and nourish her soil so she can bare her beautiful fruit. When our Secret Bad Girl is welcomed back into the care of our inner adult, not only does she feel safer, but so does our adult self.

Secret Bad Girl Soul Seed Support

When I first told Tina about the possibility of calling home her Secret Bad Girl—re-parenting her most neglected inner-kid—she wept with shame. She was embarrassed that her young survival strategies of not needing anything at all, of taking care of everything on her own, hadn't worked as well as she thought they had. In true dysregulated Soul Seed fashion, she blamed herself for all the ways her family hadn't met her needs. *Maybe it's me. Maybe I wasn't doing things right, wasn't that worthy.*

As a guide for brave souls in these times, awed by their courage and vulnerability, my usual response is a welling of tears. I can't help it. There's a beloved before me who doesn't quite see how much she matters, how much her medicine was always meant to be tended to and developed into something phenomenal and robust, full of trust and greatness.

That's not something they'll teach you at most coaching or trauma resolution training programs—to tear up on behalf of your clients, to fall in love with their wholeness, their worthiness, the phenomenon of their potential. It's not something I can teach you either. But I can plant the idea that if you want to change someone's life forever, love them from the very seed of their soul to their most tender sprout—from their wildest, wisest bloom to the weeds that try to ravish their roots, from their medicine to their poison, from their highest visions to their crippling self-doubt. Love yourself in that way, too, and you'll begin to experience what transformation is all about—the possibility of your trauma alchemizing and your soul embodying in utter, glorious surrender, from head-to-toe.

Tina looked up at me, her chest opening, her eyes empathizing with mine that were empathizing with hers. Entranced by the mirror neurons of care, we sat there and let something deep inside her change.

"Seeing you truly care about me is making me realize that I'm worthy," she whispered shyly.

"Beyond worthy," I whispered back, still teary.

"Thank you."

"You're welcome."

We sat quietly in that soft space for a while until she shot over a feisty smile, like a child ready to play.

"So what were you going to say about the Secret Bad Girl practice? I think I wanna do it!"

"Okay!," I replied, matching her aliveness. "Fair warning, though. This might not be the most fun practice. Let me tell you about it first."

"Sounds good."

"Basically, there's an age or stage from your past that you're most afraid or ashamed of, most avoidant of or dissociated from...because something hard as hell was happening during that time. The idea of this practice is to come into intimate contact with that age in you, then to begin understanding and meeting her most unmet needs. Still something you want to do?"

"Oooof," she replied. "That sounds scary."

"Tell me about it," I nodded back. "The first time I did this practice, it was pretty emotional."

"Ohh, will you tell me about it?" she asked from a young part inside.

"Sure," I replied. "I was about to go on my Secret Bad Girl book tour, and I was going through a box at my parents' house, when I found a photo of my 13-year-old self. The 13-year-old who'd experienced some not-great things," I said with a sideways frown.

"I'm so sorry," she nodded. "Thanks," I nodded back.

"The thing is, in the photo I was in a tight black dress, full makeup on my face, seductively gazing into the camera. I was sexual. Lusty. Desirous. And that terrified me. Immediately, my heart dropped to my gut. Even though I'd written a whole damn memoir about what happened to this girl, I was still afraid of her. Afraid she'd lead me right into the mouth of a lion on this book tour. Afraid I couldn't trust her. Afraid she was gonna get me into trouble again."

"Damn. So what'd you do?!" Tina asked.

"I decided to get curious about that girl. I decided to consider that maybe nothing was flawed or fucked up about her, but possibly…probably…she just needed some things she wasn't getting. And all of that unmet needing was part of what got her into trouble in the first place."

"Damn."

"Uh huh. So with that picture in hand, I looked into the eyes of that girl and asked her…what do you need the most?"

"Then I got out a piece of paper, wrote that question in the center, scribbled a brainstorm bubble around it, and began mapping all the things she needed."

"Finally, I thought, what if I focus on just 10 of these things for the next 40 days? Just read myself a little daily vow and see what happens?"

"And that was the beginning of calling home my Secret Bad Girl."

"Wow…so what ended up happening?"

"Well, I thought that re-parenting my Secret Bad Girl was gonna mean keeping everything in my life suuuuper PG, extra safe, and maybe even kinda boring ('cause the things she wanted and needed were the sweetest, most innocent ones on the list). But the reality was far more exciting!"

"I ended up having the BEST tour. I had adventures with strangers. I felt fully alive and safe in my self-expression. I stayed out late. I fed myself awesome foods."

"By acknowledging the essence of my Secret Bad Girl and taking care of her, by listening to and getting curious about the parts of my Soul Seed that were most hurt, scary-to-me, and repressed, I re-established trust in my whole system. When my inner-kid felt safe, my adult did, too. The things that woulda triggered me before? Way simpler. The things I woulda veered away from out of fear? I was able to walk toward them. It was as if by taking care of my inner-kid, my adult got to play full out."

"I want that," Tina said with a bit of eager courage.

"Great."

And then, I invited her to close her eyes, remember an age from her childhood or adolescence that felt shameful, embarrassing, scary, or hard…a time that she'd rather turn away from, hide in the closet, or erase from her memory. I asked her to do so with tender care, and to pause if it ever felt like too much.

"Paint a picture of this age and stage," I invited. "What did she look like? How did she dress? What did she sound like? How did she carry herself?"

Tina went through the same process I had, the same process I'd seen transform countless clients. She identified an age in her that she was struggling to be with, then listened in real close. What did she need the most that she wasn't getting?

She wrote her 40-day vow and said it each morning and night after brushing her teeth. Naturally, without any extra effort besides saying the vow, she began caring for herself and calling in care, in ways that she'd never quite been able to before. Of course, we'd also been doing lots of body-based co-regulation together in sessions, so Tina's physiology was more primed for receptivity. With the combination of embodied and relational coherence, Tina's Soul Seed began to ReBloom.

The 3-Part Path to Reblooming Worthiness and Receptivity

1. Sensing your needs

- Growing a felt-sense relationship to regulation, satiation, and wellness.
- Growing a felt-sense relationship to when things are feeling off or dysregulated, as a cue to pause and check in with yourself.
- Growing a felt-sense capacity to attune to what you need in order to feel safe, nourished, and cared for in terms of:
  - Romantic relationships and sexuality
  - Friendships
  - Community
  - Physical rhythms and routines (food, sleep, hydration)
  - Home
  - Purpose / Work
  - Responding to difficulty

2. Speaking, acknowledging or requesting your needs

- Once you can sense your needs in your body, the next step is communicating them (to both yourself and others)

- Being able to name, in words, your needs
- Being able to sense who, where, or how those needs could get met
- Being able to move toward the conditions that will meet your needs
- Being able to request what you need from others

3. Meeting, responding to or receiving your needs

- Once you can sense and name your needs, then it's about moving into greater receptivity
- Can you respond to your awareness with aligned motion?
- Can you allow someone else to respond to your request with aligned action?
- Can you experience receptivity on a felt-sense level when your needs are, in fact, being met?

Essential Soul Seed Practices

Soul Seed Coherence Practice

If you only teach your clients one practice for each archetype, let it be the Coherence Practice. It's the quickest and simplest—and gets straight to the point. Often, my clients weep or get choked up the first time they do the Soul Seed

Coherence Practice. It's deceptively deep.

Standing, sitting or lying down, with your eyes open or closed, put your hands on your belly, and begin noticing any sensations that possibly arise.

Remember that this is the place in your body where you were first designed to receive everything you needed, effortlessly. No proving, striving or trying necessary. Notice what comes up for you with that awareness.

If it feels nourishing, you can rub in circles around your belly. If you're standing, you might like to sway from side to side to help anchor into a nurturing presence.

Then, say either inwardly or outwardly, pausing between affirmations to allow your body to digest, sense and integrate:

I am here.
I am now.
I matter.
I am worthy of feeding my needs.
I am designed to grow and thrive.
I need ____.
I need ____.
I need ____.
I am receiving.
I am receiving.
I am receiving.

Speak to as many needs as you sense in the moment, or in relationship to the topic that you're seeking coherence around. Then, at the end, as you speak the affirmation, "I am receiving," imagine how it would look and feel at an embodied level to receive the very needs you just claimed. Give your body time to catch up with your mind. See how much you can sense yourself opening up to and letting in your needs.

It's okay if it feels challenging, or you only feel somewhat receptive. As you practice more and more with your Soul Seed, your awareness of and receptivity to your needs will increase.

To receive free video guidance through the Soul Seed Coherence Practice, head to rebloomtogether.com / coherence.

Reparenting Your Inner Kid

All humans have the same needs for safety, food, water, shelter, love and belonging. As we grow older, the core needs that went unmet as children can become ground zero for hyper or hypo reactions.

One of the most important components of developmental trauma resolution is helping our clients identify their specific core needs, and then supporting a re-parenting process where they learn to sense, speak and respond to those needs in regulated, nourishing ways.

Most of us have an inner child that's secretly running some part of our lives. The inner-child that was most neglected, abandoned, unmet, unmatched, unseen or untended to—wise as they were—likely found ways to defend against the feeling and experience of neglect; found ways to be in charge of feeling safe and protected, fed and fulfilled. Of course, because that child was only a child, their skills and capacity to do this in a sustainable, regenerative way were likely low.

Reparenting our inner kid is about restoring a healthy order of nurturance, within which the adult is caring for the child, not the other way around.

Think back to an age or stage of your life where you felt as though you experienced some level of physical or emotional neglect. What were the circumstances? What was the situation like? Picture yourself at this age. How did you dress? How did you hold yourself physically? What were you thinking and feeling on the regular?

Now imagine your wisest inner-parent sitting side-by-side with this younger self, listening with great care and love. Imagine this inner-parent asking the inner-kid, "What are alllll the things you really need?"

Let your inner kid list them out around a brainstorm bubble like this:

Then, circle the most emotionally charged things from your brainstorm bubble. Perhaps 4-5.

For each of the most emotionally charged things that you circle, make a new brainstorm bubble.

For example, if you write and circle "A mom that protects her," in the middle of your next brainstorm bubble would be, "The kind of mothering my inner-kid needs is…." Then, list THOSE things out around the bubble…

If you write and circle "safe sober men," you'd make another brainstorm bubble with *that* in the center. Then write the kinds of things safe, sober men would provide your inner kid around that bubble…

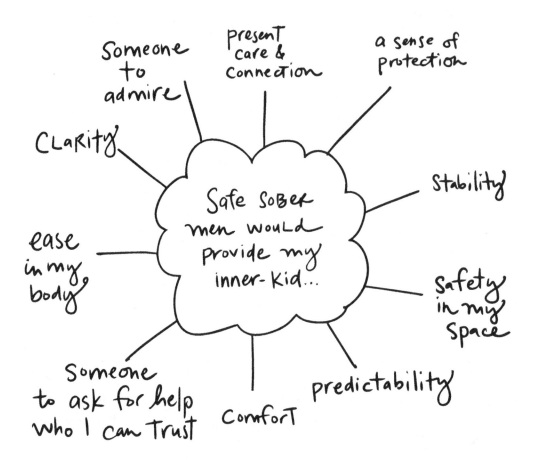

Once your brainstorm bubbles are made, circle a few needs that feel the most emotionally charged from each one; the needs your inner kid is most crying out for. Those are the core needs you'll be working with for this particular age and stage of inner-child healing.

Once you have your core needs identified, write yourself a 30-day vow that you'll read every morning.

For the next 30-days I vow to do my best to support my inner child by...

Then translate the things you circled into things you can do now. For example, if you needed a mother to protect you by validating your experience, you'd write,

"...by validating her experiences and emotions with care."

Or if you needed down time in nature you'd write, "...by taking her into nature for rest and recharge."

Or if you needed attunement to healthy masculinity, you'd write, "...by being open to and inviting of healthy masculinity in her presence."

All in all, there should be about 15-20 things on the list.

Then, here's the big secret! Once your vow is written, put it somewhere that you visit daily: an altar, on your bathroom mirror, etc, then do your best to simply read the vow every day for 30 days.

It's important with this exercise that you don't pressure or force yourself to DO the things on the list. That could incite pressure, shame, and shut down. Rather, just read the list every day as an act of commitment and care. This act alone will put your inner-child at ease and help to heal the order of nurturance. When your younger self begins to hear your daily devotion to her, a sense of safety and trust will grow. She won't feel as though she has to run the show, because she'll feel that your adult self is showing up to do the work for her.

This rearranging of nurturance allows for your inner-child to feel more safe playing and experimenting, while also allowing for your inner-adult to step up, feeling more confident and self-assured.

Cycle of Regulation Star Chart

One of my faaaaavorite practices, in my own life and for clients, is making and keeping star charts! Remember when you were a kid and you got gold stars for doing your chores? This is like that...for adults. (Or maybe our inner kids.)

Remember, what makes self-regulation possible is enough co-regulation with other supportive sources. Nature, community, close friends, family, or beloveds. When our bodies receive the deep impression that we are not isolated or alone in the world, but rather connected with nourishing and loving people or places, we can more easily drop into safe, steady connection with ourselves. In order to rest we need to digest, and for millions of years, we've been digesting—food *and* experiences—together.

Consider making for yourself or your clients a Cycle of Regulation Star Chart that encourages daily connection with all four sources: self, others, community, and nature.

ReBloom my Regulation STAR CHART

1				
2				
3				
4				
5				
6				
7				
8				
9				
10				
11				
12				
13				
14				

The idea of Star Charts isn't to always get 4-star days. Rather, it's to help build a new momentum in the direction of greater health. I like to do 2-week Star Charts. I find that it's just enough time to help establish new habits, but not too long that it feels overwhelming.

Some of us may be more introverted, and the idea of daily community-regulation could be too much. Some of us may not live close to nature, and the effort of getting there may be too much. Feel free to edit this as needed.

Examples of possible moves in each category include:

- Self-Regulation: meditation, walk outside, nap, bath, movement practice, reading, journaling, praying, divination
- Co-Regulation: quiet time with another, eating a meal together, sharing about your day, taking a walk together, snuggling, synced up breathing, playing music, dancing, or praying together
- Nature-Regulation: spending time communing with house plants or animals, walks outside, staring out the window at the rustling leaves, laying on the earth, collecting rocks, working with seasons or moon cycles
- Community-Regulation: attending a potluck, visiting your local barista, going to a local movement class, book club or full-moon circle, making dinner with friends, doing crafts together, co-working or collaborating on a creative project, eating lunch with your favorite co-worker

What are the things that bring you regulation and a full-body exhale in each category? Which regulation practices feel most doable and enjoyable for you? If you were to choose four to focus on—one from each category over the next two weeks, what would they be? What would you have to arrange or plan so that you could engage these muscles with greater ease and flow?

Understanding Intimacy Needs

Getting comfortable with having needs, then growing the capacity to voice and receive those needs, is the foundation upon which deep, fulfilling intimacy is built.

When your clients are ready to explore the realms of sex or love, here's a core question for them to consider:

What makes you FEEL physically & emotionally SAFE in bed?

Oftentimes, our struggle around safe sexual experiences is rooted in a secret developmental history of emotional neglect. Yep—the early childhood experiences we had of either receiving the interpersonal nourishment we needed, or not, wire us into embodied expectations around what's normal in bed.

Having a regulated relationship to knowing, expressing, and receiving our needs can be incredibly hard—foreign-feeling, even. That's why it's so common for many of us to instead end up in sexual experiences that mirror our developmental experience of not mattering.

As adults wanting healthy, nourishing, and fulfilling sex lives, beginning to identify our needs and leaning into the vulnerability of voicing them is crucial.

Do your clients know what physical and emotional safety feels like in a relationship? How about in bed? Do you?

If these questions stump your clients (or you), I'm here to share how normal that is.

Over the years, I've asked this question to client after client, group after group, and am often met with timid shut-down. When this happens, I like to brainstorm answers together. Hearing one another's responses helps awaken our own.

Here are some things my groups have come up with together about what makes us feel physically and emotionally safe in bed:

- Easy communication before, during and after any intimacy
- Body praise and worship
- Mutual emotional admiration and respect
- Love!
- Sharing STD statuses
- Talking about contraception methods
- Trusting I feel comfortable enough to pause if needed
- Trusting they'll honor my pause
- Feeling free to be wild or tender or sad or soft or totally rolling in ecstasy
- Openness and alignment around sexual orientations and gender identities, as well as relationship status and styles
- Honesty

- Curiosity
- Good listening
- Compassion
- Physical care
- Openness for repair
- Some level of sobriety (or no addiction)
- Emotional availability
- Attention

Identifying what we need in order to feel safe is the first step to truly fulfilling sex. Voicing needs is the second. And then, of course, mmmm…receiving.

If you or a client would like to go further with cultivating greater physically and emotionally safe sex, I've made a free Safer Sex Foreplay Worksheet that has a ton of questions you can ask yourself (and your partner) about sex, to help things feel more delicious for everyone. Head to rebloomtogether.com/safesex to scoop it.

Chapter 5

GATEKEEPER

FROM EXPLOITATION to SOVEREIGNTY

The Blueprint

Gatekeeper is a sovereign force of healthy choice surrounding Soul Seed, discerning what comes in and what stays out. A mature decision-maker. A parental figure that loves and adores Soul Seed's every need, sensitivity, and desire—and takes great pride and joy in both protecting and providing for the other archetypes in the garden.

When Gatekeeper was a young child, still maturing, still finding his sense of safe limits and boundaries he had adult Gatekeepers around him, showing him with accuracy what was healthy and what was not, what would nourish him and what would weaken him, what would help him grow and what would stunt his soul.

This initiation into healthy boundaries made it so Gatekeeper could sense on his own what nurtures life and what doesn't.

A mature Gatekeeper is not afraid to say "no." In fact, Gatekeeper says "no" every day in a whole lot of ways, over and over again, all in service to his "yes." Gatekeeper has tasted the beautiful erotic glory that's only possible inside his safekeeping. He is a proud patriot of his beautiful territory. He greets what comes to meet him and feels into his sacral truth. Is this safe? Is this healthy? Is this going to nourish and replenish me and my whole inner-ecology?

Gatekeeper adores Soul Seed and all their sensitive needs like a precious, worthy baby. He worships Expressionista's wild, radiant heart like his most cherished lover. His singular motivator is keeping all the other archetypes protected and honored.

Connected to the hips and pelvis, genitals, and womb space, Gatekeeper does the sacred dance of opening or closing according to embodied resonance and penetrating or hanging back based on what arouses in a safe and healthy way.

Within each of us there also lives a Collective Gatekeeper in service to the health of humanity. We have the capacity to sense through our pelvis what's wrong or right, what's safe or unsafe for the most sensitive, sacred parts of our human family and planet. When the Collective Gatekeeper is awakened in us, it looks like protecting the land, insisting on care for the children, and drawing clear boundaries around what goes into our food, watershed, and oceans.

The Collective Gatekeeper worships the wellness of all living things—and is not afraid to protect or defend the sacred.

Gatekeeper at a Glance

Body Connection: Pelvis, Hips, Genitals

Your sexual organs are designed to expand in the presence of emotional and physical safety, care, and praise, and contract in the presence of emotional or physical uncertainty, danger, or force. Your pelvis epitomizes the wisdom of letting healthy things in and keeping unhealthy things out, as well as moving toward what it desires and hanging back from what uninspires.

Your sex organs—in their Blueprint form—open or close, penetrate or pull out, according to right relationship. They feel pleasure, arousal, desire, and groundedness when they're in nourishing environments, relationships, and situations. They feel pain, tightness, numbness, insatiable impulsiveness, or agitation when dynamics are less-than-ideal.

When the pelvis or hips are tight, they might be protecting the more inward sexual organs from perceived or actual threat. When the sexual organs are numb or experiencing chronic pain, disease, or infection, they might be expressing an ongoing desire for safer, consensual relationships to self and others.

When pleasure, orgasm, and flexibility are available, there's likely a sense of sovereignty, safety, care, and dominion within intimacy and exchange.

The pelvis and jaw mirror each other's anatomy; akin to the vaginal opening and throat. Each of these places in the body act as a physiological indicator of how safe a situation is—how empowered you feel to sense, speak, and honor your truth—or not.

Natural Blueprint of Health: Sovereignty

You are comfortable with the give and take of energy, time, money, love, lust, resources and ideas. You know what's yours, what's others' and what's shared. You practice discernment around what's healthy or unhealthy to let into your space, and you choose your greatest thriving as often as possible—for the sake of awakening your most enlivening medicine.

Traumatic Imprint: Exploitation

You are taken from without consent, stolen from, used, capitalized on, taken advantage of, harnessed for another's gain, exposed at a cost to you, trespassed upon or extracted from. Exploitation can be emotional, physical, sexual, financial, or energetic.

Hyper-Response to Exploitation: Impenetrable Boundaries

- Walling off entry to any parts of your core self as a defense against being non-consensually taken from

- Positioning yourself to come out on top of any negotiation
- Avoiding negotiations all together—deciding you're a no before giving something a chance so you don't have to endure the vulnerability or perceived risk of deliberation
- Self-isolating to avoid navigating interpersonal negotiations
- Always being ready to fire in case of an attack
- Always watching for trespassers or violators

When someone's embodying Impenetrable Boundaries, it can often feel threatening to their system to trust themselves and others in the process of negotiating boundaries (especially if the situation is complex in any way).

Common fears and inner dialogues include:

- "They're going to try to convince me to do something I don't want to do… let me just avoid them instead."
- "…let me be VERY clear what I'm NOT okay with. There is ZERO room for discussion on this."
- "People can't be trusted with _____ [other people's hearts', my emotional needs, my body…]"
- "I don't want to get screwed over."
- "That'll be too tiring to navigate… I'll just opt out."
- "Oh, I'm going to set a VERY clear boundary so that no one fucks with me."
- "I don't let ANYONE _____ [into my heart, borrow money, live with me, etc]."

Hypo-Response to Exploitation: Flimsy Boundaries

- Giving more away than is sustainable or healthy for the nourishment of your body, mind, heart, finances or energy
- Being blindsided about people taking from you
- Always getting the short end of the stick
- Not receiving back in equal proportions to what you put in (with work, relationships, money, sex)

- Defenselessness
- No fences or sense of personal space
- Not feeling, sensing or noticing your own limits, and thus, overriding them or letting them be overridden by others (then perhaps resenting that others didn't Gatekeep for you)

When someone's embodying Flimsy Boundaries, it can often feel threatening to their system to withhold or draw limits around their resources out of fear of losing connection or belonging.

Common fears and inner dialogues include:

- "If I tell someone *no*, they're NOT going to be happy with me."
- "I committed, so now I have to."
- "Is it really okay to change my mind?"
- "They'll think I'm selfish and hate me if I put myself first."
- "Why does everyone always fuck me over?? What's wrong with me?"
- "I've worked so hard and got nothing in return! Ugh, that person is such a taker."

Portrait of a Flimsy Gatekeeper

I'd just moved to San Diego and was short on friends and familiarity. I met a charismatic musician who was handsome and witty, challenging and charming. Let's just call him Jake. He was connected to community and happy to share his friends. We hit it off and quickly developed a romantic interest in one another.

But as we made our way to the bedroom, I just as quickly discovered that this man was not someone I wanted touching my body. He'd fall asleep while we were hooking up, then wake up and demand I be more vocal with my desires. Uncomfortable but still hungry for connection, I'd try to oblige by squeaking out my hopes and dreams.

"Not seductive enough," he'd critique. And half of me would disappear, the other half upping my performance to try to woo him into adoring me.

This less-than-impressive erotic evening was enough to have me dump Jake sexually, but I still needed to make new friends, and Jake loved to be depended on. "If you're lonely, call me," he'd insist. "Let me introduce you to so-and-so, let me take you to a cool music show."

I was grateful for the connection and felt too vulnerable to not depend on him. The thing about being short on what we need is it makes us more susceptible to slipping up on our sovereignty.

The trouble was, this man and I had a dynamic that was riddled with power struggle and emotional turmoil. Some part of me, still attracted to him physically, still holding out for him to become some version of what I wanted, was always disappointed that he wasn't more sensitive or soft. Some part of him, perhaps threatened by my leadership, was always trying to assert dominance over me. We fought incessantly. But no matter. I still let him into my space, my psyche, my energy field.

At the end of our relationship, I finally had a big come-to-Jesus moment. I wasn't honoring my true needs for emotional sensitivity, positivity, or a real romantic partnership, rather than some pseudo-relationship rife with arguments and lacking nourishing intimacy.

Why? Why is it that I could go so far down the road with someone who clearly did not nourish my soil or contribute to the overall health of my garden?

Again, the thing about being short on what we need is it makes us more susceptible to slipping up on our sovereignty.

Flimsy boundaries are almost always a result of unmet needs. When we've been entrained to think our needs don't matter (perhaps due to developmental or complex neglect), our animal instinct is to reach out beyond the "safe family unit" into the mystery of something that just might feed us.

So often, Gatekeeper challenges can be traced back to Soul Seed. As adults, we're less likely to take a stand for the parts of us that were neglected as kids. The parts of us that we weren't properly provided for as young ones—our needs for care, attention, food, safety or nurturance—later become leaky valves in our energetic boundaries, the same places we struggle to have protection or limits.

In my case, as a child, my emotionality, sensitivity, spirituality and sensuality were treated as either inconvenient, or gold mines of feminine delight to extract from. Culturally, like many people with female bodies, I was entrained with the collective trauma spell of self-erasure plus sexualization for masculine pleasure. It begs the question: why would my body or soul, later on, expect that I could be met and honored in my most worthy, needy places, as my most authentic, whole self?

When I was 11, I was pushed to my knees by a guy a few years older than me. "You know what to do—now do it." *This makes sense*, my body told me. *To give more than I want. To be overridden, overlooked. To oblige for the sake of pleasing. My muscle memory knows this trope. Nothing new here, nothing surprising.*

When I was 13, I was anally raped by a 26-year-old. *This makes sense*, my soul signaled to me. *To be taken from without care or concern. To have my sensitivity and emotionality ignored. To think it's normal to hold the secret as if it's mine to carry. After all, I've been handed this weight. Of course, I'm going to shoulder it.*

When I was 16, I had an affair with someone off-limits and much older. *This makes sense*, my heart whispered. *To be someone's covert vice. To get racy bouts of attention, but nothing too fulfilling.*

Then, tired of being taken from, when I was 18, I entered into a sweet but sexless 8-year marriage. *This makes sense*, my mind told me. *No one's taking from me. I'm finally safe. Who cares that I'm not receiving anything juicy? Who cares that he can't meet me in my spiritual seductress or mystical sorceress? Who needs those parts, anyway, when they're the ones that everyone takes from, the parts that got me burned at the stake?*

In most of these instances, I thought I was to blame, the culprit Secret Bad Girl, the scarlet letter shame.

Maybe you or your clients are also blaming yourselves for the series of difficulties that came like dominoes, one after the other. Maybe you, like me, thought it was all your fault and you couldn't tell anyone, could barely even look at it yourself. Maybe you didn't realize you were living under a secret trauma spell of nervous system wiring designed for revictimization, disempowerment, and dissatisfaction. I didn't. I just thought I was *bad*.

Maybe, bloated with secret self-blame and shame for the ways your Gatekeeper was never properly initiated, and your boundaries were blown right past, you've begun to subconsciously fear your aliveness. You fear the power of what you'll grow into if you're actually well-fed, resourced, nourished. You fear it because you don't trust yourself or Life to protect you from being exploited, taken advantage of, or harmed. You fear becoming the same corrupt force that once overpowered you.

Instead, you stay weak by starving yourself of your needs. You hope you'll be safer in your smallness. But starved of your voluminous power, your energetic sovereignty weakens, becoming more prone to others exploiting, taking advantage of, or harming you.

Carrying Collective Exploitation

No matter how sovereign you are, sometimes life shits on us all. Especially if you're in a more marginalized body or pushing up against racism, sexism, toxic capitalism, homophobia, fatphobia, ableism, or all the other -isms.

The question isn't: How can I escape oppression on my own? It's: How can we change the culture together? How can we create momentums of health as individuals and communities—health that spreads like magic seeds throughout the garden of our human family?

As coaches, healers, and guides, it's important that we address with our clients both the personal and cultural trauma spells of exploitation to help combat the tendency to hyper-personalize all our problems.

Personal trauma spell: That night drunk in the backseat when way more went down than you wanted.

Collective trauma spell: The cultural conditions that disconnect men from their hearts and that entrain women to sexually over-perform.

Personal trauma spell: You're a broke life coach. You just signed up for a $25,000 mastermind on credit cards. You've been sold the idea that your money issues are because you don't believe in yourself.

Collective trauma spell: Fuckin' capitalism. We think we're supposed to get rich on our own. We forget that real abundance has and always will live in our collective soil.

Personal trauma spell: You're a lesbian and all your straight girl friends want to sexually experiment with you.

Collective trauma spell: There's no cultural context or coming of age processes for experimenting and discovering the layers of your most authentic sexual self. Homophobia closets authenticity. Non-heteronormative relationships are less represented, spoken of, understood, and honored as holy and good.

Personal trauma spell: You've been sexualized and fetishized for your skin color, gender expression, body shape or size, heritage, age, or accent.

Collective trauma spell: The extraction of the holy. Power-over by force. Domination so as to not have to humble yourself and co-create with the wild mystery of eros, sensuality and desire. The opportunity to exploit is most often given to stronger, bigger men, white people, people with money, people in positions of power, people who are older when you are young.

When we interpret the boundary violations we've experienced as solely personal problems, then draw the conclusion that they have only personal solutions, we privatize the pain that has roots in our shared soil. We disconnect from the necessary solidarity that comes from seeing the ways systems of oppression hurt us all at varying levels.

But when we understand that reclaiming sovereignty is both a personal and political act of healing, legions of angels swoop behind us and the Earth becomes our ally. You realize that the more you come into your personal Sovereignty, the more power you have to stand for our Collective Sovereignty. You realize the interchangeability of healing yourself and healing the world. You become more resourced to serve our Collective Garden.

The Foundation of Sustainable Sovereignty

Deeper than Consent with Another is consent with yourself.

Self-Consent is the foundation of Sovereignty.

When we've had histories of flimsy boundaries—when we're trying to serve the collective from an imprint of martyrdom and over-giving—it's easy to override our limits and neglect our deepest needs. I've seen it a thousand times with coaches, healers, and activists: we violate our own consent in an attempt to save the world.

We think consent is about saying "yes" or "no" and being honored, heard, respected. And it is.

Except, from what foundation are you giving your yes or no? Deeper than consent with another is consent with yourself. Self-consent is the foundation of Sovereignty.

For most of my life and probably many lifetimes before, I was excellent at saying "yes" when I meant "no." The challenging part was, my incoherence was only half-conscious. It was like I had a hazy gauze over my true-alignment locator. Most of the time, I could barely tell that I was out of consent with myself.

Maybe something felt sort of uncomfortable—but like…isn't that normal? Maybe I knew it was a bad idea—but like…I bet it'll be okay. I can pull off anything!

If I'm honest, my Gatekeeper muscles are just coming into their peak performance state. Not because I got super obsessed with Gatekeeping…with honoring my boundaries, drawing a line in the sand and defending it. *No.* My Gatekeeper muscles are coming into more beautiful form because I got super obsessed with whole-system coherence.

I started asking myself:

What's my medicine—the magic that only comes into full bloom when I tend to all my parts?

When I honor my needy animal-self?

When I'm realistic about my capacity?

When I revere my tender heart?

When I stop pretending that I don't know what I know?

When I admit how much something's gonna cost me, and then plan accordingly?

When I insist on the pleasure of togetherness?

When I tune into the higher calling?

As I learned to answer these questions—with friends, roommates, lovers, in my business, with my choices about food, sleep, movement, and meditation—boundaries stopped being walls I had to build and constantly secure, or rules I had to firm up and follow. Boundaries evolved into self-consent, and self-consent evolved into Sovereignty: the ability to choose my greatest thriving, for the sake of awakening my most enlivening medicine. So I could give it, take it, and receive it. So I could revel in the gifts I was born to share, and love the experience of sharing and receive nourishment from the generosity of being in my own full bloom.

Your medicine isn't medicinal if it isn't also serving you. But figuring out how to line up all your parts so you can receive back from your own luminous love? So you can embody sovereign regenerative relational coherence? That's a challenge. A challenge I love to help people with.

The Four Energetic Competencies of Healthy Sovereignty

Penetration

- Saying *yes* to what's fully aligned
- Moving toward what you desire
- Investing your energy, money, time, emotional resources, and intellectual resources into things that regenerate you, your relationships and our world
- Making and keeping commitments

Hanging back

- Saying *no* to what's not fully coherent
- Moving away from what you don't desire
- Divesting your energy, money, time, emotional resources, or intellectual resources from places that feel non-reciprocal, undesirable, or out of alignment
- Reassessing and canceling commitments from a compassionate, aligned, transparent place

Letting in and receiving

- Saying *yes* and allowing entry to that which turns you on
- Enjoying the delight of what's healthy in your space
- Saying *yes, thank you, more please* to the good things that are in your life
- Having clarity about your needs and desires: sensing, speaking, and receiving them

Keeping out and removing

- Saying *no* and denying entry to that which diminishes your lifeforce
- Sensing what will detract from your space (physical, emotional, energetic, mental), and not allowing it to come in
- Changing your mind about something that's in your space, and asking it to leave
- Saying *no* to things that don't turn you on or add to your capacity, aliveness or coherence

The Four Shadow Habits of Unhealthy Sovereignty

Shadow penetration

- Committing and offering your energy to things you're not a wholehearted *yes* to, then resenting or feeling victimized by others afterwards
- Penetrating things that don't desire your penetration and victimizing others as a result

Shadow hanging back

- Over-committing then ghosting because you're beyond your capacity
- Not committing (even in places where you're deeply needed or deeply desire to commit) out of fear of too much pressure, failing, not being able to meet another's needs, or not feeling worth the reward of showing up for yourself or others

Shadow letting in and receiving

- Allowing something entry that you don't feel fully safe with, nourished by or okay about
- Taking things that are not being offered consensually
- Using others for their gifts even though you don't feel fully aligned with them

Shadow keeping out and removing

- Denying something entry, as an invulnerable protection mechanism
- Being closed off to healthy things
- Attacking others so as to not feel attacked

A Love-Affair with Limits

To grow healthy, plump, empowering sovereignty, you gotta get into limits. Closing the doors to your temple. Withdrawing your energy, attention, care or concern. Pulling out, backing down, turning around, steering clear.

Embodying the tension of our no is the magical heat that alchemizes space for our *yes*.

We don't always trust the process of owning our *no*. We fear loss of belonging. We avoid the risk of having to live in the center of our unmet longings, the empty space after the loss, before the rebirth. We also fear danger, the consequences of someone being displeased with our sovereignty then violating, manipulating, or badmouthing us as a result. Deep down, many of us have a part of us that doesn't trust our own capacity to struggle our way into safety, doesn't know if it's truly okay to disappoint, insist, hold out, or wait for it.

When we've experienced exploitation either in a one-time event, systemically, or developmentally, and our nervous systems haven't had the chance to heal, our body's perception of threat—our neuroception—can often sense danger in places where it doesn't exist, or totally miss obvious cues that something is, in fact, unsafe. A faulty neuroception is a key symptom of the trauma spell—one that can be healed and changed. As we're affirmed relationally for the limits we insist upon, our neuroception muscles begin to strengthen with power and effectiveness. There's a positive feedback loop that grows when we can sense our most healthy limits, speak and enact them, and be honored, loved, and respected for them.

We can practice this process with trusted others, but we can also practice with ourselves. We all have those habits of override—staying up too late on our phones, eating past the point of feeling full, ignoring the ache of your body that screams, "Enough sitting! Please get up and stretch me!" Every time we sense and listen to a limit of our own body, we are revering our sovereignty. When we are sovereign with our relationship to ourselves, our joy and aliveness grows, and we become less willing to compromise our healthy sovereignty with others.

Fun fact: even pleasure requires limits. The epistemology of the word pleasure is *what pleases us in a measured way*. Pleasure is not gluttony. It's not overindulgence in delight. That would create pain, like a stomachache from eating too much cake. Pleasure is also not deprivation or starvation. That would create a different kind of pain—the headache that comes with dehydrating your body or soul. Pleasure is the hot summer day that ends with a cool, colorful sunset. Pleasure is the wild orgasmic night that drifts into sleep at 11 PM. Pleasure is your favorite new song on repeat five times, but not twenty. Pleasure is a whole season of darkness where the soil can rest and replenish before new flowers shoot up and bloom. Pleasure is watering the house plants just enough, but not too much, so their leaves sing happy and bright.

Limits and boundaries are part of nature's grand master plan to regenerate Life, as is the impulse to feed the needs of our soil. When we ignore that we're part of the grand master nature plan—overriding our limits or under-feeding our needs—anger rises in us. Anger is a sacred clue that a *no* has been unheeded, and a need has gone unfed. Anger is a fire asking for your rightful attention, a holy messenger wanting to offer you an oracle of change. *It doesn't have to be this way. Things can come back into right-order.*

Sometimes, when we're too anxious with unmet need or too overwhelmed by exploitation, our bodies can't sustain the heat of our own agitation and we collapse down into a depressive freeze. *Forget it,* we weep. We stop feeling the ache of the over-give. We start getting used to the dehydration of no nourishment coming in.

Until something triggers our anger again, and we feel it for a hot moment, just before hopelessness clouds our senses.

If you or your clients find yourselves stuck in cycles of hot-cold-hot-cold-hot, it usually means you haven't had enough proof that your boundaries can work on your behalf, that your desires could really be fed.

Our bodies long to growl and penetrate, push back or push away with healthy aggression—fierce, powerful energy that moves us toward our aliveness, or stops what's unwanted. When we're regrowing our Gatekeepers, we need to renew our sometimes-dormant neurobiological networks of passion that assert limits and howl for care.

When passion and healthy aggression are stifled, they turn into toxic anger. Here are some stories of possibility to help unclog the drain and open your channel to the aliveness of healthy aggression.

The Angry Banana Peel Throw Tactic for Women Who Think They Have No Anger

A few years back, I was on week three of crippling pain in my lower back. Luckily, Leo was in town, and he piled me into the car and drove me to a cabin in the woods by a beautiful creek. The first morning there, I woke up with a face full of grief and a heart hot with something a lot like fury.

"I think you're angry," he told me, matter-of-factly.

"Angry??" I scoffed back. "I'm not angry. It takes a LOT for me to be angry."

"Don't you think that maybe you've been through a lot? That even just right now all the pain you're feeling is, in fact… a lot?" He asked with a sweet concern on his face. I sat there very still, the way we sometimes do when an entire volcano of emotion wants to move through us and we gotta decide if it's safe to erupt, or not.

He gave me a moment, then winked and asked, "Wanna banana?"

The paralyzed volcano of me squeaked out a sigh. "Sure."

He leapt out of bed and retrieved two bananas. One for him, one for me. We ate together in silence, me under the covers, him over. We both knew what was coming.

You see, a week prior, we were FaceTiming over breakfast, and I was expressing some… emotions. About my friend Katie dying. About my ceaseless stomachache. About Donald Trump. About needing someone to cuddle with—now.

"Sounds like you've got some anger there, babe," he said.

"No no, I'm not angry," I defended. "I'm just sad and frustrated."

"So what you're saying is that you're sad and frustrated… but not angry?" he repeated back, a bit skeptical with a jesting vibe.

Then I went into the speech I hear so many of my clients give about their anger. "Well, the anger's in there, I'm sure. But like, it's not *accessible*."

"Huh," he said. "Can I give you some advice?"

"Sure. Lay it on me."

"I think you should work on that."

I laughed. "Oh yeah? I should work on it? What should I do…?" I retorted with a playful fire rising in me, "Throw this banana peel at the phone screen? Is that what I should do right now?"

"Yeah! That sounds like a great idea!"

God bless friends who push the right buttons.

And so it began—the Angry Banana Peel Throw Tactic for Women Who Think They Have No Anger.

I threw that goopy, floppy banana peel at my propped iPhone screen four times. With each gratifying smack against the glass, the heat of my volcanic mid-line stirred and bubbled and spewed little bits of fury.

"Phew! That was a lot to do over breakfast," I said, sweaty and smiling from the emotional intensity, "but it felt…good. Really good."

"Good," he grinned back. "I'd love to hold space for you to do more of that when we're together."

"I'M IN."

"You deserve it," he said. "To feel your anger, you know? To not have to hold it all in."

Faaaast forward back to the cabin. Banana peel in hand. Him over the covers, me under.

"So…you wanna throw that thing at the wall, or what?"

And suddenly, my volcano erupted—not in anger, nor in banana peel throws... but in tears. In huge, ugly, childlike tears emerging from the depths of my pelvic bowl.

"Why do humans do such horrendous things?" I wailed.

And I cried for the earth. And I cried for the sweatshop workers. And I cried for the child sex slaves. And I cried for the native genocide. And I cried for the young adults who die of cancer. And I cried for all my clients and all of the money and time and energy they spend healing something they never broke. I cried, and cried, and cried for all my younger selves who'd been taken from without care or concern. I cried for thirty minutes, sometimes with words, sometimes just wails.

Then, exasperated but not quite done, I wiped the snot off my face and threw that banana peel against the wall as hard as I could.

"Did you like that?" Leo asked.

"I did," I whispered.

Leo played ball boy, fetching my slowly-disintegrating banana peel toss, after toss, after toss.

Thirty throws later, plus a handful of hefty roars, I could feel the buoyancy of my soul lifting, and my whole body erupted once more, this time—in laughter. My fire had awakened. The fire in me that wanted to protect, defend, and stand in fierce solidarity with all the things it deeply loved—it was no longer frozen or numb. It was alive. Roaring. Hissing. Throwing. Laughing. INSISTING. Insisting that we can do better as a human family, and that somehow, I would do my part. I wouldn't—couldn't—let my *no* store as somatized pain in my body any longer. It would be heard. It would be effectual. It would be *power*.

A Thousand Ways to Say No

If you think you have no anger—if your *no* is frozen inside you, building concrete walls of mistrust where you'd like to loosen into more intimate receptivity—this story's for you.

Of the hundreds of women I've worked with, pretty much every single one of them has struggled with saying *no*.

There's a fire in the fierceness of denying access or withdrawing energy that women are not socialized to use. But without our fire, what's protecting our pleasure, innocence, or aliveness?

Picture this:

A group of women have been gathering for months to call home their lost power, pleasure and purpose after trauma. I'm their facilitator, coach, and guide, and at the end of our time together, we join for a retreat of rituals, games, and experiences to punctuate our healing. These women are well versed in self-consent, in leaning in or out according to their true capacity, and they've been getting reminders to only do what's doable for the last four months.

We're on day two of our retreat, and the theme is boundary repairs. We begin an exercise where I turn on emotional music then invite them to brainstorm in their journals all things in their life they never got to say *no* to. The small ways they were forced or pressured. The big ways they were never given choice. The cultural or systemic structures they most certainly didn't create. The violations. Transgressions. Big and little traumas.

If it feels doable for you, you might pause and jot some of those things down yourself. As you do, you might notice that it doesn't take long before heat begins to form on your face, in your hands, at the bottom of your heart—or grief begins to swell in your throat, chest, and soul.

Imagine that after journaling, I play two songs for the group, inviting the women who feel aligned to allow themselves to move the expression of their *no* in whatever ways feel safe and doable. We go slow. Real slow.

"Notice, as you're invited to connect with the embodiment of your *no*...does your body want to move? Does it want to curl into a ball? Does it want to kick, hiss, hide, stomp, hold, push or leave? Does it want to voice "no" loudly, or in a firm but certain whisper? *No... No... No... No...*Whatever you do, do your best to maintain presence, as that's what will keep the experience most safe and effective."

Imagine the *nos* in the room beginning to whisper and wail, speak and sing, roar and silently take up space within. Imagine tears and fierceness. Discomfort and release. Power and fear. Electricity.

Imagine after some time, music still playing, each person invited to listen for the one thing—thematic or specific—that she's finally and fully ready to say *no* to today.

"As this thing begins to reveal itself to you, locate where the *no* is living in your body. Wherever it is, perhaps let it flow from that place, through your blood, into your arms and down into your hands. When you feel your *no* in the palms of your hands, cup them out in front of you. If you don't feel a *no* in your hands, that's okay, too. Whatever you're feeling works."

Imagine me placing cool eggs in hot hands. "Let the heat of your *no* move into the egg. Every bit of stored shame, ache, grief, rage that feels ready to release… allow it to flood into the egg."

Imagine us circling around a ritual candle with reverence and awe, knowing we're about to do something sacred for ourselves, our ancestors, our lineage. I spread newspaper on the floor and pass out Sharpies.

"What's the word or phrase that wants to land on that egg, that you are ready to say *no* to today?"

Imagine them writing their words like devotional divorce papers. Some people crying. Others confident and fierce. When everyone's looking up, I invite them to take a seat, and then I say a prayer to call in the lineage of freedom fighters, suffragists, abolitionists, high priestesses, and witches who've walked before us, making our work possible. I call in the elders, ancestors and angels of every individual in the room. Then I tell them, *This is your line*:

Today, and every day moving FORWARD, for all the times I DIDN'T OR CouLDN'T... I AM NOW SAYING "NO" to...

"You're invited to say these words, then finish the sentence with what you've written on your egg. After you say your statement, we will all shout "NO" with you, as you smash your egg onto the floor under your hand."

"This will be messy. Leave your mess. We will make a collective mess with our *nos*. We will witness the long overdue dismantling of the silence that harms, violates and oppresses. Whatever you claim will be a *no* for us all, for our whole human family."

"Afterward, we will silently wash our hands like a baptism, then come back and free write with the mess still on the floor."

"Who'd like to begin?"

And one by one, their courage rises.

"Today, and every day moving forward, for all the times I didn't or couldn't, I am now saying NO to UNWANTED TOUCH."

"NO!" We shout together, as the egg smashes and splatters like liberation on the floor.

"Today, and every day moving forward, for all the times I didn't or couldn't, I am now saying NO to SHAME IN MY POWER."

"NO!" We roar together, a pack of protectors, fierce and feline.

"Today, and every day moving forward, for all the times I didn't or couldn't, I am now saying NO to PRETENDING TO LIKE IT."

"NO!" We holler, loud enough for all the ancestors to hear.

"Today, and every day moving forward, for all the times I didn't or couldn't, I am now saying NO to HATING MY BODY."

"NO!" We insist from the center of our bones, the guts of our collective soul.

Imagine this goes on and on until the whole circle has declared "no." Until we can feel how your *no* and my *no* are really a shared *no*—a no for all of humanity against the immorality of violence. Until we can feel our shared energy sphere, our collective torus, repairing, rebuilding, renewing, nourishing, and fertilizing a healthy home where new life can finally grow.

Imagine us taking a sacred moment of silence together, then getting up slowly and washing our hands with holy reverence before returning to the circle to write the poems in our souls.

Imagine us cackling and crying and sighing with sweet relief, sharing our words into a circle of new possibility.

Then, together, dignified, cleaning up our beautiful mess.

A Holistic Approach to Alchemy

Both the story of throwing the banana peel and the story of smashing our eggs are examples of embodied rituals in which the traumatized physiology of exploitation can shift and heal. The key commonality in these experiences isn't just that we're saying "no." (Or that we're using food!) It's that we're taking a *holistic approach* that engages body, emotion, spirit, and mind in a slow-enough, consensual-enough but also charged-enough way that allows for all-encompassing alchemy to happen.

We can't heal trauma with the mind alone. The nervous system needs the experience of safety, capacity, resilience, or power in the places where it once experienced danger, limitation, choicelessness, or voicelessness.

When I worked with my teacher Brigit, one thing we did together was a simulation of her as a predator and me pushing her off my body all the way across the room until, *thump!*—her back hit the wall. Through the process of pushing someone's unwanted touch off my body, I reawakened the power of protecting myself. Not just mentally, but emotionally, physically, and spiritually, as well. We did this in super slow motion so all my parts would have time to sync up into an embodied and energetic expression of sovereign coherence.

Throughout the rituals of reclamation I do with my clients and students, I make an ongoing invitation to subtly attune to their bodies, energy and emotions. Remember, if your clients have histories of being exploited, they may say "yes" to things they don't really want to do, then end up dissociating when they've accidentally gone too far. This can happen even in healing environments, amidst practices or experiences that are designed to help, not hurt.

It's important when we're doing boundary repair work to move slowly and give clients ample choice and permission to opt-out if the experience might be intense or overwhelming. A slower speed also allows for clients to interocept or perceive with witness consciousness what's happening inside their bodies. This ability to observe oneself sensationally requires the use of the neocortex, limbic, *and* reptilian brain. It's one of the most integrative, healing mind-body processes we can employ when working to resolve trauma.

"But I don't want my anger to turn me into a perpetrator..."

If your clients are nervous that awakening their Gatekeeper will turn them into a perpetrator—by unleashing an anger they can't lock back up, by giving permission to spew hate or to violate others in the same ways others once violated them—if they're nervous that their anger will be so big it'll never end, remind them:

You can take baby steps. You don't have to throw yourself in.

You can imagine yourself as a cub, letting out the smallest, squealing roar, calling in a mama bear to support you when you're feeling shy. You can slightly tilt open your jaw, let a warm energy lift gently from your belly out of your mouth. You don't have to shout. You don't have to catharsis it all out.

In fact, you might want to contain some of that fierce fire energy and let it warm your frozen parts. Hold the charge, grow your relationship to healthy aggression, let it live in you and mobilize you, speak through you and direct you.

Now, if even after all those reminders, your client's response to reclaiming their *no* or accessing their Gatekeeper is, *Ahhhhh! Do I have to? I don't wanna!* That's fair. There's no need to rush the process. The body has its own unique timeline for healing and repair.

I didn't like reigniting my fire, either. I would've rather stayed in a brutal habit of appeasing and freezing than awaken my fierceness. My nervous system was wired to fear my power. But the cost of avoiding my wholeness was tremendous.

While there's no need to force or push healing (that'd be counter to the process, yeah?) here's the thing about unresolved trauma: managing its expression won't do. Forcing yourself to behave better isn't effective. You can only fake niceness for so long. Trying to keep your cool over and over again is a dangerous long-term strategy.

We need ceremonial, intentional, embodied ways of naming pain AND claiming strength; physiological, energetic rituals that act as thresholds for moving from the underworld of our toxic soil into the health of our truest rebloom. We need embodied proof of what we're capable of etched into our psyches and energy bodies, so that when the world tries to test our limits with unjust intrusions, we'll know ourselves as full-throttle embodiments of sovereignty, trust and power.

And then...when you're existing inside a personal space that's defined and protected, when you know you can always say "no," when you trust your embodied choice and self-loving voice, you'll have so much more space to claim the beauty, joy and aliveness that's yours.

In my work with clients, rituals of reclaiming *no* are always followed up with rituals of embracing *yes*—calling in health, safety, pleasure, light, wholeness, expression. Again, on the levels of body, emotion, spirit, and mind. Because

Gatekeeping isn't only about protecting—keeping unwanted things out. It's also about providing—bringing healthy, wanted things in. The goal isn't to only weed invasive species from your garden. It's to plant new trees that bear beautiful fruits. It's to shine light on what you want to grow. It's to revel in your harvest, with friends and beloveds alike. It's to feast on the beauty together.

Essential Gatekeeper Practices

Gatekeeper Coherence Practice

Standing, sitting, or lying down, with your eyes open or closed, allow your hands to connect with your hips, womb-space, lower back, or genitals. For the Gatekeeper Coherence Practice, I find it helpful to ask my hips what kind of awakening they desire. Do they wish to embody a defensive stance, like a ready basketball player? Do they crave figure-eight sways or seductive hip circles? Is stillness desired, with no pressure at all for movement? I sometimes like to do motions with my hands that reflect the sentiment of letting some things in and keeping other things out.

Remember, this part of the body is where decisions are made in service to protecting and providing for our Soul Seed's needs. It's where we either penetrate or hang back, open up to allow entry, or close off to deny it. It's the portal to Expressionista, as well—our heart's true fulfillment—so we also use this part of our bodies to take into consideration the effect that our choices will have on our heart's most authentic expression.

As you begin anchoring and embodying these ideas and movements, say inwardly or outwardly:

> *I get to decide what comes in and what stays out.*
> *I get to decide what comes in and what stays out.*
> *I get to decide what comes in and what stays out.*
> *I keep my temple healthy, happy and holy.*
> *I feed my Seed what it needs.*
> *I say yes to _____.*
> *I say yes to _____.*
> *I say yes to _____.*
> *I say no to _____.*
> *I say no to _____.*
> *I say no to _____.*
> *I get to decide what comes in and what stays out.*

What are you a genuine *yes* to, the allowing of which will feed your Soul Seed's needs and inspire your Expressionista's heart? What are you a firm *no* to, the denying of which will protect your Soul Seed's needs and honor your Expressionista's heart? Can you own your truths? Can you feel the power in your body that grows as you do?

If sovereignty feels a bit dangerous or uncomfortable for you, that's par for the course. As with Soul Seed Coherence, as you allow yourself to slowly integrate the medicine of Gatekeeper's blueprint, the embodiment becomes easier, safer, and simpler. It just takes a little bit of time and ongoing practice.

Resourcing the Protector & Provider Energies of the Gatekeeper

Before diving into the often-charged territory of Gatekeeper, it can be helpful to create extra resource and stability in the nervous system.

For this exercise, you can either move into a visualization or a dialogue to help your client access the supportive "protector" and "provider" energies that make up a healthy Gatekeeper.

If your client is a bit challenged by the Gatekeeper, it might be easier to do this exercise as a dialogue, stopping to talk about the experience and having them attune to their physiology and emotions as they go.

If they prefer to move into their inner worlds, perhaps allow your client to explore this territory through visualization or drawing.

Whichever route you take, invite your client to tune into the energy of *healthy protection*. Invite them to sense, feel or visualize either a person from their past, a character from a movie, show or book, an archetype, animal, ancestor, or celestial being that embodies *healthy protection* from their perspective. Be sure to emphasize the "healthy" part, as many people have negative connotations of protection.

Then invite them to imagine where they'd like for that healthy protective energy to be in relationship to them—either inside of them or around them. (Front, back, beside, above, below?) As they tune into this healthy protection energy, what do they feel, notice, see, hear or sense inside? Allow them to be with these feelings or sensations for a few moments.

If your client struggles to identify a healthy protector, perhaps suggest emphasis on non-human protectors, such as animals or elements of nature. Human-like beings can carry with them associations to human complexities or difficulties, while animals and nature can be less emotionally or psychologically charged.

From there, invite your client to tune into an energy of being *healthily provided for*. Invite them to sense, feel or visualize either a person from their past, a character from a movie, show or book, an archetype, animal, ancestor, or celestial being that to them embodies a *healthy provider*. Perhaps have them speak about it, and/or visualize it in great detail.

Then invite them to imagine that that healthy provider character or energy is either inside of them or around them, offering them full and unconditional provisions. What do they feel, notice, see, hear or sense as they tune into this energy? Again, hang out with this experience, supporting them along the way if need be.

Finally, once both the protector and provider are identified and felt, invite your client to imagine both energies supporting and resourcing them (either inside or around them) at the same time. What do they feel, notice, see, hear, or sense as they tune into this experience?

Sometimes, inviting the Blueprint can shed light on the imprint or trauma. If that happens, reassure your client that it's totally okay, and work with what arises. Often, this practice can make way for feelings of deep relief, restfulness, safety and inner-ease—the physiological resource that grows capacity for deeper and more thorough boundary repair work.

For a free guided visualization, head to rebloomtogether.com/provideprotect.

Reclaiming Your No: Egg Ritual

Hundreds of humans have gotten so much out of this ritual. It is best done in a circle of others, with care and lots of permission to engage gently, in small, doable ways. Remember: no one needs to be forced to look at where they've been overridden if they're not ready. No one needs to push themselves through a process that pummels them into freeze. Invite your clients to ask, *Does it feel doable to engage this ritual?* If not, witnessing is also a powerful form of participation.

Here are the simple instructions to the Reclaiming Your No Egg Ritual:

1. Write a list of all the things you never got to say *no* to—personally, interpersonally, culturally, systemically. Perhaps in your family growing up. Perhaps in relation to your body. If you're feeling stuck around what you never got to say *no* to, you could also tune into the things you haven't yet forgiven. Give yourself about 10 minutes to do this.

2. Afterwards, turn on a few songs that embody the energy of saying *no*. Let your body move, sound, dance or breathe in any way it desires. Consider that hissing, kicking, air punching, crawling into a ball, hiding under the covers, crying, or asserting your personal space could all be ways of embodying your *no*. Remember that smaller movements with greater awareness can be more digestible for the nervous system, so don't feel like you need to overdo it or express in huge ways.

3. As you move with your *no*, notice if there's one *no* that keeps popping in,

that keeps asking to be declared with more definition. Begin moving with or embodying that specific *no* more and more.

4. Hold an egg in your hand. Let the energy of your specific *no* flow from your heart, your blood and your cells, down your arms into your hands, then into the egg.

5. With a Sharpie marker, write a short phrase on your egg that represents what you're now saying *no* to.

6. Gather around a candle in a circle. Call in your ancestors, angels, guides, and the powerful Gatekeepers from all of time.

7. When you're ready, make this declaration: "Today and every day moving forward, for all the times I didn't or couldn't, I am now saying NO to _____." Finish the sentence.

8. Shout "NO," and smash your egg on the floor under your hand.

9. Let everyone in the circle take a turn.

10. Hold a silent, sacred, ceremonial space as you do this.

11. Leave the mess on the floor and wash your hands with a baptismal energy, releasing all the times you didn't get to say *no*.

12. Free write for a few songs.

13. Share your prose or poems with the circle.

14. Clean up the mess.

15. Rest and digest.

If you'd like an audio accompaniment to this ritual, you can find one for free at rebloomtogether.com/eggritual.

Red light, Green light, Reverse

Nurturing self-consent is a core part of post-traumatic growth. How do you know what a neutral *yes* feels like in your body? How about an exciting *yes*? How do you know what a neutral *no* feels like in your body? How about a charged *no*? Can you sense your *yeses* and *nos* both with yourself and when engaged relationally? Can you act in alignment with what you sense—honor your embodied truth—both when you're alone and when you're with others? When you voice your truth in a relationship, do you trust that connection can be maintained, even when you say *no*?

The following practice helps you live into these questions and grow the muscles of self-sensing and self-honoring, specifically in relationship to another. It helps increase capacity for interpersonal intensity in a small, doable, embodied way.

How to Play Red Light, Green Light, Reverse

In this game, one person will be the "driver" and one person will be the "car." Both people throughout the game will be invited to feel into their bodies for felt-sense experiences of safety, ease, neutrality, stability, and desire.

Before getting into partners, have each person tune into their own body and the environment around them. Invite them to look for something (inside or outside of themselves) that feels like a resource—something they can tune into that grows their presence and sense of inner trust. Have them anchor into that feeling, then invite them to find a partner.

The "driver" has three invitations they can make. Red light, green light, and reverse. Red light means the person who's playing "car" stays where they are. Green light means they take one step forward. Reverse means they take one step backward. As the driver, you're invited to make these invitations based on your physiological desire.

Do you desire safety? Do you desire to test your limits of intimacy? Do you desire neutrality or groundedness? Do you desire the feeling of being in charge, noticing what it's like to move someone else around?

You can experiment with bringing someone super close in, or moving them super far away. Notice how you feel in your body as your partner is at different distances from you. Notice what it's like for you to get to invite your partner into different forms of intimacy.

As the "car," you have two tasks. The first is feeling into your own body at each instruction the driver gives. Does it feel doable for you or not? If it feels doable, you can oblige. If it doesn't, you say "veto." The "veto" part of this practice is a critical component of what makes it more real. In relationships, no one ever has total control over anyone else. Introducing the power of "veto" makes space for an experience of negotiation that is true to real life dynamics.

To reinforce permission for the "car" to "veto," at the beginning of the practice, invite the "driver" to say to the "car," *You have total and utter permission to veto me at any moment.*

The only thing the "car" can't veto is the driver's request for you to move further away.

The most important part of this practice is growing embodied trust around feeling and honoring your truth in relationship. Being honest with yourself and your partner—to the best of your ability—is the heart of the experience.

To begin, partner up and stand facing one another at a comfortable distance. Decide who will be the "driver" first and who will be the "car."

Set a four-minute timer. There is no talking other than the words "red light," "green light," "reverse," or "veto." If at any point the game feels too intense, you can also "pause" and stop playing.

After the four minutes are up, you'll take one minute in silence to go back into your own energetic space and reconnect with that original resource of stability.

Then each partner will get one minute to share what that experience was like for them.

After both partners share, there's another minute in silence to reconnect with your personal space and resource.

Then the roles reverse, and the same rules apply.

As the facilitator, keeping the time and form is an important component to the process that gives it structure, doability and predictability for the participants.

After both partners get a chance to play and reflect on both roles, come back into the group and ask for the big lessons people learned. I like to talk about what was surprisingly awesome about the practice and what was surprisingly difficult. So many gems arise from this seemingly simple practice!

Boundaries and Belonging: A Best Buddy Game

In intimacy, most of us want to know two big things: that we can embody our true preferences *and* still belong. When we have histories of being disregarded, overridden or shamed for our honest *nos* (or *yeses*), we can cultivate habits of acquiescing to others' preferences or fighting with feral fangs to defend our own.

If we fear that our boundaries will kick us out of the club of belonging; if we sense that asserting our *no* will mean being left without connection, is it any surprise that we people-please ourselves out of integrity?

It doesn't have to be this way. *Boundaries and Belonging: A Best Buddy Game* is a way to practice saying *no* and receiving *no* with honor, care and secure attachment. It's a way of entraining our nervous systems, hearts, and souls to expect interpersonal regard around our boundaries, rather than disapproval.

How to play Boundaries and Belonging: A Best Buddy Game

Find a friend who you really trust, who you know wants the best for you, always. Together, you'll practice the art of saying *no*, receiving *no*, and thanking someone for their *no* in two rounds. Round one is a bit easier, while round two is a bit more challenging.

In round one, have one friend make an outlandish request of another friend. It doesn't have to be real, but it also could be within the realm of possibility. For example, "Sarah, will you pay off my $200,000 of student loans with the inheritance you just received?"

Sarah would then practice saying the most powerful one-word sentence on Earth—"No."

You can say more if you'd like, give a reason if you feel inclined. But the idea here isn't to apologize for your *no*. So you might say, "No, that doesn't feel good in my body." Or, "No, I have other dreams and plans for the use of that money." But not, "I'm so sorry, I don't think I can." Stand in your *no*. Let the knife-edge truth live a little.

Then pause. Both take a moment to feel what's happening in your bodies—for one of you to say *no* and for the other to receive *no*.

After the pause, the person who receives *no* simply says back, "Thank you for your *no*." This entrains a feeling of belonging for you both—you can make a request and receive *no*, and still care about the person who said *no* to you. On the other hand, can say *no* to someone and not lose connection or closeness.

Again, pause here. Notice what it feels like—to give a thank you to someone's *no* or to receive a thank you for your *no*.

That's round one! Simple and extraordinarily powerful.

In round two, we up the stakes a tiny bit by making a request that's more realistic—something you would ask for from the heart, maybe something that would even be vulnerable to request.

For example, "Sarah, I'm having the worst day. Would you be up for picking up my kid from school? I could use the extra thirty minutes to myself." Imagine, if you're Sarah, that you would genuinely love to help your friend, but it would mean overriding your own capacity and dishonoring your own self-consent. Let yourself in this moment say a simple and honest, "No." You might add some humanness by saying, "I wish I could, but it's too much for me today, so I'm a *no*."

Pause, notice how it feels for you both. Then again, the person who just received *no* thanks their friend for the authenticity of their *no*. Pause here, too, to notice how it feels.

That's the heart of the game. Be sure to switch and give everyone the opportunity to make requests, say *no*, and thank the other for their *no*.

Here's the magical truth of interpersonal sovereignty: the more you know you can always say *no*, the freer you feel to stay and play. *No* is essential to real intimacy, because it's the foundation of embodied freedom. Knowing you have your *no* gives you the safety to grow genuinely close.

Chapter 6

EXPRESSIONISTA

FROM SHAME & REPRESSION to WHOLE SELF EXPRESSION

The Blueprint

Expressionista is the heart of Soul Seed coming into vibrant, authentic identity. Exploratory and playful, Expressionista wants to know who she is from soil to soul and share herself, let everyone know. She is of the garden, a young bloom finding her way through her heart. In kinship with the teenage years of life, Expressionista is asking the questions, "Who am I?" and "Who am I *really*?" and experimenting, rebelling, and flirting her way toward answers.

The biggest directive of Expressionista is to share her truest essence with full, uninhibited authenticity—as an act of love and creativity. Expressionista regards her essence not as burdensome or shameful, but as needed, glorious and medicinal. Affirmed for who she is, Expressionista dares to discover how to make her medicine even more potent.

Expressionista is unafraid of her various shades, moods, powers, and truths. But she's also intentional with how and where she shares her fullness. She knows the medicine of her essence doesn't work for all people or situations. Expressionista seeks environments where she'll thrive, where her medicine is needed and will be heeded, and where Gatekeeper can keep her safe, lush, and loved.

In healthy environments, Expressionista shares her majesty shamelessly, fully and exquisitely. In unhealthy environments, Expressionista communicates exactly what's off in order to restore functionality and fertility to the soil. Expressionista is a living litmus test of wellness in the garden and wears her feelings about how she's doing on her petals for all to see.

She'll howl to be watered, weeded, protected, counseled, and guided back to plump aliveness. She'll share the inconvenient message when the garden isn't a safe place for everyone. These expressions, while sometimes less popular, are brilliant, life-preserving, and unifying ones. They get everyone working together again for the sake of a thriving habitat.

In full trust and communion with the truth of her heart, Expressionista is devoted to embodying and sharing her fullest bloom—to making divine medicine from her essence, and to reveling in the pleasure of her own potency while she's at it.

Expressionista comes to life at the collective level through celebration, amplification, and inclusion of all identities in the garden, knowing everyone's unique essence is needed for the full medicinal potential of our collective garden to be realized.

Expressionista at a Glance

Body Connection: Heart, Chest, Breasts, Throat

The heart is your epicenter of connection with the world around you. When it feels safe, it expands and shares its love in a vast array of generous expressions.

The heart is your emotional source, the place from which love, disgust, grief, anger, celebration, or care spring forth. When your heart feels threatened and criticized—especially over time—it hardens and freezes, calling in its own special Gatekeeper (the heart protector) to keep out threats. With prolonged experiences of shame or repression, your instinct to share your true self could also harden over.

For mothers, the heart sources the breasts, and the breasts become a literal source of nourishment, nutrients, and medicine. The breasts can also be a source of pleasure. When they are praised, massaged, and given loving attention, they delight in sensual aliveness.

The throat is your communication source—the place from which you share the truth of both your heart and your intuition. When your heart feels protected and empowered your whole system relaxes and your throat gives voice to your divine truth inside.

Natural Blueprint of Health: Whole-Self Expression

You share the truth of who you are, how you feel, what you think and what you want with authenticity, compassion and confidence. You care about your expression's impact, and your intention is to liberate—not harm—yourself and others. You are resilient in the face of being misunderstood. You shine bright and true in the world, regardless of criticism or others attempts to shame or repress you.

Traumatic Imprint: Shame and Repression

You are wronged, made bad, quieted, hushed, covered up, hidden, made secret, silenced, hyper-criticized, blamed, name-called, ostracized, or told you're a sinner or sinning for your core way of being.

Hyper-Response to Shame and Repression: Toxic Defiance

- Saying "fuck the man" to everything and everyone who's ever tried to hold you back—including healthy Gatekeepers who are simply employing safe limits
- Expressing yourself without regard to the effect your expression has on others—even those who never actually shamed or repressed you

- Reckless self-expression
- Vindictive language

When someone's embodying Toxic Defiance, it can often feel threatening to their system to be voiceless or to give space to others' voices. There's an all-or-nothing energy around self-expression, and the core fear is if they don't say everything on their mind or heart, they'll be silenced.

Common fears and inner dialogues include:

- "I'm not going to let them shame or repress me ever again!"
- "No one gets to speak on my behalf—ever!"
- "I'll say whatever I want. I've been silenced enough!"
- "If I don't say it loud or direct enough, no one will hear me."
- "I'm never hiding my true self in any way, ever again."
- "You can't shame me if I shame you first."
- "Oh...I'm going to express myself fully...on my anonymous Instagram account that goes viral!"

Hypo-Response to Shame and Repression: Dimming

- Internalizing negative messaging and shame in a way that leads you to shut down your voice, truth, and power
- Fear of who you really are, your true identity
- Significantly dimming your authentic volume
- Evaporating your medicine
- Depressive frozenness around bringing your heart, gifts, talents, or creativity forward

When someone's embodying Dimming, it can often feel threatening to their system to be seen, heard, or known in their authenticity. Showing their true self and creations can feel vulnerable, unsafe and like it runs the risk of further shame or repression.

Common fears and inner dialogues include:

- "I'm going to look or sound really stupid…"
- "I don't know how to _____ [express my creativity in some form or another, share my gifts, start a business…]"
- "Everyone will judge me and think I'm untalented, bad, or dumb if I share what's deep inside."
- "They're going to reject me."
- "I have nothing original to share. So-and-so shares it better, so why bother."
- "I will literally die if I _____ [sing, share my art, share my writing, step into my calling, or come out.]"
- "I have NO IDEA what I'm good at, what direction I should take with my life, what my purpose is."
- "If I assert or share my heart, it will be trampled on…so it's better to stay small."

From Private Shame to Public Emancipation

I remember my sixth-grade school dance, sweating in skin-tight, black spandex, booty grinding into a prepubescent boy an inch or two shorter than me to the tune of "Back That Ass Up." My eroticism was turned ON, and I was ready to play. Despite all the small, insidious ways culture tried to shame my aliveness—telling me how to dress, how to sit, how to speak, how to breathe—I couldn't help it; I was raunchy.

Tell a thing not to be a thing enough times, and that repression may turn into a deep, rigid freeze encasing true expression or identity. On the other hand, that thing may become defiant; sharing all it wishes with an edge of fierce resentment. Worst yet, it may go in both directions at once. Hazy cognition and less access to full, authentic expression, and—over-sharing without caring about impact. This is the science of how we respond to shame; the way we move from toxic defiance to dimming, hyper-arousal to hypo, until eventually the hypo becomes too heavy and thick, such as a cold sickness to the soul, we can't thaw it out on our own, so we just don't.

In my case, as a sixth grader swallowing ongoing cultural shame pills while simultaneously coming of age as an erotic creature, I took my raunchy grinding into dark corners, hidden bathrooms and backseats of hand-me-down cars. I hyper-expressed my wildness in the shadows where no authorities could catch me. It was part organic wildness, part over-righteous resistance, and part shame-induced dissociation. In the dark, on a mission to prove my freedom, but without the skills, full cognitive reasoning, or initiations of power to do so, I eclipsed my true tongue, my real needs. With Soul Seed and Gatekeeper both offline, I had no voice to name and find my real hungers or limits. I performed deeds and had deeds done to me that shocked my system into even more shame, shoving me further into hidden-away caverns of dissociated carelessness.

When you're working with clients who have severe or even minor histories of being shamed or repressed for their true nature, they'll often come to you in a deep state of physiological fear around whole-self expression. They might wonder what's wrong with them for being so damn stuck and why they can't seem to muster the courage to show up and shine. They may blame themselves for all the ways their honest dance has led them to a series of bad romances. They probably don't trust the safety of their true nature. And it makes sense. It's likely that their true nature has been compromised and clouded by the dissociative effects of shame.

Shame and repression are like straightjackets on honest expression. At first, you go mad trying to hiss your way out, but when you're met with more shouts of denigration, eventually, you give up on trying to get free. If you sense your true expression will stifle connection, it becomes difficult to share your authentic heart.

Scientifically, the limbic portion of the human brain seeks attachment, connection, and meaning. We are familial creatures, and we crave the feeling of belonging as a core survival need. When we sense a threat to our belonging, our nervous system sends signals to our reptilian brain to protect and defend us from that loss. The trouble is, the reptilian brain is disconnected from language, and as emergency responses of hypersocialization, fight, flight, or freeze come more *online*, clear logic, creativity, reasoning, meaning making, and voice go more *offline*.

Shame is a direct threat to our feeling of belonging as mammals. Often, when we experience shame or repression, we lose access to the clear truth of our identity, it becomes harder to integrate our feelings, thoughts and voice, and we struggle to express ourselves from the genuineness of our heart.

In my case, I was in a cycle that I've seen many clients suffer inside as well. Toxic cultural shame around female sexuality led to a dissociative relationship to it, which led to unsafe experiences and violations, which led to even deeper shame, which led to even deeper freeze. By the time I got to college, I'd experienced enough exploitation in intimate places that shining shamelessly felt like a surefire path to danger. Instead, I nearly extinguished my erotic light with hyper-Gatekeeping of my sensuality. If bits of my natural eroticism seeped out of me, I quickly caught myself, and blushing with embarrassment, covered-up. Sex at the time felt like a weird side dish I could just as easily leave off my plate. No biggie.

My life went on like this for almost a decade, until I'd had enough time, enough safety, enough no-pressure relating to my very sweet husband that I finally regrew my sexual appetite. When my sex started to wake up again, which coincided with my divorce, I had no real clue how to wield my sensual, wild life-force. My boundaries were super wonky. My worthiness was especially low. And my desires were off the charts. My heart and pussy were not talking to each other. At all.

I was in the land of Soul Seed and Gatekeeper, trying to find my footing, my roots, my needs, my embodied truth. During this time, I was drawn to ecstatic dance. For three years, twice a week, I let my feet hit the floor to the beat of the music. My body searched for safety in its expression, hints of respectful attention, and the ability to communicate wordlessly when I wasn't interested, without having to run away from unwanted moves.

Fast forward six years. I had devoted endless time to learning my embodied worth, sovereignty and whole-self expression. Now, I found myself at a magical place called Tamera, a "Healing Biotope" in Southern Portugal where most people in the village had been practicing polyamory for over forty years. It was the fifth day of "Intro Week," and we'd split up by gender. Twenty women all lounged around the edges of a mystical pond sharing visions of their most erotic fantasies, when a snake slithered up between my legs, stared me straight in the eyes, and practically smiled. The whole group of women *oohed* and *ahhed*. "It's good luck!" one hooted. "A symbol of awakened eros!" another giggled.

I smirked, real joyful and certain. "Uh huh…sure is." Then I went on to share my most erotic fantasy. One of multiple men, maybe six or seven, that I'd approved of, all *paying me* to pleasure me, worship me from head-to-toe, body, heart, and soul. It was the ultimate turn-the-patriarchy-on-its-head-fantasy, and I was ready for it—ready to embrace the energetic of just how completely receptive I could be, just how much I could let my sexuality feed me, just how valuable I could view my eroticism and shamelessly own my sensual medicine.

Later, as we were walking back to the main grounds for dinner, I saw out of the corner of my eyes a small group of three beautiful men dancing together in a courtyard. I slipped away from the pack and pranced up to them. Like synchronized swimmers, they turned gracefully toward me. Then one, a dark, handsome Indian man, whispered playfully, "Well, well, well, if it isn't Shakti herself!"

I smiled with coy recognition then began to sway and dip my hips, letting my arms travel up toward the sky, their bodies beginning to encircle mine with a reverent, erotic ferocity. This went on for three whole songs, each of us going deeper into the fantasy I'd just described. The fantasy they knew nothing about, at least not in their minds.

These men were getting high off worshipping me kindly. My medicine was getting fed by their generous attention, their heated, respectful lust. There was so much trust in the space. Because I knew I could always leave. Because I knew they didn't need to take from me. Because they'd already been dancing happily with each other, basking in the power of erotic brotherly love. Because Tamera's was a culture of celebrating sensuality. Because I knew no one would shame me. Because this was a place where the medicine of eros was seen as just that—healthy, needed and necessary.

You might be reading this thinking, "Good for you, Rachael! You got to twirl through Heaven on Earth with sexy men who worshipped you, in an environment cultivated specifically for safety! What about me over here in the cold forest of cultural exploitation where no one's thinking about erotic emancipation?!"

I hear you. Valid. As we all know, when it comes to whole-self expression, the environment—both internal and external—matters. When we try to express our whole, holy self without a deep knowing of our worthiness, without embodying sacred sovereignty and without others there to celebrate our authenticity, we're less full of ourselves, less enlivened by our own life-force, and our wholeness can have perceptible holes for others to poke at, take from or enter into.

In trauma resolution, we talk about a toric field—the donut-like energy field around your body that's a holographic representation of your internal nervous system. If our nervous system is spinning in hyper-arousal or crashed out in hypo-arousal, that's projected outside and around our whole bodies. Our internal state is perceptible energetically. Even if someone would never consider themselves attuned to energy, our toric fields are all reading each other without our cognitive awareness. We sense the holes, the thorns, the presence and the dissociation of all living things around us.[11]

At Tamera, my toric field resonated with the collective field they'd co-created, which celebrated eroticism and sensuality. But what happens when we're living in a collective field that celebrates the opposite? When we try to grow wild and free in the soil of patriarchy, white supremacy, heteronormativity or colonization, it's more challenging for our roots to sink in. It can feel risky for our flower to rise and be seen. Hyper-competition, domination, sexism, sexualization, control, extraction and racism—these are poison to the medicine of our true nature, which

---

[11] *I learned about the toric field from Brigit Viksnins, who learned about it from Anna Chitty.*

wants to celebrate one another, share with one another, honor, regard, and uplift one another.

Blooming True in Toxic Soil

While for me, Tamera was a place of erotic liberation, my best friend Jodi—a queer lesbian who came with me—had a much different experience. Before we left for our trip, we wondered, would this be another "leading edge, spiritual, sex-positive environment" that emphasized the interplay between the "divine feminine" and "divine masculine," completely eclipsing gender and sexuality spectrums? Would Jodi's existence feel valid and valued in this environment? Would she feel safe, wanted, and welcome? Or would shame and repression, erasure and heteronormativity, pour salt in the old wounds that Jodi had accumulated as a lesbian in a homophobic culture?

Sadly, we experienced an unfortunate dose of the latter. The whole week, the leaders at Tamera referred to eros as only happening "between a man and a woman." When we brought to their attention the harm and exclusion in their language, they chuckled as if they'd heard it a million times before, and then chalked it up to their German language limitations.

Eventually, through many voices echoing the courage of Jodi's, we got through to them, and they began citing the possibility of love between a "man and a man" or a "woman and a woman."

The thing is, language matters. Representation matters. Words and images create constructs that our bodies either dance, break, bruise, or bloom inside.

In Naomi Wolf's life-changing book, *Vagina*, she talks about the effects that language has on physiology—most specifically, the vagina. "The sexual threats encoded in hostile language centered on the vagina do more than trigger stress reactions in our bodies," Wolf writes. "Cultural concepts become embedded in a woman's body and her brain perceptually…"

She goes on to share about sexuality workshops wherein she'd read to large groups of women the names and concepts for the vagina from cultures that revered it. She'd ask those women to notice how they felt in their bodies hearing the vagina referred to with phrases such as "the most sacred spot in the most sacred temple in a sacred universe," (thirteenth century Japan), or "golden lotus," "gates of paradise," or "precious pearl" (Chinese Han dynasties), or "like a flower that loves to absorb the sun's rays—that is, to be seen in daylight—and the caress of strong hands. Her juices have the fragrance of a freshly blossoming lotus flower," (Tantric texts on the yoni of the Padmini). The whole room would let out great sighs of relief, then burst into joyful, blushing cheer.

Then she'd have them share their first or most poignant memories of the ways their vaginas had been named or talked to. "Sit on my face." "Give me some of that slanted pussy." "Cockpocket." "Meat curtain." "V-hole." "Vertical seafood taco." The groups' energy shifted from sensuous delight to felt-sense shame.

Wolf writes about the way language neurally encodes differences in perception and how that perception affects the moves we make in our bodies, relationships, bedrooms, and lives. When language is positive, affirming, and representative in beautiful ways, it creates an open, inviting space within which we can grow and thrive authentically. But when language is negative, demeaning, or void of representation all together, the space inside of us shrinks.

At Tamera, in an environment that validated and gave language to the dominant orientation of my loving and fucking, I felt a sense of possibility, intrigue, flirtation, and belonging. My eros had a place to go, a people to connect with. I had spontaneous experiences of eroticism and sensual delight. I felt, viscerally—in my tits, pussy, heart, and romantic stirrings—like I belonged. My free nature, spiritual power, loving leadership, wild hair—they had a place there, no questions asked. Few parts of me went unmet or were made to feel unwelcome.

Jodi, on the other hand, didn't feel immediate connection in the areas of sex and love. Instead, from the edges looking in, she spent most of her time evaluating to see how inclusive the space would be. She was listening for representational language, to find out who else was queer, to know where she fit into this community—if at all.

When we're healing the wounds of shame and repression; when we're gathering the magic of our whole-self expression, it seems to me that a critical act is seeking out places and spaces where our core identities and specific medicines are honored and revered. And if we can't find those places and spaces, creating them becomes the call.

If our identities are more centered by culture, can we co-create spaces that include more marginalized voices in leadership roles? If we are part of more marginalized or oppressed identity groups, can we seek refuge, joy, and relief by gathering with others like us?

In preparation for this book, I interviewed almost a dozen people whose identities were different than mine. In my interview with Jodi, I asked her things I'd never asked her before, even though we've been best friends since we were twelve years old. This particular snippet of our conversation stemmed from an inquiry around language:

"You know, identifying as queer and working with kids, I was always terrified of being accused of anything," Jodi told me. "My social lens, the things I'd seen or heard, were negative views about homosexuality. *They're perverted. They're going to pray on kids.* I felt inherently more nervous working with kids and identifying as queer, because I thought people were gonna think I'd abuse their kids. I was extra cautious. Not that there was anything to be covering up or hiding, but I was hyper-aware of the dominant cultural fear."

"With sexuality, that's always been the interesting thing," she said. "It's invisible for me. I can play that to my advantage. If I'm in a situation where someone's talking poorly about gay people, I can hide and feel shame or speak out and potentially be in a dangerous situation."

As Jodi was talking, I was feeling the missing perspective of queer women of color and trans people in our conversation—those who couldn't hide who they were, but also weren't always safe to be out. I brought it up, asked what she thought about it and whether we could even speak to it as two white women.

"Yeah, that's tough. I don't think we can, really. I also don't want to gloss over the big danger that many people face in coming out. It's horrible." Jodi said, "But…" and she paused to connect with something tender and quiet inside. "I also want to highlight the dangers of shame. That's why there's so much suicide in the queer community. You're gonna hurt yourself when you're hiding, if others don't hurt you when you're out. And not like you should have to choose one danger over another, but just know, at the deepest level…every single queer person is valid."

I started to tear up with resonance. "Keep going," I whispered.

"Here's what's really important: at least having one other person in your life who sees you for who you are, who's safe to be around, to validate your existence as your most authentic self. That is critical to have. It will save you from the extremes of the world. People are still going to be shitty on Instagram, in public, in conservative towns, in your family…You might still experience your own internalized homophobia and shame…Danger might still be a reality for you based on race or location. But if you can come back to this core truth that feels like, *I'm meant to be here on the planet and the planet's meant to learn from who I am…My voice is needed for the planet's healing*, it's a very different approach. An approach that saves lives."

I remembered the interview I had with a brilliant woman named M'Kali-Hashiki earlier in the year.[12] I was seeking to better understand the way systemic oppression created and sustained trauma, and I hired her for consultation.

M'Kali-Hashiki is a self-described, "Black, fat lesbian" living in Oakland, California. She works as a tour guide to the realm of eros, a renegade sexual mystic, and a teacher of somatic erotic possibilities. She's also spent decades researching and observing the ways systems of oppression affect the body and sexuality.

I shared with M'Kali-Hashiki my model of the seven Natural Blueprints of Health and Traumatic Imprints. At the time, I had "oppression" as an imprint, but she illuminated for me that, in reality, oppression is more like our collective soil.

"Oppression," she said, "because of its systemic nature, actually can't be overcome or overturned on an individual level. The way one might go about healing from an 'incidental trauma' like rape or assault, can't be applied to the trauma of oppression. Because with oppression, we have to convince the body it's in a place of safety in order to get temporary relief and begin our healing. But how do you convince the body of a Black, fat femme that she's in a place of safety in an environment in which she's not safe? The body can't be fooled that way. How do

---

[12] *Learn more about M'Kali-Hashiki at fiercepassions.com*

we say, *you're safe in this way, but not in that way?* To the body, safety is safety—it's either totally safe, or not." I sat, quiet, with curious presence as she continued on.

"What I know is being small, being silent, will not keep us safe. If we're in danger anyway, isn't it better to be in danger being the fullness of ourselves, then to be less of ourselves?"

"Mmmmh, yes." I nodded. Then asked, "What, for you, has helped make that more possible?"

"I've been doing a lot to try to create spaces that are predominantly queer people of color. Together, at least, we can take down our guards and get some relief, some healing. Trying to do this in isolation is next-to-impossible. I'm really intentional that part of the purpose of having events is to build community; community that can have each other's backs, not just in the sense of physical safety, but in the sense of...*I'm trying to heal my erotic wounds or explore what's pleasurable for me.* That feels so hard to do alone. But here, we can do it together, in the safety of people who also experience the complexities of being in a body that's marginalized by the state."

When we got off our interview, I thought of flocking—one of the less popularly known nervous system emergency responses that creates safety through sticking together. I thought of Collective Gatekeepers, and how sometimes, groups of people need the refuge of only being with each other, so they don't have to endure the endless exhaustion of fawning off micro-aggressions or systemic threats. And I thought of how important it is for groups who aren't subject to so many intersections of oppression to respect and support the groups who are—financially, energetically, and relationally.

Whatever your true identity, whoever you are at your inner core, however you present—perhaps consider the question:

What community conditions would honor, uplift and amplify my personal medicine, and how can I devote to co-creating them?

Just this past summer, Jodi, seeking to create the world she was hungry for, decided to put together a Queer Your Living Room Candlelight Music Tour. She gathered people in private house shows across America and told stories of searching for love as a queer lesbian. She shared her heartbreak songs and her mega-feeling songs, her hopeful tunes and her angry ones, too. Magically (or not so magically), she met her next partner, a soul mate of sorts, at her very first show. Jodi being fully "out" in the wholeness of her Expressionista, baring her truest heart for all to see was the medicine that landed her the life of her dreams. Go figure.

The Weight of Words

"If you could do anything, what would you let yourself do?" I asked her. Laura was 30 years old, living with her parents, and severely stuck around her work in the world. Like a corked-up, precious bottle of wine, she had gifts inside, but was terrified to let them out.

There was a long pause.

"What's happening over there, love?" I asked.

"I'm feeling really hot all over," she began, "like I can't say the thing."

"Okay, no need," I whispered. "Can you just be with your body a bit? Notice, without needing to erase or change the heat, if perhaps any part of you feels a bit more neutral, possibly okay?"

"Okay...I can do that."

Laura grew up with a conservative, evangelical Christian, patriarchal father, who also happened to be an alcoholic and an asshole. He shamed her sexuality, warning her that if she ever had sex outside of marriage, she would be a disgrace to the whole family. He told her that girls should be seen, not heard. He doubted her intelligence and often exploded in fits of random anger, directed at her, cursing and name-calling included. Laura's mother, disconnected from her own sovereign protector, bowed to the patriarch of the family, meek as a mouse at her daughter's expense.

With all this shame and repression forced in Laura's direction, it became very hard for her to discover her true self. Laura developed what's called a *double bind*: the embodiment of two competing momentums in the nervous system. When you're in a double bind, one part of you is saying, "I must," "I have to," or "I need to,"(hyper-arousal), while the other part is insisting, "I can't," "it's impossible," "it's too dangerous." (hypo-arousal).

For Laura, one side of her double bind went like this: *I can't trust my core nature, my inherent beauty and brilliance, my wild light. I was told I'm bad my whole life. I'll get in so much trouble if I shine. Sexual self-expression? FORGET IT.*

A physiological freeze set deep over her heart and zipped the lips of her truest love—singing. Even though Laura had the most gorgeous voice, she never sang in front of anyone.

Sexually speaking, her desires were equally silenced, and in their absence, she let her partners lead the way. With her body a half-there, barely-aroused version of itself, she felt next-to-no pleasure in intimacy.

On the other side of the double bind, Laura's internal voices sounded more like: *I must break out of this motherfucking cage! I **must** express myself at all costs! I must be all of who I am and let no one and nothing hold me down! I will be a sexually liberated GODDESS!*

In tangible talk, this meant Laura was constantly feeling oppressed by her bosses, quitting her jobs, and rebelling against anyone or anything that sat in the seat of authority—whether or not that authority was, in fact, oppressive.

She was dressing to express her rebellious sexuality, but also secretly terrified of the attention she received. She didn't know how to back up her sensual expression with regulated protection, and she often found herself in sexual situations that didn't meet her heart or soul.

Double binds are like Chinese finger traps. You get stuck in the pull of opposing forces. The only way to get out is to soften the intensity of both directions until you can gently allow the pressure to loosen, and from there, allow one momentum at a time to express and resolve slowly. Like most, with no guidance or understanding about how to gently allow the pressure to loosen (both in physiological and cognitive ways), Laura took to alcohol as a handy helper.

Laura's circumstances are not unique. I've worked with countless clients who experienced deep shame and repression growing up, then later felt incessant doubt about their direction and deep fear of their power.

I like to think of shame and repression as sound waves that compress the

Blueprint of beauty that wants to burst forth. Imagine a flower, ready to bloom, being yelled into a corner. Even nature couldn't thrive under those conditions.

Dr. Masaru Emoto is famous for his experiments with the effects of words, consciousness, and music on the molecular structure of water. He published several volumes of work entitled "Messages from Water," wherein he took photographs of ice crystals under a microscope after they'd been infused with the energies of certain words or songs. Their shapes dramatically changed and took on the energy of those words or music.

If you tell a child she's bad enough times, she might begin to believe it. On the other hand, she might begin to resist it. In many cases, she'll do both at once.

In Laura's case, her double bind of refusing to join any patriarchal system as a form of defiance, coupled with her deep, traumatic fear of her own authentic expression, left her at thirty years old, penniless and still living in the cage that raised her—her parents' basement—while having a whole lot of crappy, quiet sex.

We started working together just after she sobered up. Our first step was reawakening her Soul Seed—her worthiness, her right to be as she truly is: sensual, sensitive, creative, powerful, sexual. We then moved into building the muscles of her Gatekeeper—the part that draws good things in and keeps bad things out. It took years of working together on-and-off, as well as Laura making her personal healing and empowerment her top priority, but eventually, Laura began to let her beautiful voice sing free in small spaces of safe, supportive friends.

She quit her job, but this time on the premise that her boss truly was an asshole, and she became committed to earning money in ways that honored, as opposed to exploited, her gifts. Eventually, feeling centered, safe, and expressed in her healthy power, Laura became a life coach, helping other people who felt deeply held back by shame and repression come into rightful confidence and aliveness.

Using Healthy Aggression to Break Free from Toxic Shame

When we experience chronic, toxic shame or repression—being told that our inherent nature is bad or wrong over and over again—it can put us into a deep physiological freeze, muting our voices, stiffening our movement, and stripping the vibrancy from our expression.

Healthy aggression and disgust are the antidotes to toxic shame. They're the ability to feel the ridiculousness of someone trying to harm you, then invoke an energy that strikes or pushes away from what's dangerous or harmful. Healthy aggression and disgust are impulses of mobilized protection. When they succeed interpersonally then metabolize physiologically, they settle into healthy turn-on, passion, desire, and penetration. In other words, the same part of your life force that's used to protect your preciousness is also used to claim your aliveness.

However, as we learned in the last chapter, for some, healthy aggression is not always easy to access. Often, we first need a gentle, safe space to thaw deep freeze. The warm-couch embrace of unconditional auntie-love. The celebratory shamelessness of witchy sister circles. The solidarity of the gathering with others who look, love, or fuck like you.

With enough time and space—with no pressure to come into who you really are, but just a simple invitation that you're allowed—the body may begin to feel safe enough to sing.

Healthy aggression rises when the body senses it could actually succeed at securing your desires or protecting your place in the human family. Or, when the body senses there's no other choice—the fight is necessary, and the freeze cannot be afforded.

It's worth mentioning again that we tend to move through both the hyper- and hypo-responses to traumatic imprints, in order to rebloom our Blueprint. In this case, to access healthy passionate whole-self expression, we often first thaw out the hypo experience of dimming, move through the hyper experience of toxic defiance, then finally, emerge into the radical revelation of whole-self expression. We melt the walls around our hearts, rebuild the muscles to push away harmful words and toxic shame, and then, inside the sacred space that our emergency responses created for us, a seedling emerges into a sprout; our truest medicine begins to come all the way out.

Essential Expressionista Practices

Expressionista Coherence Practice

Standing, sitting or lying down, allow yourself to bring your hands to your heart, chest or breasts, or simply orient your attention there. Take a moment to connect with the felt-sense experience in this part of your body. Perhaps bring to mind a time when you felt shamed or repressed, or on the other hand, a time when you felt totally loved and adored.

Notice how your hands feel called to connect with your body as you do this. Are you feeling open, ready to receive the world? Are you feeling like you need to hug yourself or curl inward? Or perhaps you'd like to rub or massage this part of your body?

Remember, this part of your body is the center of your emotional landscape and it's also the place from which your true identity radiates. What does the true you want to show today?

Notice your sensations, then say either inwardly or outwardly, with pausing and sensing in between affirmations:

I feel my heart fully.
I feel my heart fully.
I feel my heart fully.
I share my heart truly.
I am medicine.
I am meant to be me.
I am embodied expression.
I am shameless.

How do these words feel in your heart, your chest, your breasts, your throat? What do you sense is your medicine, in general, or in relationship to the specific situation you're focusing on?

Repeat these affirmations as many times as you'd like, perhaps giving yourself space to rest, express, or journal afterward. Remember, difficulty embodying the Blueprint is just a sign that your body needs more time allowing these truths to come online. Go slowly and be kind with yourself in this process.

Naming the Source of Your Shame

I remember the moment with exquisite clarity when Brigit told me that toxic shame is often a transference of someone else's bad behavior—internalized shame or repressed desires that gets projected onto you, and then taken into your nervous system as your own.

A necessary part of shame resolution and reclaiming whole-self expression is giving back what was never yours to hold.

When your clients are stuck under a trauma spell of shame or repression, you might gently lead them through the following journaling exercise, inviting them to stop and connect with their bodies as they engage the process.

Question 1: Who shamed or repressed you?
Question 2: What did they say or do?
Question 3: What was their own relationship to the thing they were shaming or repressing in you?

Once your client has excavated these things, have them consider writing a letter to that person, giving the shame back, or releasing it to the earth for both parties.

Here's a shame releasing letter template they can use, if it would feel supportive:

Dear _____,

This is a letter to release the shame you gave to me. The shame I never earned. The shame I don't deserve.

I have a core identity that includes _____, _____, and _____ [name qualities of your identity] and essential medicines that include _____, _____, _____ [name qualities of your goodness, talents, joys or gifts].

These parts of me are holy, wise, beautiful and good.

Once, you told me I was too _____, _____, and _____. [Cite the language that was used to tell you that you were too much.]

I see clearly now how those things are qualities you also possess and are afraid to express or embody.

Another time you told me I wasn't _____, _____, or _____ enough. [Cite the language that was used to tell you weren't enough.]

I see clearly now how afraid you are of not being enough, of being kicked out of the human family.

I release from my body and soul the words and energies that you game to me. I am not willing to carry this shame. You are no longer able to _____. [Name the boundaries you will now embody around their behavior and words.]

Here's what I need to say for myself to feel complete: _____. [Declare anything else that would affirm your goodness, your truth or your heart.]

Thanks for reading.

Sincerely,
[Your name]

Once the letter is complete, your client may wish to read it aloud to you, to burn it, to bury it, or maybe even to send it to the actual person. Invite them to feel into what would be the most empowering and affirming action for them to take with this letter, then support their instinct.

Co-Create Safe Space to Fully Express

When we're still cultivating our confidence or safety, it's important that we have people who encourage, validate, witness, celebrate, and amplify our whole-self expression. It's also important that we're in spaces or relationships that are pressure-free. The dance into whole-self expression after layers of shame and repression is often sensitive—needing both support as well as spaciousness. The following process can help your client identify, envision or co-create the right-fit relationships needed to rebloom their Expressionista.

Invite your client into the following visualization:

Consider a part of your identity that you desire to embody more full-out, but also feel a bit of shame or repression around. Perhaps close your eyes and imagine what kind of environment or community that part of you would thrive within. Who would be there? What would they be wearing? What would the space look and feel like? What music would be playing? What permission would permeate the room?

Invite your client to open their eyes and write down what they saw. Then, ask your clients the following follow-up questions:

Do you know of any spaces like the one you just imagined? If so, write them down. Do you know of any people who'd also love the space you just imagined? If so, write their names down.

Here's the part that's scary but absolutely necessary for our clients to hear:

If the space already exists—can you let yourself show up to it? Show up shyly or show up in full radiance? Show up alone or show up with a friend? Can you employ that healthy aggression that activates your drive to move toward your desire? Even just a little bit? Even just once?

Your flowers will bloom brightest in the company of others like you. Dare to step into the garden.

If the people exist (even one will do!) but the place or community container doesn't—can you reach out to those people? Make a simple phone call or send a short text.

Here's an invitation template your client can use:

"Hi! How's it going? Hey, so, I've been wanting to awaken more of my _____ [insert adjective this person also shares: witchy side, sensual side, mystical side, intuitive side, queer side, Indigenous side, polyamorous side] and you came to mind as someone who might also be into that. Would you wanna get together for a night of [insert possibilities of things to awaken said quality]?"

If your client can't think of other people or places that share their core identity trait, it might be time to do that really brave thing like Jodi and M'Kali-Hashiki did—cast a wider net.

Invite your client to envision how they might bring to life a place that honors the identity they're trying to unleash from within. Then, help them make an invite. Tell them to send it to anyone and everyone who might possibly, secretly, maybe strangely be into it.

Shame-resolution requires authentic connection and affirmation of true identity. Your clients are worthy of being seen and known, found and grown alongside others who love and lust and long in the same way. Celebrate their truest identity by helping them amplify it with like-minded friends.

What Gatekeeping is Needed for Your Expressionista's Most True Bloom?

At heart, Expressionista is the young, radiant, romantic bloom of Soul Seed. Protected and provided for in her sovereignty by Gatekeeper, advised and counseled by the older, wiser Sage, she shares herself shamelessly, with love and potency.

If your client's Expressionista is stunted—if her whole-self expression feels stifled and afraid—you might ask what Gatekeeping is missing from her inner-ecology. What protection or providing is offline, the absence of which makes it unsafe for her Soul Seed to grow and emerge?

Expressionista is the heart of the matter. If your client isn't expressing her heart's greatest love—through embodying her calling, sexuality, identity, spirituality, or creative capacity—*what does she need in order to feel safe and resourced coming all the way out?* Invite your client to sit with that question, journal on it, feel into it and vision with it. Living that question is the key to liberating Expressionista's greatest medicine and aliveness.

Chapter 7

SAGE

FROM MANIPULATION
& CONTROL
to CLARITY
& CHOICE

The Blueprint

Sage is the knower, seer, wisdom-keeper, and advisor of the garden. An age and stage beyond Expressionista—older and closer to her own decay, death, and regeneration—Sage is less afraid of change, endings, and destruction. She's not as wide-eyed or innocent as Expressionista, but she embodies the same essential heart medicine. She's lived longer and seen more, experienced persecution, coercion, manipulation, and neglect. Now, she cannot be fooled, nor does she deny her needs. She feeds them.

Sage has earned a no-nonsense approach to seeing the truth, speaking the truth, and aligning to the truth, even when doing so necessitates closure, disruption, or completion.

Sage knows everything is impermanent and infinite, dies and gets reborn. This long view imparts Sage with the courage to let go of toxicity or misalignments and move coherently into a healthy future.

Sage prioritizes sincerity and righteousness. She's committed to living utter fulfillment, so that at the end of her life she can die knowing she walked in Truth.

On one hand, Sage councils Expressionista: encourages her to embody her true bloom. On the other, she asks for help from Gatekeeper and Groundskeeper to keep her space free of anything that may muddy the potency of her medicine.

In an era of mass cultural lies and gaslighting, falsity and fascism, our Collective Sage protects the shared soil by broadcasting clarity, encouraging the masses to stay lucid and in-choice, on purpose and loyal to veracity, no matter how propagandized things become.

Sage has precise intuition about what's true and what's false. She is rarely duped. She sees through lies and calls things as they are—to herself and others. This wisdom, in service to the whole, propels humanity forward on a path of justice and peace.

Sage knows that integrity with the truth of our compassionate, humanitarian hearts is the means for personal and collective liberation. She takes a wild stand for emancipation from the manipulative, controlling lies that keep humans small, doubtful, and imprisoned.

Sage is willing to swallow the challenging medicine of leadership in order to embody and promote truth, against all odds, popular or not. She is a living, breathing exemplar of responsibility, morality, love, and alignment.

Sage at a Glance

Body Connection: Eyes, Ears, Throat, Third Eye

Your eyes are the portal through which you see yourself, others and the world. Your ears are the means through which you hear messages, learn languages, and sink into stories about what's real. Your throat is the channel by which you add your own truth and story to the messages of the world. And your third eye represents the felt-sense, intuitive perception of what can't be seen or heard in the open—but rings true under the surface, nevertheless.

As a child, your body is designed to learn through mimicry, sensing both the visible and the invisible, then repeating back what you perceive for confirmation. When you're affirmed for the truth you sense, then you develop confidence in your capacity to perceive the world around you. You trust your perception skills, even when others try to sway you in a different direction.

However, when what you sense, see or perceive doesn't line up with what's being told to you—perhaps over and over again from a young age—two things can begin to happen: you can doubt your capacity to locate what's true, causing the onset of deep confusion (swirly or clouded sight), or you can become hypervigilant and untrusting of others and the world (strained sight).

Sage has 20/20 vision and an unobstructed connection to her truth-meter. She uses her eyes to see the messages that are in plain sight, her third eye to read beneath what's being said, and her throat to share the sum of what she senses. Her clear sight is the grounds for her stability in terms of direction, authority, inner-peace, and outer volition.

Natural Blueprint of Health: Clarity and Choice

You have a clear sense of who you are, what you know, what you want, and what your options are at every moment. You make decisions from a place of alignment with your wholehearted values, embodied wisdom, and mental discernment. You are the validator of your experiences. You trust your perceptions to be true and know that your feelings and opinions matter. You take time and space to yourself or with trusted support to get clarity when you're feeling unsure or uncertain. You have inner-authority and knowing. You choose in consent with yourself, first and foremost. You trust others from a place of trusting your own integrity. You are empowered through access to the truth.

Traumatic Imprint: Manipulation and Control

You are gaslit, denied your experience, lied to, served ultimatums, given the silent treatment. You experience financial withholding, shaming, monitoring, having constant tabs kept on you, the withdrawal of affection, guilt trips, being constantly faulted, having another's extreme moodiness blamed on you. You have projections cast on you. You are bullied, not listened to, or coerced.

Hyper-Response to Manipulation and Control: Hypervigilance

- Not knowing who you can trust
- Having extreme skepticism
- Assuming that others are trying to get one over on you
- Stubbornness about going your own way
- Controlling situations and relationships
- Playing emotional games with others in order to keep the upper hand
- Doing extreme case-building about what's going on
- Being hyper-guarded
- Isolating out of fear

When someone's embodying Hypervigilance, it can often feel threatening to their system to give up control and let another lead, to close their eyes, to trust others, or the mystery of life.

Common fears and inner dialogues include:

- "Are they lying to me?"
- "I don't trust people. I trust myself. That's it."
- "I need to be extra cautious with who I listen to."
- "I'm not open to others' opinions of me. They're totally wrong."
- "I'm going to be under attack if I let them in."
- "I'll lose myself if I compromise."

Hypo-Response to Manipulation and Control: Confusion and Following

- Having blind trust or a sense of naïveté
- Looking to others for validation, approval, or direction
- Having crippling self-doubt
- Lacking in personal identity
- Seeming disconnected from reality
- Having trouble knowing what's going on
- Feeling a big draw to charismatic leaders
- Desiring to be saved by someone who knows what's going on

When someone's embodying Confusion and Following, it can often feel threatening to their system to trust themselves, to sense their own truth and then align to it, to feel safe locating and following their own guidance and inner-authority.

Common fears and inner dialogues include:

- "How can I make good decisions for myself, my life, my direction, if I can't feel what's right or wrong?"
- "I just need someone to tell me what to do."
- "I'll fuck it up if I choose."
- "It's not safe to be in charge."
- "I don't know why I can't figure things out."
- "Who can I hire to fix this for me?"
- "Can I trust anyone to really help me, or will I be lost like this forever?"

The Trauma Spell of Manipulation and Control

Many years ago, I went through a season of accidentally becoming friends with a handful of people who had narcissistic tendencies. By this I mean, people who were continuously pointing out things that were wrong with me, putting me down, defining my experience and identity for me, bullying me, and insisting that their perspective was superior to mine. They'd forget my birthday. They wouldn't ask "How are you?" at the beginning of our conversations. They'd take up all the space, until suddenly, they'd disappear.

At the time, a key rupture with an old friend had me feeling less secure about my place in the world, my decency as a human. I had what felt like a swiss cheese heart—energetic openings of uncertainty, regret and frozen remorse. I was also living in a new community and had fewer secure, in-person bonds than I was used to. My need for closeness and belonging was under-resourced. I was extra hungry for connection and validation. And I was more unconsciously desperate to receive those things—no matter the source from which they came.

In walked Samantha. A crone figure of sorts, wild with sharp wisdom, free in her sexuality, opinionated and powerful. We met during a time when she was riding high off a number of sweet successes, and we quickly developed a friendship that almost felt like romance. She showered me with praise, offered me lots of reflections about my power and pointed out all the ways she thought I was better than other people. It was a tad bit intoxicating to get that much attention from someone who embodied such command over life.

But about six months into our friendship, things turned on a dime. A swirl of challenging experiences happened at once in Samantha's life, and out came all her worst qualities.

Feeling vulnerable, she started directing crude remarks at me—telling me I was a burden to be around, but then continuing to invite me to hang out. She began insulting me in weird ways, telling me I was untrustworthy and failing the friendship test, but then wanting more from me as a friend.

As you can imagine, I was left with a trail of confusion. *What happened to that friend who was recently praising my every word? Why is she now telling me I'm a burden, then continuing to try to make plans? Why is she telling me I'm untrustworthy, then still seeking me out for trusted support?*

Let's take a small detour to talk about the physiology of the person enacting manipulation and control, which can also be considered narcissism depending on how extreme the behavior becomes. Usually, the one manipulating and controlling either inherited those behaviors or experienced severe developmental trauma that led to them.

The physiology of a narcissist is one of deep freeze and collapse, especially in the heart-space and social nervous system. The narcissist's ability to rest into safe parasympathetic social engagement (eye contact, presence, connected facial expressions, empathy, voice) is diminished. This makes it near-impossible to co-regulate with a narcissist, because they are cut off from their social regulation capacities.[13]

However, narcissists still have needs for belonging, connection, approval, validation, and mattering. Their unconscious survival strategies lead them to create a false self, a contrived persona, that can scan others for their most unmet needs, their weaknesses, their joys and their challenges—then use that information to manipulate and secure connection.

A study done by the Mayo Clinic describes narcissism as "a mental disorder in which people have an inflated sense of their own importance and a deep need for admiration. Those with narcissistic personality disorder believe that they're superior to others and have little regard for other people's feelings. But behind this mask of ultra-confidence lies a fragile self-esteem, vulnerable to the slightest criticism."[14]

Relationships with narcissists are often hallmarked by extreme praise and wooing in the beginning, then emotional abuse, power-over dynamics and gaslighting in the end. When we're under a spell of manipulation and control, the

[13] *Big thanks to trauma specialist Emily Aube for her support and insights on narcissism and the nervous system, developed from her studies with Stevel Terrell. Learn more about Emily's work at https:// emilybeatrix.com/*

[14] *https://www.psychologytoday.com/us/blog/communication-success/201507/10-signs-you-re-dating-narcissist*

disorientation from the mixed messaging can create a haze of confusion that leads to blind following or hypervigilance.

When clients who've experienced narcissistic abuse finally realize what's been going on, they often well up with shame. "But how could I be so stupid? Why couldn't I see it happening?" Then they'll follow up with more confusion. "But what's wrong with that person? Why won't they just reason with me?" Narcissism uses manipulation and control as an attempt to garner safety and power in relationships. Those most susceptible to a narcissist's spell often have their own developmental trauma; wobbly Soul Seeds hungry for love, care, emotional safety, and genuine regard.

What happens when someone close to you—say a parent, sibling, best friend, or partner—uses toxic shame as a means to control? Manipulative attacks as a way to garner power-over? Or the silent treatment as a tool of vengeance—consciously or unconsciously? What happens when you experience these things starting at infancy, in response to your innocent cries or exploratory falls? How do you grow to trust yourself in the face of so much defacing?

Developmental narcissistic abuse leaves children in a very challenging dilemma. *Do I trust myself and my own sacred truth? Or do I choose to buy into the lies of my family, so my survival needs for connection and belonging, to be fed and tended to, get met?*

The young developing human subconsciously sizes up the options and chooses survival. Even when it sucks. It's the human imperative. It's the unconscious impulse. It's the way we live through the dark.[15]

I've had many clients share stories about being belittled, shamed, manipulated, and controlled rather than tended, nurtured, encouraged, or celebrated by the people closest to them. Parents, friends, mentors, partners, lovers. In these relational cages, they lost their sense of self—their ears to hear and eyes to see the truth about their unbreakable beauty, their beloved identity, their very worthy needs.

---

[15] *Insight developed in thanks again to Emily Aube.*

Whether it happened in childhood or is happening as an adult, you can tell you've experienced the spell of manipulation and control when:

- Another person's voice, perspective, and narrative has taken the place of your own
- You can't quite make out what's really going on
- You feel belittled, less valuable, or self-doubting after hanging around that person
- You put their needs above your own
- Your friends don't like the way that person treats you, but you still somehow defend them

With Samantha, I was under the spell. I could tell because Jodi kept saying to me, "Rach...I love you, but this is really fucked up." I couldn't get Samantha's words out of my head. I was thinking everything she said was the truth, could barely make space to differentiate between her perspective and mine. I was feeling worthless while simultaneously overgiving to compensate for not receiving. Thankfully, I could tell I was under a spell, and that I needed to break it—fast.

Ritual Spell-Breaking

I went down to the ocean, put my feet in the water. With the sun shining bright upon me, I closed my eyes and silently opened a sacred, protected space around me. In Celtic traditions (and many Indigenous spiritual practices) it's custom to welcome in the seven directions—east, south, west, north, below, above, and within—along with their corresponding energies.[16]

I drew my attention eastward and welcomed in my Crone—the energy of lineage and wisdom. I drew my attention southward and welcomed in my child—the energy of innocence and play. I welcomed my adolescent in the west—the

---

[16] *I first learned about opening an energetic ritual space with the seven directions in the book Celtic Magic by D.J. Conway.*

energy of identity expression and exploration. I welcomed my adult in the north—the energy of purposeful responsibility.

I tuned into each of their unique gifts and frequencies for just a moment, then imagined a violet flame of protection forming around me. I sank my attention below me to the abundance of Mother Earth, welcoming her nourishing resources. I drifted my attention upward to the wisdom of Father Sky and welcomed his fair discernment. My violet flame was now encircling me 360 degrees, and I invoked my Soul, my most loving, present, essential self. Then I said a prayer of intention:

May this ritual be a source of forgiveness and freedom, for both myself and Samantha, so that we may move forward in powerful, loving ways.

May we be unhooked from the toxic energies of needless shame, manipulation, and control, and rather, both feel safe to connect to Life and others with love and vulnerability.

May my Gatekeeper, Sage, and Groundskeeper serve to cleanse and protect my Soul Seed and Expressionista, and may my Pollinator sow light and compassion between us.

Then, I let the phrases that were stuck in me come up to the surface one-by-one:

You're untrustworthy.

I felt where these words were living in my body, right at the front of my heart. I asked my Gatekeeper to move that phrase outside of my sacred, protected space. Then, I asked my Sage to see and speak the truth.

You're imperfect, but you're not untrustworthy, she told me. *You have limits to where you can put your energy and drawing boundaries doesn't make you bad or wrong. It makes you caring and strong. You've been honest and compassionate the whole way through—*

both about what you could and couldn't do. Samantha may be hurt and disappointed, but not because you're untrustworthy. It's okay. Forgive yourself.

I spit the energy of toxic shame out from the front of my heart into a sacred cup, then watched as my Groundskeeper swept clear the debris in that area of me. Somewhere in the energetic atmosphere, my Pollinator was transporting golden honey love from my heart to hers.

I went on from phrase to phrase, asking my Gatekeeper to remove toxic words from the land of my body, my Sage to illuminate truth and clarity, my Groundskeeper to cleanse and weed the tendrils of pain, and my Pollinator to weave healing golden love through my energetic body, hers, and the body of our relationship.

When it was all said and done, I'd released each phrase she'd used against me from my energy body. I scooped the ocean into the cup that I'd spit her words into, then tossed it out seven times (once for each of the seven directions, closing the protective ritual circle). Then I dove into the ocean, dunked my body, let my cells release it all to the big salty mama.

I went home and stripped down, sat naked at my altar where I'd prepared a clean and clear space. I did a small meditation, imagining love and compassion meeting the parts of my body that were still uncomfortable or rearranging. I anchored into my center of gravity and imagined being scrubbed by a hydrating flow of healing energy. When I opened my eyes, I felt deeply released from Samantha's words, and ready to release our friendship as well.

Reclaiming Your Sage

So many humans carry secret tendrils of shame, uncertainty, and confusion based purely on the wounded words of others. We hold back our sexuality, the way we love, the way we relate or what we create, because we're afraid of the lies that others might say. Maybe we've had a traumatic break-up or endured manipulation and shaming to the point of disorientation. Maybe we've been told something toxic so many times that we're no longer sure what's true or what's false. This is the beast of gaslighting—someone else defining your experience, identity or truth for you, in either subtle or elaborate ways. It erodes your sense of self-trust that you can name and claim reality for yourself, and that erosion of self-trust leads to insecurities around how you act, create, relate, or move through the world.

Developmental manipulation can pave a path for relational manipulation later in life. If you were reared and steered to believe someone else's truth above your own, you may later be more susceptible to coercion or persuasion, even by well-meaning people who have no ill intentions. Reclaiming your Sage is about acknowledging the ways you don't fully trust your capacity to find and know your own truth, and then, slowly but surely, finding pathways back to an inner-compass you can count on.

While there's a cerebral association with the Sage archetype, it also requires the support of the more embodied Soul Seed, Gatekeeper, and Groundskeeper archetypes. The needs of your Soul Seed must be well fed so that you're less susceptible to letting in threat. Your Gatekeeper and Groundskeeper need to feel empowered to act quickly and consistently to protect your well-being, choice, and aliveness. Perhaps you even need to know the feeling of your Expressionista dancing in her fullest joy, so that when you're feeling compressed by another's emotional violence, your heart recoils with the sacred knowing that something is wrong.

One of the most important strategies for protecting against and healing from any form of violence—physical or emotional—is creating a safe distance from unsafe behavior.

Growing up, my parents fought in equal proportions to how much they talked. When I was eighteen, I drew a line in the sand. I was exhausted by their dysfunction and unwilling to bear witness any longer. I told them neither was allowed to talk shit about the other in front of me, or to me, ever again. If either did, I'd ask them to stop. If they didn't stop, I would exit the conversation or room.

When I moved home at twenty-eight with vaginal melanoma, the same rule applied. Talk shit about the other or even fight in my presence, and I'm leaving the space—immediately. I wouldn't even ask them to stop. When they couldn't stop themselves from fighting, I'd leave, as promised, then predictably, one would yell at the other, "Look what you made happen!" Eventually though, they stopped fighting in front of me.

Ah, the miracle of effective consequences.

Sometimes, safe distance means leaving the room or not talking to someone. Other times, it means moving across the country. Other times still, it means voicing with firm certainty what is and is not okay, and creating an energetic boundary with the power of your clarity.

Is It Tolerable?

I was having a conversation with my friend Bear Hébert[17] about manipulation and control, lamenting about a difficulty I was having in an old interpersonal dynamic. I was feeling uncomfortable with someone, but wasn't sure if I should try

Do you need to EXPAND your Window of Tolerance — or is it just Intolerable?

[17] *Connect with Bear and all their brilliance at bearcoaches.com*

to be more flexible, expand my window of tolerance. Remember: the "window of tolerance" is the threshold within which one can maintain mental and physiological presence while riding waves of intensity.

Bear looked at me straight on and asked, matter of factly, "Do you need to 'expand your window of tolerance'—or is it just *intolerable*?" They went on. "You know…what if the stress you're experiencing is your body's boundary telling you it's *not okay*?"

I paused with relief and gratitude.

"I think those of us with people-pleasing tendencies have a habit of thinking it's on us when things feel off. But what if you're not supposed to become more tolerant? What if you're supposed to listen to your discomfort as an important signal, an important sign?"

When you're working with clients who are under strong manipulation and control trauma spells, one of the first things you may notice is how hard it is for them to center and trust their own discomfort. As I shared in the story above with Samantha, it's easy to prioritize someone else's narrative over your own.

As a guide in these situations, you might ask your client to consider the following questions:

What do you want to tolerate in your relationships?
What *are* you tolerating?
What would you tell your best friend it's okay to tolerate?
What would you tell your best friend *not* to tolerate?

The window of tolerance isn't supposed to change quickly or with wishful thinking. It's supposed to change slowly over time, in response to growing trust with ourselves, others and Life (as opposed to pressuring yourself to tolerate more than is healthy or good for you). If your client's window of tolerance isn't expanding to meet intolerable behavior—you might let them know that perhaps this inflexibility is a great thing. Perhaps it's their body's wisdom saying *no*. Perhaps their emotional limits are feeling safe and brave enough to show.

When we tell ourselves we're supposed to be able to tolerate more sex or less care, more emotional abuse or less emotional intimacy, it's a form of gaslighting our own needs and denying the preciousness of our truest nature. When you hear your clients defending unsafe, intolerable behavior, perhaps feed them some phrases that they might experiment with saying instead, then invite them to see how it feels in their body to speak them.

"This is intolerable for me."

"This is uncomfortable for me."

"This is painful for me."

"This is tiring for me."

"This is exhausting for me."

"This is draining for me."

"This is unpleasant for me."

"This is uninspiring to me."

"This is diminishing my self-esteem."

"This is infuriating for me."

"I don't want this."

"I don't deserve this."

"I don't need this."

"I'm not designed for this."

"I need more than this."

Give them time to breathe into these words, see if any part of them can let them land as true. A process like this is important, because when we're tolerating intolerable behavior, there's usually a strong internal narrative telling us we should be okay with what's not okay. Naming the not-okayness is a powerful spell-breaker. Giving the body time to feel and sink into an updated, more self-loving narrative can transform the whole system.

Often clients will object that the one who's hurting them is not a "bad person." I like to reassure my clients that they don't have to deem another "bad" in order to accept that they're a bad fit for intimate relating. They can simply honor their own limits.

It can be hard, sad and disappointing to walk away from what's intolerable. It can be vulnerable, tender and scary to name what you need and then wait to see if someone can show up to meet you. The more mature, reasonable and committed to interpersonal growth you are, the harder it can be to understand when some won't grow with you. But this is the secret superpower of the Sage. She believes in change. She's not afraid of endings. She can let things go, let things die. She knows the truth—that a rebloom is always coming (either with that same person, or someone new), and only ever as fast as she's willing to release to the earth what no longer works. She's okay with rising, with letting others meet her in her higher standards. She knows the truth: that she's not alone in her mature capacity, even if it can be a long or achey process finding others who meet and match her.

Speaking of awakening your Sage and honoring what's tolerable for you or choosing to walk away: this chapter has one more story of manipulation and control. Specifically, as it relates to love, sex and relationships. It's not the easiest story to read, but it does paint a very clear picture of narcissism and intimacy.

Does it feel tolerable for you to read another story? Do you just want to skip ahead to the practices? Perhaps close your eyes. Feel inside. What's your true capacity? Choose accordingly.

The Long Road to Walking Away

Scott reached out over email with a knightly air about him. "My girlfriend and I are going through some things related to her sexual trauma. She never wants to have sex with me anymore and I'm concerned about her. Do you think we could have a session?"

"Sure thing. I'm in," I wrote back. We met up a few days later, and I proceeded to witness a nauseating case of gaslighting.

I opened up the session by asking both Scott and Megan to identify and connect to a resource, something they could pause and return to if ever the energy of our session became overwhelming.

Megan rooted into her sit bones planted firmly on the ground. Scott tuned into his perception of God-consciousness and luminous, permeating light. I imagined myself inside a giant cocoon of iridescent love energy and put them each in their own cocoons as well. We breathed there for a few moments, then I let them both know my ethos for working with couples.

"My goal is to help you both marry your own most healthy aliveness and find ways to support each other in doing so. Essentially, if you leave as co-conspirators on the mission of helping each other feel more fully aligned to aliveness, I'll consider this session a success."

Then I offered the opportunity for them both to share what was going on.

"Who wants to share first?"

"How about you Megan?" he offered, in a gesture of generosity.

Megan's face crunched inwards in obvious emotional discomfort. "Are you ready for this?" she asked him, almost as if seeking permission. "I don't exactly feel safe sharing my truth," she confessed in my direction.

"That's the thing!" Scott exclaimed, gathering ammunition for his argument. "She never trusts herself. She can't trust herself. She's completely out of touch."

"Let's pause for a moment," I said, attuning to each of our iridescent cocoons. I was noticing already that Scott was defining Megan's experience for her—a key element of gaslighting that can lead to the eventual degradation of self-trust.

"What I heard Megan say is she doesn't feel safe sharing her truth, not that she doesn't know her truth. Megan, I'm curious, do you feel like you can trust yourself to know your truth?"

"I do," she said looking straight at Scott, face reddening with anger. "I trust myself completely. But he seems to like to tell me that I don't."

"What has you feeling unsafe to share your truth?" I asked her.

"Well, let me give you an example. Lately, I haven't wanted to have sex with Scott. He likes to think it's because of my sexual trauma, likes to tell me I'm so wounded, need to heal my past, should be more free in my sexuality. It's true that I have some unhealed hurts I need to deal with. But also, I don't feel connected to Scott. He flails around in emotional ups and downs all day long. When I tell him I don't want to have sex with him, he tells me it makes him so mad he could punch himself in the face. Obviously, that makes me feel unsafe!"

"I hear you," I replied with reverence. "I appreciate your ability to express your truth here. I think it's valid and normal to feel unsafe in those conditions."

I thought to myself about the intoxication of sophisticated gaslighting. How narcissists will find an empath's weakest link, then prey on it. Use one truth (in this case, that Megan has sexual trauma) to manipulate the empath with a whole slew of lies.[18]

I looked over to check in with Scott. To my surprise I saw him "calling in the light of God," then convulsing in a sexual way. "I have to move her toxic energy out of my system," he said. I averted my gaze as he did his thing.

Meanwhile, Megan was rolling her eyes, tears welling under a heavy sigh.

"Why have I bought into this shit for so long?" she asked, sending signals of desperation in my direction.

"Hmmm." I paused. "I think what might be important to ask right now is what would make you feel safe and loved?"

She was stumped. She knew she felt invalidated. She knew she felt unsafe. She knew she was buying into bullshit. But she didn't know what would cultivate the feelings she really desired.

"As you pause with curiosity," I whispered, "I wonder what you might sense in your body, below the mind, just right now?"

"I feel like I'm falling into an endless black hole," she whispered back. "Like there's nothing that can pull me out, and all I can do is scream, but even that... even my scream... is silent."

Scott had gone into his own process completely, lying on his back on the floor, t-shirt covering his face, whispering mantras in a language not his own.

I proceeded with Megan.

"Do you think you can let yourself go there for a moment... while another part of you stays here and witnesses?"

She nodded her head quietly, closed her eyes, went in. After a minute or so, I asked again, "What's there to notice now?"

"I feel like I'm in a humongous cave at the far edge of the world where no one can find me."

---

[18] *Informed by informational interviews with Emily Aube.*

"What's that like to notice...sensationally, emotionally?"

"I feel scared, shaky in my core...a bit desperate to be found, to get out."

"Ah, yes. I wonder if some kind of valiant resource might want to support you in this moment? An animal, an ancestor, something celestial, or something in nature, perhaps? As you hear me plant the seed that something on your cosmic team might want to show up and support you right now, is there anything to notice?"

She sat calmly with the offer, then I witnessed a ripple move through her spine. "What's there to notice?" I asked gently again.

"I just felt a huge black snake slither up my spine, bright green eyes coming into mine, a hiss wanting to move through my whole body."

"Wow..." I whispered in awe. "I wonder if you might allow those snake instincts to embody a bit more, perhaps in micro-movements, or even just energetically."

I witnessed as Megan swiveled the back of her neck, skull tilting left to right in what seemed like horizontal figure eights.

"It's like there's a red lava of heat gathering at the base of me, wanting to volcano its way out," she said, now with less of a whisper, more solidity.

"Great," I affirmed with matched volume and confidence. "Is there a direction the lava wants to go, a speed, and flow with which its moving?"

"It's spiraling up my spine, slow like honey, but hot and fierce. It wants to come out of my mouth, like the fire of a dragon."

"Fantastic," I replied, opening my own mouth, letting out a bit of heat. "Perhaps if you open your jaw just a bit, imagining a few inches out beyond it, the energy will sense an open pathway to travel through."

Megan did just that, and I witnessed as she allowed the energy to move up and out, up and out, up and out. A few minutes later, she opened her eyes, looking one part renewed, one-part shy. I could see her growing confidence, right alongside her still-present fear.

"How's it going now?" I asked.

She looked over at Scott, who was now looking up at her. A gentle glaze washed over her eyes. A small smile painted onto her face.

"Ummm, it's good. Yeah. I feel better. Maybe he was right all along. I think I just needed to move some energy out of me." She shook her body like a dog a bit, took a few deep breaths and put on a troubled, trying smile.

The powerful snake energy that had just been dancing up Megan's spine suddenly seemed nowhere to be found.

I wish I could tell you that I was shocked at Megan's change in demeanor, but the sad truth is, I wasn't. I was heartbroken, but not shocked. When we're under the strong spell of chronic gaslighting, our self-trust can become deeply compromised. We become accustomed to using someone else's eyes to see ourselves. It's a way to survive the frustration and exhaustion of being told over and over again what's true.

"Hmmm. Okay. I hear you. Yes. It also seems like your energy just shifted. There was a bit of a fierceness before. How do you feel now?"

"You know, I feel better. I'm glad I got that out of me."

I looked over at Scott, who was staring her down. "I'm proud of you babe. You did it," he said.

In this moment, it was clear to me that Megan was still under Scott's spell. I wasn't quite sure what to do, so I called my own Sage into the space to help navigate the situation. I knew that with Scott in the space, there wasn't enough relative safety for Megan to reconnect to her own power. I could share with them what I thought was going on, but there was no guarantee either would be able to hear it. I was concerned that directness might have negative consequences for Megan. I decided to pause the process and go a different route.

"Listen, you two. Can I be honest here and share what I see?"

They both agreed.

"Scott, it seems like you have a strong need to source your sense of value from Megan. And Megan, it seems like you have a strong need to source your sense of value from Scott. But there's also a strong thread of toxicity lacing you together that might be making you both feel unsafe. I wonder what kind of safety agreements you might be able to come up with together?"

Megan requested that Scott respect her *no* and honor her body, always. He agreed with an air of faux-enlightenment that made me a bit sick to my stomach.

We ended the session, though I knew the work was far from over. Scott went to the bathroom, and I managed to let Megan know in the safest way possible that I was available to talk to her later if she wanted.

After the session, Megan found me sitting in my car around the corner. Her energy still seemed split, but a bit more authentic.

"Listen, thanks so much for what you did in there," she said. "I know I need to leave him. I'm just trying to figure it out. It's so complicated. I really do love him. I know he really loves me. He's just got so much trauma from the church, you know? And I don't know how I'm going to pull it off. All his friends are my friends. He pays most of the rent. My whole life here depends on him. Listen, I couldn't let him see my strength in there. I'm gonna leave him, though, I swear."

"I know, I know...that was really tricky in there. I'm sorry we didn't have space to just work together one-on-one. I'm here if you need anything at all," I told her, eyes of solidarity standing fiercely on her side. "A session, two. Whatever. Just call me."

"Thanks," she said, eyes locking with mine in equal trust.

Then I took a breath, looked up, and said one more thing. "Have you heard of the term gaslighting? Do you know the symptoms of narcissistic abuse?"

She paused with an awkward smile. "Not exactly."

And then, I gave her the gentlest information I could about how narcissists will use gaslighting—a form of psychological manipulation—to make a person question their own truth or sanity.

"I'll send you an article from Psychology Today called '10 Signs You're Dating a Narcissist' by Preston Ni. It may be helpful."[19]

As coaches, we can't force our clients to align to health. Sometimes, someone's stuck really deep in a swamp. Sometimes, the most powerful thing we can do is love them in that place while also helping them see where they are. Sometimes, care is trusting in their path, as gnarly as it might be.

Six months later, Megan finally reached out to me.

---

[19] https://www.psychologytoday.com/us/blog/communication-success/201507/10-signs- you-re-dating-narcissist

"I did it. I left. That was utter hell. I should've left the day we had that session. The day he held me down in bed and told me those horrible things. The day he started using his mental health challenges as a reason for us to have sex. I feel so fucking stupid, but I finally did it. Can I come in for a session? I've been a serious mess."

When Megan came in, she had a metaphorical bowling ball stuck in her throat that had hardened into her jaw, locking it near shut. Her perception of her vagina was invisible and hollow. Her heart was spiked with thorns. Needless to say, we moved through many waves of resourcing her resilient power, resting in her tender needs for safety then growing her sacred ferocity.

We worked together for the next six months, unraveling truth from lies in both her body and her mind. At the end of our work together, she sent me this note:

I don't know what I would have done if we hadn't been miraculously connected, albeit through Scott. This was the hardest year of my life, hands down. But I have no regrets now. I discovered how to find my truth in the dark with your gentle, powerful help. Was it worth the price of admission? Fuck. Who knows. I wouldn't wish what I went through on anyone, ever. But I do know now what it means to be totally committed to myself. I don't know how you did this, woman, but you're a real angel. I could cry with gratitude.

I wrote back thanking Megan for her kind words and assuring her that we did it together. It was a long road to leaving, but she did it. She regathered her clarity, little-by-little over time. She refound her footing—her ability to get safe distance from unsafe behavior. She collected resources over months, stashed them away in secret places, all to make the leaving possible. It wasn't easy. She often felt crazy. But below the uncertainty was the lucidity of her Sage, which stayed with her despite all the eroding and degrading she endured.

Now, Megan's traveling around the country hosting workshops for women to embody their most powerful callings. Her Sage is leading her life. She knows the power of possibility in seemingly impossible situations, and she helps awaken faith in other women who've somehow lost their footing.

Essential Sage Practices

Sage Coherence Practice

Standing, sitting or lying down, allow yourself to rub the back of your neck and the base of your cranium. If you'd like, massage your entire scalp, behind your ears, then your jaw, temples and forehead. Then either place gentle fingers on your third eye or look yourself in the mirror. Notice the sensations of your brain, head, scalp and face. Perhaps take an inhale and imagine a golden light traveling up from your perineum (in between your anus and genitals) through the midline of your body, illuminating your pineal gland (just above your brain stem, straight back from your third eye, in the center of your brain).

Say inwardly or outwardly the following affirmations over and over again, with time in between, pausing for sensations and visions.

I see the truth.
I speak the truth.
I align to the truth.
I am clarity.
I am choice.
I am integrity.
I trust myself.

Notice any images, impulses, or sensations you may be experiencing. What is the truth you imagine yourself seeing, speaking, aligning to? What clarity lives inside of you? What choices would that clarity have you make? If you were in total integrity, what would you do? What kind of leadership is wanting to emerge in you? Notice if perhaps by connecting to your Sage, an energy of self-trust grows inside.

Remember, baby steps are key. If you have a history of hearing but not heeding your own internal wisdom (a hypo response to manipulation and control), you might feel insecure around your integrity. If that's the case, perhaps start by asking: how can I begin embodying my truth in a small and doable way? Who can I invite to support and celebrate my emerging inner-authority?

Show Me Something Doable Practice

When clients begin reconnecting to truth, they can often fear what they'll be shown. Often, on some level, there's a fear that seeing anything at all means seeing everything at once.

For some of us, the fear of seeing something uncomfortable or scary—that one memory, just how much you've abandoned yourself at times, or the potency of the elephant in the room that no one ever likes for you to say—stops you from seeing at all. Your third eye goes partially blind, your truth-meter hazy. *What if I see something that will mean I need to make a change that I'm not ready to make?*

If your clients are afraid of seeing too much and it's keeping them from seeing truth at all, I recommend you support them with a "Show Me Something Doable" practice.

Invite your client to tune into the sensations of their third eye or forehead and notice what's happening in terms of temperature, color, speed, density, lucidity. Invite them to notice the rest of their body as well. *What sensations are similar? What sensations are different?*

Then, for about two minutes, consider an invocation that centers around showing your client what's safe or doable for them to see.

For instance, if your client feels like no one can be trusted, you might invite them to say a few times...

Show me what trust looks like.

If your client is in a spell of feeling like everyone's dangerous, you might invite them to say a few times...

Show me safe humans.

If your client doesn't want to see a traumatic memory from their past, and this fear is keeping them from seeing any childhood memories at all, you might invite them to say a few times...

Show me something beautiful about being a child.

It doesn't have to be something beautiful from *their* childhood. Just the state of being a child at all.

If your client is trying to embrace her power, but keeps getting fixated on minor offenses she's done in her past, you might invite her to say a few times...

Show me all the ways my power is good for the world.

After about a minute or two of "trying on" a right-fit invocation, invite your client to tune into their third eye or forehead again. *Notice what sensations are present now. It's okay if a challenge arises here.*

A few minutes of this practice is more than enough. In the spirit of titration, this practice isn't about flooding your client's system but rather, making mindful choices about what they see and when.

Your client can tell their body what they're ready for. They can do what's doable, in consent with their wholehearted yes. Remember, trauma is often classified by "too much, too soon, too fast." Your clients can start to counter that pattern in their systems by intentionally choosing a less-is-more approach to their healing process. And you, as their guide, can help pace the process by inviting doability as often as possible.

Seeing and Believing Practice

Oftentimes, when your clients have experienced enough manipulation and control, their self-trust erodes, and it's hard to believe the messages they hear, the visions they see, the feelings they feel.

What even happened? What was fake and what was real? Am I making it all up?
Is there something I can do to check for what was true and what was false?

It's easy to get into a state of frustrated disorientation when your client's been in a relationship with someone with narcissistic tendencies. When their agitation gets dismissed, denied, or downplayed enough, they might collapse into a deep, exasperated freeze. Then, regaining their sense of reality becomes an incremental process.

I encourage clients to begin with a practice of seeing and acknowledging what's real for them, shifting away from the focus on another and into a focus on self. Helping clients move from basing reality on another's narrative, to basing reality on their own somatic, emotional, and cognitive experience—as well as input from trusted others—can be world-changing.

Part 1—Diagnostic

To flex the muscle of seeing and believing your client's own experiences, invite them to list out 3-5 people with whom they've experienced difficulty in close relationships. Partners, parents, lovers, bosses, close friends.

One person at a time, put their name at the top of a piece of paper, then complete the following sentence starters with the honest truth about how the relationship actually is or was.

In relationship to this person, I see myself looking like...

In relationship to this person, I see myself feeling...and...and...

In relationship to this person, I see myself thinking…and…and…

In relationship to this person, I see my body feeling…and…and…

Then write:

I trust what I see as true.

How does this feel for you? Comfortable? Uncomfortable? Tolerable? Intolerable? If it feels honest but awkward, tune into your body and ask, *If my body were in charge right now, what would it have me do?* Perhaps follow a bit of your physical impulses in the moment to allow some energy to move through.

Then, if you feel ready, continue with the following inquiry:

Seeing and trusting these things, I'm inclined to…(What would you like to say or do?)

Part 2—Aligning to Potential Blueprint

Now that your client feels clearer about their experience inside this relationship, invite them to be honest about what they *want* to experience.

Have your client imagine they were talking to a friend or child they love dearly. How would they want them to look, think and feel while relating to others? Can your client let themselves want those things for their own life, too?

In relationship, I want to see myself looking like…

In relationship, I want to see myself feeling…

I want to see myself thinking…

I want to see my body feeling…

If these sentences feel especially powerful or important for your clients, perhaps invite them to write them as "I am" statements and put them on their refrigerator.

For example:

In relationship…

I am exhaling with deep joy and big grins.

I feel loved, free, confident and adored.

I think clearly and trust my own perspective.

I am relaxed and digesting all my food with ease.

Finally, have your clients do an assessment of their current or past relationships. When or where did they possibly feel more like the potential Blueprint they just imagined? What qualities were present in the people with whom they felt those ways? What conditions were present in the relational dynamics in which they felt those ways? How was your client showing up that contributed to trust in the space?

As your client tunes into the positive Blueprint experiences they've had or seek to have, they can begin creating a bit of a Manifesto for Trust, naming the qualities and conditions that help cultivate relational health and trust. They can return to this Manifesto when they're feeling worried or uncertain entering into a new relationship.

In-Sourcing with Clients in Sessions

Often clients who've experienced a lot of manipulation and control will look to me to be their Sage, their inner-knowing keeper. When I notice this dynamic happening, I'm extra careful to not take it on. It's important for someone who's reclaiming their Sage to have the opportunity to access their own truth, first—to relearn the skill of self-connection rather than outsourcing their authority to try to win connection.

As a coach, you can do this in small, doable ways. For instance, by inviting your clients to feel and name their sensations, identify any possible animal instincts, or describe the room around them.

Another thing I like to do in these moments is to help my clients clarify, "What's the question you really want an answer to?" Then I invite them to write that question at the top of their journal page. I set a five-minute timer. "Let your Sage spill all the wisest answers she knows to be true. Then we can talk about it afterwards. If you're still unclear, then I'll share with you what I see."

Affirming the inner-wisdom of a client who's gotten used to outsourcing for answers is an essential step in helping them begin to trust themselves again.

Chapter 8

GROUNDSKEEPER

FROM VIOLENCE & CHAOS to EMPOWERED SAFETY & VITALITY

The Blueprint

Groundskeeper is the wise, embodied elder of the village. She wakes up with the sun, walks the whole garden grounds, weeds, waters, feeds the animals, peeks into Soul Seed's room and coos at the sleeping baby. She does her morning practices—both embodied and energetic, then makes coffee for the parents who are about to leave for work. She loves the role of tending the rhythms of healthy aliveness; the chipper morning, noon and nighttime rituals that give melody to a family, a community, a life.

One-part cheerful grandmother energy, another part tai-chi ninja, Groundskeeper is responsible for tending to the health and fertility of the soil, garden, and all that's growing there within. She weeds, waters, harvests, composts, re-pots, transplants and rearranges—all for the sake of ensuring the most vibrant growth possible. She rises with the sun and sleeps with the moon in daily, consistent, reliable cycles, devoting her energy to the sanctity of the space and the vitality of all living things.

Groundskeeper knows that it's not enough to plant a garden then let it grow reckless and rampant. A fertile garden is tended, decluttered, kept tidy and fresh—daily. It's easier to remove a weed if it hasn't grown ten feet tall. Groundskeeper is intimate with this truth and devotes to adding or subtracting in order to cultivate strong, fertile soil.

Groundskeeper is not afraid to move things that need to be moved in order to help them thrive in fullness. She's not afraid to prune or cut things off completely, especially if Sage has counseled her to do so. She'll even move the entire garden if that's what will yield the most wellness.

The goal of Groundskeeper is to create a stable, safe environment that empowers every other archetype in the garden to grow into its fullest potential.

Groundskeeper has a sixth sense for danger and violence. She knows when the environment isn't sound—when the water has been poisoned, when the land has been fracked. She can feel the need for empowered safety wherever it's missing. With powerful physical valor, she rearranges what's out of order. She brings into clean, sacred alignment anything that's been muddied by addiction or violence.

Our Collective Groundskeeper is the guardian of our collective soil. She keeps a steady eye on systemic violence and devotes herself, night and day, to realigning our culture toward health and safety. She knows that what she does to herself she does to the whole, and what she does to the whole she does to herself.

Our Collective Groundskeeper isn't afraid to clear up the messes of our human family. She looks at the landfill and asks, how can I turn this into compost one small step at a time? She rolls up her sleeves and gets dirty with the work at hand—daily. She utilizes new and ancient tools: the tools of communion with nature, trust in the rhythms of life, and full, humble responsibility for doing her part to nourish the world in the same ways the world nourishes her.

Groundskeeper at a Glance

Body Connection: Hands and Feet, Arms and Legs

Your hands, feet, arms and legs allow you to move through the world, and move the world around you. Realign. Adjust. Pick up. Put down. Feed. Weed. Water. Move closer. Move farther.

With empowered mobility—whether physical, emotional or energetic—you can choose to move yourself and others into right relationship; connections in service to the thriving of all. When unsafe or unhealthy things are too close in, your hands and arms weed them out and replace them with what feeds and nourishes life. Your feet and legs move you away from danger and toward the remembrance of reverence.

You can use your physical, emotional or energetic mobility to till miracles into the land of your being. You can scoop fistfuls of compost onto the brittle stretches of your body. You can move your flesh into the full summer sun. You can lather eucalyptus onto anything infected or diseased.

Your Groundskeeper devotes to tending vitality through touching, pushing, pulling, lifting, letting go, holding on, removing, moving toward, moving away, and transplanting.

Natural Blueprint of Health: Vitality & Empowered Safety

You devote regular care to your health, wellness and thriving. You prioritize your physical, emotional, mental and spiritual well-being for the sake of blessing our shared relations and your own body. You keep yourself at safe distances from unsafe behavior, situations, locations and people. You remove what plagues health, and plant miracles that heal on all levels. You have vitality that empowers you to share your medicine fully and freely, to transform environments of illness and violence into those of peace and prosperity.

Traumatic Imprint: Violence or Chaos

You are physically harmed, injured, beaten, hit, caged, strangled, choked, forced, pressured, put down, told mean words. You have your possessions threatened or stolen, have things broken around you. You experience war-torn environment, genocide, environmental disaster, or chaotic displacement.

Hyper-Response to Violence: Outbursts or Addiction

- Outbursts of anger, aggression, or frustration
- Self-harming
- Extreme highs and lows
- Temper tantrums
- Recklessness
- Speed
- Addictions to sex, uppers, work, dysfunctional relationships
- Bullying
- Carelessness
- Moving toward chaos/danger
- Bypassing pain and insisting on only positive perspectives

When someone's embodying Outbursts or Addiction, it can often feel threatening to their system to be present to the intensity, pain, or complexity of what they've experienced or are currently experiencing. Slowing down and feeling their feelings can feel threatening, vulnerable, unsafe, overwhelming, or destabilizing.

Common fears and inner dialogues include:
- "I'll be weak or susceptible if I feel my feelings."
- "Nope, can't feel that—way too much."
- "Fuck it, this is some bullshit. Let's get wild."
- "What's the point of processing? Nothing really changes."
- "If I start to feel, it'll be a never-ending flood. Not going there."

- "Shit, I slipped up on that responsibility again. Oh well. Might as well party harder."
- "If I slow down all my unprocessed trauma will catch up with me. Nooope."
- "How about I fuck with them before they fuck with me?"

Hypo-Response to Violence: Numbing or Addiction

- Addictions to food, alcohol, cannabis, prescription, or non-prescription drugs, technology, or video games
- Depression
- Chronic illness
- Chronic pain
- Hiding out inside safe environments, relationships, people or jobs for a sense of security, even if they're not aligned
- Cycles of internalized violence

When someone's embodying Numbing or Addiction, it can often feel threatening to their system to be present to the intensity, pain or complexity of what they've experienced, or are currently experiencing. Mobilizing and metabolizing trauma feels overwhelming, too big, too much, and shameful.

Common fears and inner dialogues include:

- "I don't have the capacity to process that."
- "I'm so exhausted. I'm always so exhausted. I can't cope."
- "There's nowhere safe enough to be vulnerable."
- "I'm just gonna joke this one off then get high and watch Netflix."
- "I'm such a piece of shit that I can't get out of this funk. What's wrong with me?"
- "Yeah, it's not that great. But what can I expect? It's stable enough."
- "Things feel meaningless but changing feels impossible."

Growing Yourself into a Healthy Jedi

When I first met my teacher Brigit, I remember thinking, this is the healthiest person I've ever encountered. To me, Brigit is the living, breathing embodiment of the Groundskeeper. In class, she tells stories of her hour-long morning routines, her love affair with martial arts, and keeping her energetic and physical spaces spruced and tidy. One time, I approached her office, and she was sweeping the sidewalk of autumn leaves with a chipper smile and radiant energy! This image got etched into my mind as a signature Brigit meme.

Despite her Latvian family's history of war (or perhaps, in part, thanks to it), Brigit's Groundskeeper is alive and well. She's got post-traumatic superpowers that support the upkeep of her internal and external spaces day after day.

Relating to Brigit and witnessing the vitality, resiliency, and aliveness of her Groundskeeper was a big wake up call for me. When I first started working in the field of trauma resolution, I used to finish client sessions feeling drained and exhausted, questioning if this work was even for me. But seeing the way Brigit tended to herself modeled for me how I could be. The more I grew my own wide base of physical and spiritual support—every morning, every night, and before every client—the more capacity I grew to feel enlivened even after meeting clients in some of their most difficult physical and emotional states.

The term "secondary trauma" describes the cumulation of stress and energy that a practitioner, therapist, coach, or even loved one can experience, hold, or carry after exposure to another's trauma—either intimately over time, or quickly in a flash of emergency.

When I published my first book, *Secret Bad Girl*, the wave of trauma stories

I received in return hit me like a freight train. For months on end, email after email landed in my inbox, and story after story about just how bad it had been— childhood memories, abusive relationships, moments of overwhelming terror— became my pastime reading.

At the end of my days, I'd lay flattened and frozen. I hadn't prepared for the weight of what came. I hadn't increased my capacity for that much intensity, that quickly. I hadn't set up proper boundaries to keep my system healthy. I was naive before I published that book. I had no idea what was coming. And although mobility, movement, and healthy release of emotions weren't foreign to me, I was caught off guard. I was overwhelmed, distraught, and dazed by the volume of trauma arriving at my door. Panicked and trying my best to meet and feed the cries, I relied on the deep reserves of my embodied energy and gave too much from my personal well.

Eventually, my Groundskeeper shut down into a collapse between pain and numbing. In my moments of desperation, I'd fantasize about moving to the sunny, ocean-breeze city of San Diego. I'd never been there, but my body felt physically called. Some part of me sensed that a warm environment could help nourish and replenish me as I embraced the demands of my professional life.

I ended up moving to San Diego, and magically landed myself a house a block from the ocean with the sweetest elderly landlord who rented it to me for a ridiculously good price. Night after night, the sound of ocean waves helped soothe my traumatic stress away. Morning after morning, I walked a quiet 30-minute stroll, then meditated on seven-million-year-old rocks. Evening after evening, I watched the sun set dramatically upon the sea. My favorite pastime became lying on my bed with just a candle lit, watching the sky get dark after sunset.

In my work life I was meeting emergency after emergency, intensity after intensity. But in my home life, in my personal space, I was letting nature nurture me, teach me how to regulate my rhythms, remind me that even the sky rests every single night—and longer, much longer in the winter. Over the years, I've come to revere my dance with natural rhythms as one of the most important relationships in my life. It keeps me spruced and centered, nourished and filled.

The thing about working with trauma is that there's almost always a momentum of emergency or dysregulation that other people are bringing to your doorstep. Like Brigit, we want to be metaphorically and actually sweeping the space, preparing the field with an energy of stability, resourcefulness, vitality and health. Because whichever momentum is bigger—regulation or emergency—will "win" in the interpersonal dance of energy. If someone brings you a tsunami of intensity and you haven't been practicing your surf skills, that wave will knock you both over and out. But if you've been growing your capacity to ride waves of intensity with majesty, together, you can surf the hard moments like pros.

If you want to be able to sustain your health and vitality guiding people from trauma to trust, you've gotta grow into your greatest imaginable Groundskeeper. You don't have to live a block from the ocean to do this, or even have immediate access to nature. But you do need to have ways of weeding your physical body of toxicity (dancing things out, taking salt-filled baths, resting in some kind of sacred space, shaking, hissing, boxing, running) and watering your health for greater aliveness (saturating yourself with beauty, having rituals of sensory delight, eating foods that rejuvenate your body and soul).

If you're sitting there thinking, *mayyyybe I'd rather not work with trauma, this sounds like a lot to take on!* I'll let you in on what I often tell my coach trainees:

You don't have to promote that you work with trauma, especially not at the beginning. You can simply have the skills and resources to meet it when it walks in the room. No need to call it in. It's pretty damn rampant, and it's coming either way.

If you don't explicitly invite clients with trauma into your practice, the bigger waves might not grace your space so quickly. As your capacity increases in a titrated way, you can become more public and inviting of the greater levels of complexity or challenge you feel called to serve.

Lesson learned from the trenches of offering trauma-informed care!

Addiction as a Coping Mechanism to Violence

Violence overwhelms our nervous system's capacity to cope with reality. Prolonged violence—due to complex interpersonal trauma, systemic trauma, living in war zones, intergenerational family addiction patterns, displacement from homeland, and beyond—can leave a client with a chronic sense that they don't have control over their body, emotions, life, or world.

This out-of-control feeling will reach for anything that might offer a sense of a predictably soothing outcome—whether that soothing is sustainable in the long term, or not. We reach for food, sex, drugs, alcohol, consumerism, social media, porn, Netflix, or video games when the violence or chaos around us or within us feels too big to tame.

A client who's experiencing extreme anxiety or panic might reason that nightly drinking could soothe their system into relaxation. While there might be temporary relief in a nightly half-bottle of wine, the cumulative effect is further dysregulation of the nervous system, more eventual anxiety, and additional depression.

On the other hand, someone who's experiencing chronic exhaustion or hopelessness about life, might seek out a stimulant like cocaine to give them a boost of life-force energy. Again, while they might receive a wild momentary high, the cumulative effect only further dysregulates their system.

It matters little whether someone's seeking stimulants or depressants—both are attempts to soothe discomfort and create an experience of perceived control and safety. We don't need to name these things as wrong or right, good, or bad. It's a challenging world to live in at times. Our culture invites disconnection, normalizes toxic individualism, is founded on oppression and sells screens as replacements for community. We know in our souls this is bullshit—that connection is the real medicine we're missing. But all the systems are designed to keep us confined and consuming.

The radical medicine of Groundskeeper is knowing how to create the missing conditions for consistent connection—to self, Earth, and each other. Taking down the walls of separation. Building community gardens in their place. Cultivating safe space where all the parts of your personhood can thrive. These are the signs that your Groundskeeper is alive.

If ADDICTION happens in ISOLATION, ALIVENESS happens in CONNECTION.

Yes, it's helpful if some of that connection happens between you and yourself—in regular meditation, journaling or tending to your physical body…if some of that connection happens between you and the Earth—gardening, walking, swimming in the river, watching the ants walk their mighty line.

But solitude alone is not enough. Humans are creatures of togetherness. We need regular, doable connections—the kind that let our bodies know it's safe to show up and rest, play, feast, or cry in the company of another. We need connections that show us it's safe to need. It's safe to be seen. It's safe to want. It's safe to weep. It's safe to be all of you—broken and beautiful, undone by this life. You can still belong like that. You can still be loved.

Without safe-enough connection to others (and perhaps lineage, and original culture), addiction is the ever-present temptation lurking in the corners of the lonely room of isolation.

"But what if I'm afraid of connection? What if it doesn't feel safe? What if I don't trust myself or anyone else?"

I once had a man ask me these things, weeping that his Soul Seed felt terrified of genuine care. I told him he might need a regulated but non-intrusive Groundskeeper, a grandmother-like love that would sing to him nightly lullabies outside his bedroom door. A love that could know he was tender, skittish, and afraid. A love that could respect that he couldn't do closeness right away. A love that could play peekaboo with his disbelieving hope. A love that could let him grow trust slowly, over time, until he was able to find a feeling of relief in the sweet, miraculous truth that love wasn't there to overwhelm or hurt him; that instead of blocking it, he could depend on it. He could really let it in.

He asked me where he could find a love like that. I told him it lived inside of him and was also all around him, waiting for him to see and receive its quiet blessings. I told him maybe, in small ways, he could start to look for the tiny clues of that grandmotherly love singing him her nightly devotions, unwavering with tender care; the way it's been hiding there, perhaps in plain sight, perhaps in the persistency of starlight, perhaps in the humming of the breeze, perhaps in the sweet barista, perhaps in the friendly toddler neighbor who never asks for much, just smiles with delight so happy to see you, so happy you're there.

When we're beginning to remember the melodies of interbeing, the harmonies of belonging, it can help to look for clues that they've been there all along. When we have histories of developmental or complex trauma, we can tend to look for and resonate with what's challenging, hard, unsafe, or not working as a way of staying alert to possible danger. Our attachment receptors can be injured, in need of gentle healing. Looking for connections of care and consistency, when we're expecting to see chaos or aloneness, is a radical act of tender vulnerability that can open you to new life, new beginnings, new experiences, new endings.

Healing a Lineage of Violence

Rhea worked with me as a one-on-one client on and off for four years. During most of those four years, we moved slowly through the first four archetypes.

We did inner-kid healing and called home her Soul Seed's Secret Bad Girl. We reawakened the sovereign strength of her Gatekeeper. We encouraged her most erotic, creative Expressionista's bloom. And we fostered the leadership of her wise and brave Sage to take center stage in her life.

But there was one thing that Rhea did not want to touch. The topic of her dad.

Rhea is a first-generation Vietnamese American. Before her parents came to the U.S., her dad was a ship driver for refugees fleeing from Vietnam to Thailand, en route to the states. On his eighth trip from Vietnam to Thailand, after unloading the boat full of passengers, he decided it was his turn to get outta dodge. He shot a hole in the floor of the boat and boldly sank the ship. No turning back.

On that eighth trip, he met Rhea's mom. Together, with faith, smarts, and defiance, they made their way to the United States.

Unfortunately, their story didn't end happily ever after. Rhea's dad had a temper and a drinking problem. He'd go on alcohol binges that ended in physical and emotional violence toward Rhea's mom.

When Rhea was four years old, her dad almost hit her in a missed swing intended for her mom, and that was her mother's last straw. In an instant, her mom found the courage to make the call and leave once and for all. She raised Rhea as a single immigrant mom from that moment on.

In elementary school, Rhea was very shy and extremely afraid of men. She'd sometimes get in trouble at school for having huge outbursts that seemed to come out of nowhere.

As she got older, Rhea took to heavy drinking. She slept around in ways that left her feeling shitty. She looped in emotionally unstable and abusive relationships and pretended to enjoy things that didn't bring her pleasure in attempts to win the approval and attention of men. She was often overtaken by extreme jealousy and rage. And she had no idea what to do about any of it.

When we started working together, Rhea didn't realize that she had inherited, systemic, developmental, or sexual trauma. She didn't think her story was a big deal. She knew it was kinda fucked up, but definitely didn't want to go there.

As a rule of thumb, I follow my client's lead, trusting that their soul and physiology has a unique timeline of energetic and emotional capacity to cope, heal and transform. In this case, I followed Rhea's lead, working with what was directly in front of her, rather than pressing into the issues of her past.

One time, we had a whole session about a temper tantrum she'd had in an alley after accidentally dropping a trash bag. She couldn't stop screaming and crying. Although, clearly, dropping a trash bag wasn't worthy of this kind of outburst, a feeling of being left alone with no "man" to do the "manly things," while she was overstressed about other interpersonal dynamics—well, those were the perfect conditions for her unresolved trauma to explode in feral distress.

Still, in this session, we didn't directly address her past. Instead, I helped her move through the energetic embodied layers of grief, helplessness and desire that had amassed a 20-year fire in her belly, without ever talking about what struck the match of that flame. We were, in fact, addressing her father-trauma, without exposing or dissecting it under a fluorescent light.

After four years of this kind of work, Rhea's capacity for intensity grew bigger and bigger. One day, her mom, who'd been holding and carrying so much for so long, finally feeling just how strong her daughter had grown, decided to tell Rhea all her worst stories. Stories of what it was like when Rhea was a kid—the fights, the hitting, the heartbreak.

Rhea called me in a panic. Suddenly, like rushing lava, a wave of all the ways she had been holding others' pain came tumbling through her body. She was terrified of the rage unleashing inside of her after hearing her mother's stories.

"What does your body want to do right now?" I asked.

"My mind is telling me I should stay and listen to my mother more. To be a good daughter," she whispered. "But my body? My body wants to run. Run far and fast, and not come back."

"Okay, I hear you. What if you trust that your desire to be a good daughter isn't going anywhere? And then what if we momentarily let your system run—as far and fast as it wants to?" I asked, knowing that if we overrode her instincts, they'd get stuffed and stuck inside of her.

"Yeah, I think I need that," she whispered again.

Then we let her run—run in her mind, run in micro movements, run like a wild cheetah, until right-distance made a safe space for young Rhea to cry, and cry, and cry, releasing years of held in grief and hot, disturbed depression. After a pause, she looked up quiet and concerned.

"What's happening over there?" I asked.

"I feel guilty, like I should go back to that bedroom and help my parents in their violent flares."

"Mmmm. That's such a sweet intention from little-Rhea," I acknowledged. "Can I offer another possibility?" I asked. Rhea nodded, so I continued. "What if perhaps adult-Rhea decides to keep little-Rhea safe instead? Just right now, just for a few minutes longer? What if she could build a safe space for the little one to feel and heal and play? Then what if perhaps your Mom could come into this sacred, safe space, too, rather than little-Rhea going over there into that darkness where the whole family sinks?"

Rhea sighed a combination of relief and remorse. Relief that, maybe just maybe, she didn't have to put out an impossible fire. Remorse that she'd been raised inside of one, and now had to build something steady and stable for herself instead. We made space for both things—relief and remorse—and after a few minutes of this deep allowing, her physiology began to melt into a warm metal-like substance. She breathed with the sublime experience of her nervous system rearranging, then looked up at me again, this time with steady certainty.

"I can build a healthy home, a healthy life, a safe space. I get it. That's how I heal my lineage. That's how I say thank you to my mom. That's how I embody real care."

We teared up together in a holy moment of knowing.

Rhea's tendency to caretake danger didn't change overnight. But over time, she began focusing less on saving others and more on cultivating fertile ground. With this subtle but important distinction, Rhea's energy body grew into a luminous pillar of light. I'm not kidding. You should see the way she shines. The way she wears pleasure on her skin. The way she calls others into her den of deliciousness. The way she trusts herself to take care of herself first, as a radical act of care for the world.

In the self-development industry, there's a common false belief that changing our minds can change our lives—overnight. But the truth is, with developmental, systemic, and inherited trauma, we need time. We need time for long-term physiological shifts to aggregate. We need time to form new synapses and patterns in our nervous systems and brains. We need time for our identities to rearrange from stuck and stifled to full and whole.

The pace of nervous system transformation is both slower and more efficient than cognitive behavioral shifts. As we respect the sensitivity of our neurobiology, working with it at doable paces, in gentle ways, powerful changes can happen quickly. But not because we rushed. Rather, because we slowed down. Not because we pushed, but because we listened closely.

Rhea and I have still never had a session about her dad. Some hurts are so deep and big that they don't need to be opened up, interrogated or investigated. They can be the quiet *why?* too tender to talk about. They can be the sacred wound that we revere by only hovering near, not picking it apart. We can let those wounds tip-toe toward us, in their own secret ways, with their own right timing, on their own holy accord.

Meanwhile, when working with clients, we can invite them into the essential practices that build strength and resilience in the dark. We can help them learn to nurture doable aliveness, call in valiant resources, create safe distance from unsafe behavior, and tend to their fertile grounds with epic care.

Essential Groundskeeper Practices

Groundskeeper Coherence Practice

Standing, sitting, or lying down, with cupped hands, allow yourself to pat down each of your arms and legs and the entirety of your body—belly and back, sides and chest. Shake out your hands and arms, feet, and legs. Then if you'd like, let yourself move through your space in any way that feels enlivening or empowering. Embody your sense of empowered safety and vitality. Feel whatever degree of aliveness is accessible to you just right now.

Then, perhaps as you're still moving, say inwardly or outwardly the following affirmations over and over again, pausing between each to notice what you sense or see:

I am fertile ground.
I tend to all of me.
I move things where they need to be.
I weed and water accordingly.
I keep rhythms that revitalize me.
I am empowered safety.
I am so alive!

What parts of you want to be moved and where do they want to go? What in your life, your space or your relationships wants to be rearranged? What movements might empower you to trust that you can move things where they need to go in order to renew health and vitality in your life and body?

Fertile Grounds Star Chart

If dysregulated Groundskeeper has a life of high highs and low lows, as well as addiction and chaos, then regulated Groundskeeper has a one of steady, predictable rhythms and routines that cultivate an inner-fertility and wellness. Since connection is the antidote to addiction, and because re-regulating from violence and chaos can be so challenging to do alone, a Fertile Grounds Star Chart can be a lovely exercise to do with family, close friends, or in community. Daily check-ins and support can make the process more appealing and achievable. Simply support each other in finding personalized right-fit Star Chart moves, then have a quick text, phone, or dinner check-in to see how it's all going. Or if you live together or nearby, do some of the moves together—especially if they're challenging for you.

Remember, the idea with Star Charts isn't to be perfect, or to force yourself

FERTILE GROUNDS STAR CHART

1				
2				
3				
4				
5				
6				
7				
8				
9				
10				
11				
12				
13				
14				

to get four stars each day. Rather, it's to let yourself play with the possibility that it could be fun and simple to grow and heal. This is really important, because if you're using your Star Chart to measure your worth, you may end up punishing yourself when you don't get four stars.

So often, we set unattainable goals for ourselves that we then fail to reach. With aggregate failures stacking up like piles of undone laundry, we can feel daunted by a sense of powerlessness or hopelessness.

Let's not do that with this. No need. Instead, make the things on your Fertile Grounds Star Chart as simple and easy as possible. I do Star Charts religiously, and often include things like, "drink eight glasses of water a day." "10 minutes of movement." "10 minutes of reading," "bathe," "morning smoothie," "make a plan or see a friend," or "evening prayers."

These moves are easy for me to make, but they also make a dramatic difference in the momentum of my personal health. But just because they're easy doesn't mean I've always been in the habit of doing them. Truth be told, I need fun and playful systems to help me reinforce healthy habits. I need *friends* to do these things with, to not expect myself to be able to only ever self-regulate my way back to stabilization. That's just the way I'm wired. How about you?

If you find yourself unable to complete the tasks on your Star Chart with ease, they're the wrong tasks (or you might need more co-regulation!). The idea is that your tasks should be easy enough that you can do them without force. For example, if it's hard for you to do your dishes, instead of telling yourself you have to do them all every day, your Star Chart could say, "Five minutes of dishes while chatting on the phone or listening to my fave song." Set a timer or play one song, then call it done, even if there are still more dishes in the sink. Small win.

You can make Star Charts for any archetype by focusing on the particular developmental muscles required to grow into that archetype's healthy blueprint. In the case of Groundskeeper, the developmental muscles are related to consistent tending of body, space, and self in ways that amplify health, safety, empowerment, and vitality. What small, doable moves could help grow your coherence to these energies?

Some great Groundskeeper Star Chart moves could include:

- 10 minutes of mindful movement every morning
- Morning altar tending
- Daily bathing, hair care, or skin care
- Daily energetic hygiene practice like cutting cords, qi gong, lighting sage, etc.
- Cooking a delicious, healthy breakfast for yourself and your beloveds
- Five minutes tidying right before bed
- Making your bed first thing in the morning
- Tending plants like friends, weeding, and watering accordingly

What grows a feeling of safety, stability, and power in your physical and physiological space? What small ways can you grow that connection?

Safe Distance from Unsafe Behavior

When your client is in a situation of ongoing physical or emotional violence and it becomes especially challenging for the nervous system to regulate, bounce back, or heal, cultivating safe distance from unsafe behavior becomes of utmost importance.

It may be supportive to ask your client the following questions:

- What would be a safe distance from this unsafe behavior?
- How would it feel to be at that distance?
- What do you notice in your body or emotions as you consider the possibility that you could be that far away?
- What might be the first small, doable step in securing that safe distance?

If your client begins to feel shame, fear or powerlessness—like they cannot get themselves to that distance—invite them to be curious about the most realistic way of creating just a bit more distance, and what they might do to grow strength and power when they're in that environment of increased relative safety.

It might take time for your client to create right-distance from violence or threat, so it's important to help them remember that lots of small baby steps create big momentums of change over time. It's also important to note that systemic and state violence—racism, classism, sexism, ableism, etc.—are harder to escape. In these cases, being in affinity group healing spaces is often a big relief, even if it's only temporary.

Find a Safe Place in Nature that Becomes Yours

If your client is able to access nature, invite them to go on a sacred walk in search of a piece of nature that feels especially supportive or loving—like a safe haven of grandmotherly care. Even living in the city, a client could do this practice. Once your client finds that safe nature space—a beautiful tree, a sturdy rock, a small opening of grass that feels as though it's inviting them to sit upon it—encourage your client to name it or listen for the name it would like to have. (The name may be as simple as "Safe Rock." It doesn't have to be super special.)

Encourage your client to begin visiting this place in nature often. Tell them they can go there when they're feeling sad, happy, celebratory or in need of support; that nature will always be there for them—all they have to do is show up. Through this process of co-regulation with nature, your client can develop a feeling of connection to safe space and stable ground, both inside and outside themself.

Receiving Safe, Doable Touch

If your client is stuck in parasympathetic shut-down—freeze, chronic pain, chronic illness, or depression, or if they're stuck looping in fight, flight, or hypervigilance—working with a touch-based practitioner who's trained in the nervous system can be a life-changing experience.

The following modalities couldn't be more helpful for reviving a healthy Groundskeeper:

Somatic Experiencing

Cranial Sacral Therapy

Trauma-Sensitive Yoga

Alchemical Alignment

Organic Intelligence

When a compromised nervous system has the chance to co-regulate with a more regulated one, old imprints rise to the surface to complete and resolve. The presence of stationary touch can be incredibly supportive in this alchemical nervous system rewiring. If you'd like to do touch-work with your clients, I highly recommend training in one of the above modalities to ensure a trauma-informed and safe approach.

Chapter 9

POLLINATOR

FROM ISOLATION & ALIENATION to INTIMATE BELONGING

The Blueprint

Pollinator is the mystical, sensual archetype of sex, lineage, community, ritual, and belonging. Pollinator isn't bound by time or age, but rather, graces the garden when the environment is safe. She weaves from flower to flower, home to home, throughout the land, carrying and sharing the sweetness of life.

Pollinator embodies pleasure. Spreads it, too. Through sex, song, and dance. Through texture and touch. Through tender, holy lust. Though community, intimacy, tradition, and trust.

Pollinator thrives off of knowing her place in the village and helping others find belonging as well. She's got a knack for bringing the ancestors back—through rituals and recipes, spells and poetry. Pollinator carries the heartbeat of her bloodline from one place and time to another.

The aliveness of the garden, its ability to reproduce, depends on Pollinator's presence. But the trouble is, Pollinator cannot survive in toxic or unsafe gardens. She requires a healthy flow of reciprocity—where the garden gives to her just as much as she gives to it. There's no nourishment for Pollinator in a garden that's been genetically modified. Stripped of care and connection, wisdom and traditions—these traumatized gardens feel like graveyards for the ghosts of sensuality.

Pollinator has many purposes, all centered around intimate belonging. She buzzes through the garden asking, "Is this a safe place for my sex to bloom? For community to bloom? For all identities and unique purposes to bloom? For lineage and traditions to bloom? For cooperation to bloom?"

It's no mistake that these things—sex, community, identity, lineage, and cooperation—go together. Pleasure without cooperation isn't pleasurable at all. Procreation without community strains and stresses the family. Lineage that's lost its song and dance has a hollow ache in the center of its bones. Identity without a witness, without togetherness, ends up feeling like hopelessness.

The first five archetypes are focused on personal and interpersonal healing. Pollinator and Sacred Gardener—the last two archetypes—open us to the wider sphere of lineage, community, and collective healing. They cannot heal on their own, or even in intimate relationships, alone. They require togetherness, movements, and change at systemic, interconnected levels.

Pollinator is a litmus test for individual and collective liberation. How much sweetness can we experience together? How much honey can we drip from spoon to tongue, unafraid of what others will say? Unafraid of what someone might take in our moments of tender submission? How much can we bring our wild medicine forward? Can every flower be devoured with reverence? Can every song have a chance to be sung? Can everyone find their place in the mysterious circle of life? Can we know the land we live on like the back of our hand? Can we honor its original people? Can we remember the language of our ancestors? Can we weave their Indigenous Earth Alchemy into the wind and sea of wherever we find ourselves living now?

Pollinator at a Glance

Body Connection: Eyes and Lips, Face and Skin, Social Nervous System

Your eyes and lips, face and skin, are the portals of connection between you and others, between you and Life. The sensory sensuality with which you can touch, see, feel, taste, and energetically brush up against the world, let the world brush up against you.

When you feel safe, you can look others in the eyes and smile, flirt, dance. You can trace the softness of another's skin; you can let their warmth touch yours. You can kiss. You can make love. You can even, if you feel like it, fuck.

When you feel unsafe, isolated or alienated, shame might shroud your face or avert your gaze. Sweaters might cover your skin and you might find yourself in clothes you definitely can't dance in.

In belonging, we connect eye-to-eye with curiosity, compassion, healthy critique, or care. We trust the semi-permeable membranes of our personal boundaries and borders. We sense that others respect our selfhood, and an intersovereign dance is possible between the me and the we. In isolation, we hide the points of connection, the ways in. We're not so sure we can maintain a safe sense of self amidst interconnection.

Natural Blueprint of Health: Intimate Belonging

You are surrounded by people who know, love, and respect you for who you are, how you present and where you come from. You are connected to the land and culture in which you reside, as well as the land and culture of your lineage. You have opportunities to contribute and do your part in our human family. You have quality care, touch, partnership, and friendship available to you. Your gifts, Eros and love have a place and are put to good use in the world. You belong in a way that's healthy for you and healthy for others. You can adventure on your own and come back to your people and place with trust and security. Your full self, sexuality and gender expression is welcomed, acknowledged and valued.

Traumatic Imprint: Isolation and Alienation

You are ostracized, incarcerated, separated, quarantined, segregated, made to feel different or Other (for your personality, looks, size, ability, race, class, gender, sexuality...), friendless, without community, without family, in it all alone. You are experiencing digital addiction without fleshy connection, no touch. You are a refugee, placeless, or closeted. You have extreme privilege or extreme poverty. You are on the fringe or edges of society, feeling that you do not belong or have a place or way to contribute your true gifts, your honest heart.

Hyper-Response to Isolation and Alienation: Ride-or-Die

- Being a part of gangs, extreme loyalties, cults
- Clinging to who you have even if they're unhealthy or not aligned
- Exclusivity
- Hazing for entry
- Us against them mentality
- Lacking compassion for people outside your group
- Fear of outside threats
- Feeling only safe in the pack

When someone's embodying Ride-or-Die, it can often feel threatening to their system to relate to people outside of their known or perceived "safety" group. Past experiences of isolation, alienation, ostracization, abuse, or cultural and systemic pressures or oppression creates a group-level fear that contributes to an extreme banning together with others like them.

Common fears and inner-dialogues include:
- "I'm only safe with people like me."
- "Everyone else is out to get me."
- "Our way is THE way, and everyone else is nuts."
- "It's so exhausting relating to people different than me...why would I put myself through that?"

- "Thank God I've got my crew. Everyone else can suck it."
- "We're the only ones we can depend on."

Hypo-Response to Isolation and Alienation: In-It-Alone

- Depression
- Relational collapse
- Self-imposed isolation or alienation
- Existential crises
- Perpetual nomad
- Commitment-phobe
- Unsafe in spaces with others
- Chronically Othered
- Deep feeling of being an outsider
- Hopelessness around belonging
- Closeted
- Endless search for your people
- Making do without others
- Solitary living
- Work without connection to others

When someone's embodying In-It-Alone, it can often feel threatening to their system to join groups. Past experiences of difficulty or trauma in the group setting, or even the interpersonal realms, leads to a lack of trust or perceived safety in group, community or cultural settings, and isolation or alienation becomes a more secure base to operate from.

Common fears and inner dialogues include:

- "I've been ousted so many times…why bother trying to join?"
- "I can't be my real self anywhere, so I might as well be alone."
- "Where are my people? Do they even exist? Maybe I'll just do more self-improvement to try to get out of feeling so lonely."

- "I keep fantasizing about the perfect community, but it feels so out of reach."
- "When I try to relate deeply to others, it's a total drain. People are so unhealthy."
- "How will I ever be less lonely if I can't trust people to meet and match me?"
- "I don't want to drop the friends I have because then I'll be REALLY alone, but they're not meeting my needs, at all."

Starved for Community

It was a Thursday night when I received this tender email from a woman on my mailing list.

Hi Rachael,

This feels like kind of a long shot because I live in Portland, Oregon, and I don't have tons of extra money so it seems a bit crazy to be doing this, but I'm wondering if you're still accepting people for brunch this weekend? I just feel so alone. Maybe we can hop on the phone real quick and talk more about it?

Thanks so much!

There was something about receiving this email that felt cosmic—as if dear-mailing-list-soul-sister was a hologram of my past self, reaching out to her future for support. I'd been in her shoes, ready to spend my last dime, travel across the country at a moment's notice, do whatever it took—just to feel less alone. My heart took to her call.

Hey there,

Feeling you. I'm happy to hop on a 20-minute call with you tonight. 7pm?

She sent over her number, and soon, like the fates themselves had arranged it, we were Past and Future dancing in divine dialogue.

"So what's really drawing you to come?" I asked her, after exchanging some gentle hellos. She started to weep about her loneliness, the horrid hole of isolation she found herself in, couldn't find her way out of. I empathized with her pain, then asked if I could tell her the words I knew I needed to hear when I was crying my own tears of isolation.

"Please. Tell me. I'm listening. I'm ready."

"Okay," I replied. "This is a hard pill to swallow. It's something I still have to tell myself almost every day. I'm gonna share it with you from a place of love, okay?"

"Uh huh, please," she whispered into the other end of the phone.

"There's no community out there that's gonna whisk you away on a magic carpet ride of togetherness. No one is going to hand you belonging. Not these days. Not in this culture. You have to grow it with intentional care, slowly, over time. You have to make consistent invitations. You have to respond to the invitations of others. Over, and over, and over again."

"I'm saying this for you as much as I'm saying it for myself," I told her. "Intimate belonging rarely knocks on our doors. We have to bust that door down—every day, week after week, month after month, year after year. Until eventually something forms that has its own rhythms and rituals, roots, and ceremonies. Until we've cultivated relationships strong enough to sustain themselves.

"I think it takes at least two years of regularly showing up to form secure community attachment. It's a big undertaking. Don't underestimate the commitment required. It's a long game. You gotta be willing to go all in."

She thanked me so much for the wider context, for calling her into her devotion. I thanked her for helping me get crystal clear on the truth I hadn't before spoken with such volition. We hung up the phone renewed with passion and gratitude.

If you're fearing you don't know where to begin, how to call community in, how to respond to the call, please know you're not alone. The longing for intimate belonging can bring up all kinds of barriers.

But I'm so different, so sensitive, emotional, deep, creative, you might think. *Who could I possibly belong to?*

Why the sensitive, emotional, deep and creative people, of course!

But those people don't exist where I live! you might object. *I'll never find them. I live in the wrong city.*

Okay. But if they did exist, where would they want to gather? What would the garden of belonging look and feel like in your town? Can you make it? For a night? For a weekend? Could you find it or grow it online, if not in person?

It's easy to feel like a victim in our isolating culture. Most of us are, after all, living on colonized land, orphaned from the trees and rivers, foods and recipes, rituals and songs our way-back-people once knew. I've stretched years at a time grieving the architecture of disconnection. But eventually, that grief gave way to creation. I decided the story couldn't end there if I wanted to experience togetherness or sweet belonging.

What if your gifts are needed in order to create what you're wanting? What if you're meant to be the Queen Bee of a hive that's yet to form? What if there's a Queen Bee out there tryna call in her colony, and you just gotta put your antennae out to find her?

You might be reading this thinking, "Yeah—but people don't feel safe to me." When we've had histories that violate our sense of safety, we become less trusting in others, in the decency of humanity. A good friend of mine was in an abusive relationship with a narcissist for three years. After they broke up, it took her almost two years to feel safe in community again.

When I was in the acute process of healing my sexual trauma, there was a period of time when I became more afraid of strangers than ever before in my life. Going to the grocery store was riddled with anxiety. Getting dinner with friends? Exhausting. I was open, exposed, raw. I needed cocooning to help me feel safe while I healed.

I hear this same thing from clients over and over again—the fear of others while we do our sacred work, the need for way more time alone, resting under covers. Sometimes, spending time alone is needed like a dressing over the wound that separates raw flesh from the outside world while new skin is still reforming.

While there are times when going inward supports our process, sometimes that very solitude can turn into chronic isolation when it becomes a new habit or coping mechanism. It's hard to know what's what sometimes—if you're in a necessary phase of solo recovery, or if that phase has passed and you need support re-emerging into safe relationships in small baby steps.

There's no right timeline for how long a recovery process should take. This is really important to say, especially because it can be hard and lonely in those necessary cocoons. When your body and heart start to long for reconnection, if you open and listen, life will show you doorways back into new and safe togetherness.

Erotic Waste

I was lying in bed, double-armed with my tools. Chakrub[20] in one hand, Womanizer[21] in the other. I don't know how long it'd been since I'd felt a body of love melt into mine and dance with me toward ecstasy, but my vulva was aching—literally aching—and I was going to rub that ache out.

Of course, I was doing my best to be a self-loving masturbator. I'd already taken coconut oil in the palms of my hands and given myself a generous breast massage, circling my nipples in one direction then the next, then circling in broader strokes

[20] Chakrubs are sex toys made from natural crystal that bring a sense of sacredness to your playtime. These beautiful, hand-crafted tools are created with the intention of opening oneself up to the healing properties crystals provide." In other words, magical crystal dildos. Head to chakrubs.com to check 'em out.

[21] The Womanizer, despite it's… well, interesting name… is quite the experience. Use it for next-level clitoris stimulation and orgasms. womanizer.com

around all my soft flesh, shaking and waking up my vitality. I was whispering, "I love you" aloud to myself and listening for where my hands wanted to go.

I wasn't quite crying, but the grief in my heart had moved into my breasts, creating a half-numb density of remorse. When I couldn't take the feelings anymore, I pressed go on the vibrator, and the quiet buzz got louder and louder as I increased its speed to max capacity. In went the Chakrub, and the walls of my vagina engorged and convulsed. A long moment later, I began to orgasm, sad and soft.

I believe in self-pleasure. I'm a regular practitioner. It shows us where we really are with the state of our hearts and bodies. Grieving, angry, hungry, at peace. When we show up to practice enough, it's like daily journaling. Your mood shows through. Your ache points to the places where your life is unfulfilled. You confront yourself. Intimately.

In this moment, I was in a rut of isolation, living in a location where I felt invisible and disconnected, without a lover, without a Beloved, without a community to dance and romance. My erotic gifts felt wasted. Not because I couldn't give them to myself, but because even when I woke them and turned them into creativity or service, dance or poetry—somehow, the feedback loop of fulfillment wasn't hitting me. I'd spent so much time self-sustained and self-directed, self-satisfied, and self-sufficient, walled off so that nobody could hurt me or disappoint me, that my body was revolting. *No more isolation!*, it practically screamed in pain and heartache.

In a culture that convinces us to internalize the cost of personal distress, we forget the essential humanity of intimate belonging. We forget that we didn't come to earth as individual bubbles meant to fend for ourselves our whole lives. We forget that we're part of a long lineage birthed from sex, kept healthy through rituals and community care.

We forget how to cultivate this kind of intimate belonging. We forget to fight for it in healthy ways. We either gorge ourselves on false versions of it (porn, meaningless hookups, social media, Netflix), or lose the impulse to hunger for it altogether. (*Who needs love or connection?! I've learned how to make do on my own.*)

Lost, we spiral in internal debates about whether our gifts are enough or too much, if our needs are weak or reasonable. We wonder if we're the only ones struggling and everyone else somehow has what they need. We lie to ourselves, saying we're just highly sensitive, super-hungry love freaks, because maybe then we can stop longing for a different world—a world that feels so far out of reach.

I've been lost in the spell of isolation more times than I can count. But what if my neediness for connection is a sign that I haven't resigned myself to the lonely self-sufficiency of scrolling hour after hour? What if my courage to grieve is how I break into the community I need?

In community, I chime in where I'm needed and offer my gifts in the gaps of the whole system.
In isolation, I think I have to hold it all alone.

In community, I snuggle with my girlfriends on the couch and hip bump while doing the dishes.
In isolation, I scroll Instagram and leave plates in piles higher than the sink.

In community, I reflect to you your brilliance and power, and you reflect mine back to me.
In isolation, I forget what I have to offer; I lose my connection to purpose.

In community, I flirt.
In isolation, I dim.

In community, I connect eye-to-eye, letting the cues of our bodies guide us toward compassionate connection, or not.
In isolation, I read words on a screen that divide you and me or attract us without the humanity of flesh.

In community, I have social proof that you're a safe person to have sex with.
In isolation, I rely solely on pheromones and one-on-one negotiations.

Wasted Gifts

The less community intimacy we cultivate, the easier it is to neglect, exploit, shame, repress, manipulate, control, violate, alienate and colonize each other. In a healthy community, you know your gifts and how they're meant to be used. You're celebrated for your place in the circle of the collective. Your role has been carried on from generation to generation. You've apprenticed with an elder who's helped show you the way. Nobody's gifts are seen as valueless.

With deep reverence for each person's unique call, a healthy community has zero waste of human resources. In turn, the whole village is better cared for. There's a regenerative abundance born of true togetherness. Everyone matters. No one is wasted.

You, the doula.

You, the witch.

You, the poetess.

You, the songstress.

You, the ritual keeper.

You, the medicine tender.

You, the Mother.

You, the Father.

You, the initiator.

You, the sorcerer.

You, the Elder.

You, the Child.

You, the genderqueer.

You, the mistress.

You, the trickster.

You, the teacher of the young.

You, the one we can tell our secrets to.

You, who keeps the rules.

You, who tracks the moon.

You, who chops wood and carries water.

You, who tends the land.

You, who keeps the bees.

You, who communes with the animals.

You, who builds the houses.

You, who drums and you, who dances.

You, who heals the sick.

You, who ushers the dying.

You, who catches the babies.

You, who tells the stories.

You. You. You. Whoever you are—in a healthy community, you have a place. You are needed. You belong as an essential cord of connection to the greater whole. Your role matters. You matter.

In communities stuck under personal and collective trauma spells, you lose the sense that your unique medicine matters to the whole. Your Soul Seed experiences a sort of existential orphaning, and you do all kinds of things to try to make up for the loss of belonging. Amp up your ego. Make more money. Play your expected role—no matter if it doesn't lead to where you wanna go. And in this garden, you lose your place. Your gifts—unknown, unheeded or misdirected—turn to waste.

What happens to the parts of you that were meant to belong all along—the parts left unrealized, like seeds stored in a jar somewhere on the top shelf of a dark garage? How much of the true you feel wasted? And where does that waste go? Where in your body is it stored? On whom does it get taken out? What's bought or consumed to hold, carry or replace it?

When I got back from that trip to Tamera Healing Biotope, I could feel just how much of me was being *wasted*. Not only my sex, but my soul. I felt like a walking myth, an invisible goddess, a secret ancient sex mistress in a sea of disconnected cyborgs. I didn't care that I wasn't seen. I cared that I was wasted.

After all, maybe the desire to be "seen" is really the desire to be put to use. To have a place where your gifts aren't discarded like the extra packaging of your Amazon delivery. To belong in the most felt-sense way. To be part of a bigger symbiotic relationship that points toward regenerative health.

Maybe the desire to awaken your sexuality comes from a secret whisper inside telling you something essential is getting tossed to the landfill. Something that could be cycled through your breath and blood, your cells and soul, from head to toe: like solar energy—sustaining, renewable, sane, powerful vitality.

Maybe you're more like the bees, wanting to move from flower to flower, spread the pollen, collect the sweetness. Maybe the Soul of your Seed only comes to life when it's put to use in the greater garden.

Sex is the energy of creation. Am I creating something sustaining or something wasteful? Something generative or something destructive? Something in coherence with the bigness of my true nature, or something shrouded in the smallness of fear? Am I even creating at all?

Am I consuming and calling that belonging? At whose expense do I consume? The further away we get from the source, the easier it is to exploit and be exploited. Is my consumption exploiting someone else? Am I somehow exploiting myself?

Have I told myself I can do without? That I don't need to create or consume? Am I numb to the flow of life? Is the pain (or pleasure) of aliveness too big for me to bear?

These questions fuel my calling to do this work. They sustain my attention, because they are so much bigger than sex. But they are also as intimate as sex. Because how we regard sex—both personally and culturally—overlaps with how we regard creation, consumption, waste, exploitation, extraction, and dissociation on a global scale. It's all relationship.

The Toxic Soil that Endangers Pollinator

The further away we get from the source, the easier it is to exploit and be exploited. The source of humanity is community—intimate belonging, reputation, place among the group and shared knowledge of one another. The further away we get from relational accountability—the less we value the necessity of the Pollinator—the easier it is to leave each other in shitty conditions.

The shiny new tech we use that's a world away from the sweatshop conditions in China where it was created. The drunk stranger at the bar who, having watched so much superficial porn, objectifies you for your sex. The oil and gas we pump into our cars and warm our homes with, so automatically. Nevermind the Indigenous land from which the resources are fracked and the communities dying in the wake of our waste. The animals we eat whose cages we dare not see. The dying elderly, displaced from family.

We didn't create these genetically modified hives of disconnection. We didn't pray for them. We didn't intend for them. But these are the homes we live inside, the land we feed off of, the air we breathe.

If we're awake, surely we must grieve. Given the glory of our gorgeous Earth, we as humans have betrayed it—and ourselves, as a result. We have used it. We have fracked and mountain-top removed it. We have polluted it. We have killed many of its precious creatures. We have gravely disrespected it, at our own peril. Earth will survive us by employing the superpower of a deep, long-lasting freeze, then thawing again in a few hundred million years. But will we?

Disconnection is the great endangerment of Humanity. It can be overwhelming to see the real damage of disconnection. But even when we close our eyes, we still feel it. In the bedroom. In the body. In the psyche. We still eat it and can't digest it.[22] We're still watching the news reel of destruction on the very screen that's causing the collapse. We can sense from far away the dying song and dance, the lost romance of Pollinator. We can sense it real close in, too—the song we no longer sing, the hollow void, the quiet, horrible longing.

What could be more transformative than a critical mass of people, so full of grief and hunger, committed—together—to reblooming our collective garden?

What if just enough of us could awaken from the spell of dissociation and recycle our wasted gifts into pleasurable creation? What if we knew we could access our fullest magic? In the bedroom? In the boardroom? In the courtroom? On the land? How many of us would it take to make psychic ripples across the world?

We could culture-fuck the norms that overthrow our natural health. We could revive the spiritual wealth encoded in our design. What if we dared to be so audacious? What would we find?

[22]*A 2020 study in the Environmental Research Journal found that microplastics are being found in apples and carrots due to the root systems picking up the microplastics from rainwater. https://www.bbc.co.uk/ newsround/53195056*

Oh, with that much honey love, sex magic, sensual erotic care, we'd be sourced from the greatest life-force of belonging. We could co-create and innovate all that our human family is longing for. We could shoot the moon. We could save the oceans. We could feed the hungry. We could become the prayers we've been praying for. And if it all goes to shit, we could feel okay about it. We could know in our souls we did our best. Let us die and be reborn, try again next time—in this universe or another. Fuck it. No regrets.

I know I've gone too far. I can't turn back. I'm on track to a whole new world, whether it ever comes into full bloom or not. You don't have to be, but if you are, too, I hope you take my confession as a blessing of solidarity. We are together. Radically. Whether we ever meet, mix, mingle, or not.

This is the mystical call of the Pollinator, the highest expression of deep belonging, the inquiry that consecrates you to serve the invisible and inextricable interconnectedness of Life.

Let no gift be wasted. Let no move happen in isolation. Find your footing by diving into purposeful communion with the whole.

Let it be pleasurable. Let it be delicious. Let it be divine. Let it carefully unravel the cultural lies that have been stitched into your skin. Let yourself begin to remember the big home your soul belongs to: the hive of our togetherness.

Roots first, then the bloom

Wanna have the best sex ever?

Forget about sex. Focus on sovereignty. Focus on self-connection and honoring your truth. Focus on finding people who affirm your soul's goodness and getting used to the balm of their blessing. Focus on unshaming all the shades of your feeling-body. Focus on knowing you're your own most important Gatekeeper. Focus on celebrating your *no*. Focus on finding your hot, holy, ecstatic *yes*—outside of sex, where there's less risk, more play. Focus on your heart and what it needs to feel seen, known, loved. Focus on just how worthy you are, and if you can't feel that or if you think that's a dumb idea, focus on the possibility that feeling good is revolutionary—and you were born to make waves in this world. Focus on taking deep breaths and saying the words, "I need to pause" when you feel yourself trailing away from your center.

After working with hundreds of people on sexual post-traumatic growth… I'm tellin' you now: self-honor is the secret elixir.

No matter how many jade egg or tantric breathing practices you do, if you're overriding your limits, pushing when your body is saying no, or forcing yourself to perform—the high isn't gonna last.

Sexuality can be one of the most challenging places to honor yourself if root-level self-reverence isn't a thing you're familiar with.

Sexual post-TRaumaTic growth is a BoTTom UP QuesT.

Sexual post-traumatic growth is a bottom-up quest. It's about knowing what you need to feel physically and emotionally safe—with yourself, first. In relationships, second. In intimacy, third.

Then it's about slowly regrowing your capacity to honor what you know…

Roots first, then the bloom.

And the bloom? THIS bloom? When it comes, you're gonna feel it from head to toe, from soil to soul, from the inside out—alllll over. Over and over and overrrr again.

Roots first, then the bloom.

Your Longing Holds the Keys to Our Belonging

For years, a quiet nag invaded my psyche when clients would cry about how alone they felt, then consequently blame themselves for not being able to figure out a true sense of belonging. The same nag scratched away at me when clients who were oriented toward collectivism and sharing were trying to make it on their own—working for themselves, by themselves. The nag whispered something sacred and essential in my ear:

We can't heal collective problems at the level of the individual. We must heal them together, through community and culture. And if we don't…if we keep blaming ourselves as individuals, the collective trauma spell siloes us into weaker isolated parts—and wins.

I've given many private speeches along the lines of, "Nothing's wrong with you. You're built to move like a bee, in a world that insists you can only win if you're a hawk. It's not true. But pollinating isn't something you can do on your own. And it's possible that your togetherness muscles have atrophied in a world that makes it hard to exercise them. So how can we start to rebuild them? Because they're in there, and they're the answer."

One spring, feeling sick with my own case of digital isolation, I got fed up with the invisible weight of our collective trauma spell overwhelming my capacity to hope, love, or envision a future humanity. My clients were echoing similar malaise. I could hear it, though no one dared say it—our hive was dying from hyper-individualism. We needed to come together.

I took my ache to the trusty Coherence Practice. The through line was clear: be a bold stand for what you need, what *we* need. Make an invitation into the most beautiful possibility. And get the fuck off social media.

So I threw spaghetti against the wall. I wrote an email to my list sharing all the ways I felt trapped under the Collective Trauma Spell of hyper-individualism, all the ways I had a hunch I wasn't the only one. At the end, I made a sincere invitation:

I'd like to have a 3-day workshop at my lil brown house by the sea called ReBloom Together. For coaches, artists, mystics, and healers withering in the world of individualism, designed for a more collective way. We can live the questions of our time. We can commit to breaking the spell of isolation together. If eight people reply saying yes, I'll do it.

Fifteen people signed up within five days. Coherence. It does that.

I coulda charged a lot of money, but money wasn't the point. I needed the feeling that we cared about one another more than cash transactions or exchange. I needed us to do the dishes together and hold each other and sing songs and say prayers. I needed it to be simple and small and full of raw humanness…and it was…and it meant everything.

In three days' time, we bore witness to our personal and collective grief, we amplified our personal and collective medicine, and we visioned our way out of isolation. Funny enough—on the third day of the workshop, woman after woman began strutting erotic dance moves. "I feel so turned on!" one shouted while striking a pose on top of a chair. "Me too!" laughed another.

There was zero focus on sexuality at this workshop. But in a safe community space centered around collective wellness, whole-self expression and honorable sovereignty, the natural juices of eroticism re-emerged in women who'd felt dry and turned off for years. In a garden with nourished Soul Seeds, Gatekeepers upholding healthy boundaries, Expressionistas feeling free to be themselves, Sages center stage with their wisdom, and Groundskeepers weeding and watering the plot…the Pollinator naturally shows up. Pleasure, turn-on, cackle, song, and dance are the organic outpourings of a robust interior ecosystem and safe cultural context. The sweetest romance is never forced, but an emergent spring from the source of a healthy environment.

This is the secret the sexual development industry doesn't always get: while feelin' yourself is important—feeling *safe* to feel yourself, as yourself, in the company of others, is the greatest turn-on of all.

The relational, community, and cultural context of your sexual expression affects your access to feeling pleasure. In other words, the safer the relational space, the greater the gorge, the wetter the temple doors, the more moaning, owning, delighting, and inviting. And safe spaces are created by healthy humans.

So often we want to rush to pleasure like an outcome that can make everything better. *If I just orgasm! If I just get laid! If only I could own my sensuality, see myself as pretty…then, then, then…all my problems will disappear.* I've had endless clients come to me wanting to work on sex, thinking the outcome of a healthy sex life comes from focusing on sex alone. While that might seem logical, it's not what I've seen to be the most sustainable way.

Focus on the soil, focus on the roots—and the flower naturally blooms. The pollinator naturally chooses to buzz into the lushest garden. Fertile soil grows fertile crops. Healthy sex doesn't bloom from the top down, it emerges from the bottom up.

At the end of ReBloom Together, we made star charts to cultivate deeper momentums of community connection. I had people partner up and schedule integration and accountability calls for the coming weeks and months, so they wouldn't just go home to the same problem they were trying to escape—so things would actually change.

ReBloom together was decentralized, collaborative, and rooted in the ideology that a shared solution could only be found in our shared soil—the space we had to tend and cultivate together. It didn't depend on me saving, fixing, or healing anyone. It was co-created by the *we*. It was the right medicine to meet our shared difficulty.

Here's the thing: it's not easy to transition out of the world of hyper-individualism. Even when our values align to togetherness, so many of us are still operating from a paradigm of isolation and competition. Sadly, systems of patriarchy, white supremacy and capitalism breed us to be this way.

But this isn't the end of our story. We can regrow the muscles to become we-people in an era ripe with me-fears, me-focuses and me-goals—all perpetuated by me-systems. We can envision we-systems, contribute to we-cultures, read and write we-literature, birth we-businesses and run we-trainings.

I think of effective personal and cultural evolution as a pendulation or weaving back and forth between me-development and we-development.[23] A certain level of personal healing, emotional maturity, and self-regulation is required in order to effectively collaborate in we-spaces. The more personal and interpersonal healing happens in the first five archetypes, the more resourced you become to effectively work at the wider cultural levels of the last two archetypes. Then, the more you co-create with others healthier micro-cultures, the more your body, heart and soul can relax into safety and security.

Often, it's within the most safe and secure relationships and communities that our deepest wounds surface to be felt and healed. Inside safe spaces, deeper, more buried personal traumas often show themselves momentarily, seeking care and resolution. As those older personal traumas alchemize and integrate, even greater layers of creativity, wisdom and life-force spring forth from you, life-force that can be channeled into the next cycle of cultural renovations.

ReBloom is a system for awakening the regenerative spiral of personal and collective healing. Can you see the interwoven nature of the *me* and the *we*, how they depend on each other for holistic thriving, for true liberation? Can you embrace that it's not an either/or, but a necessary pendulation between the two, that grows true hope in the collective heart?

---

[23] *Dan Siegel is one person who's talked about the dance between the me and the we. He calls it "mwe."*

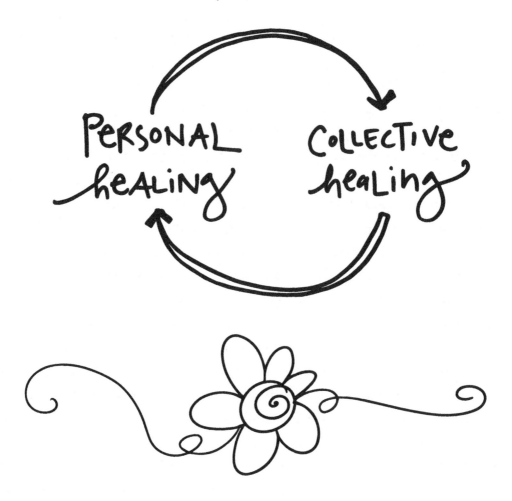

Essential Pollinator Practices

Pollinator Coherence Practice

Allow yourself to move in a way that delights your body, excites your skin. Perhaps grazing your fingers over your arms, belly, or face; perhaps dancing and swirling about; perhaps allowing something erotic to come out. Imagine yourself free to embody your greatest pleasure, your most sincere excitement. Wink at yourself in the mirror. Make seductive faces. Smile lovingly in your own direction.

Say inwardly or outwardly the following affirmations over and over again, pausing in between to sense what's happening inside and noticing any visions that arise.

I am sensual.
My sensuality belongs.
I mix and mingle.
I flirt with life.
I embody pleasure.
I am super excited.
I am needed.
I am wanted.
I belong.

As you engage the movements and mantras of the Pollinator, what truth comes to you about your belonging, pleasure, excitement, and place in the wider family of things?

This coherence practice is designed to connect you to the Blueprint of intimate belonging, in which you have enough personal resources to feel safe in your sensual expression, as well as exist inside a cultural or community context where your greatest medicine is fully welcomed.

If this coherence practice is hard for you, that's okay. It may be that the earlier archetypes are more needed right now to grow a sense of self-empowerment, then as they develop, you'll experience greater ease in erotic territories. Or it may be that a safe community is the medicine you need to help create a space of solidarity where your fullest self is welcome and celebrated.

Pretending You're a Pollinator

Pollinators slurp from the sweetest, most high-vibration flowers. They delight in the deliciousness of life. They sing and dance their way through the garden. They rub up against what's soft and smells good. They're completely sensual with no shame or inhibition. And they do all of this in community.

How might you be more like a Pollinator? How might you make your environment more beautiful and enlivening to the part of you who's turned on by sensuality? Would the Pollinator in you dim the lights, light the candles, fill the house with flowers or plants, turn on the music, freshen the space?

What materials and colors does your inner-Pollinator wear? What smells do you delight in? What textures turn you on? What foods fully satiate your deepest hungers?

How does your Pollinator dance or romance? How do you sing? How do you flirt? Inside which hive does your inner-Pollinator most thrive? With whom do you intimately belong?

Write it out like a scene, then take a day to see how much of your fantasy you can turn into reality.

Star Chart for Pleasurable Connection

What if reawakening your Pollinator could happen little-by-little, over time, in ways that feel exciting, sweet, or like a big relief? When we focus on small and doable healthy habits and do those things with relative consistency—then celebrate our efforts—we create energy and movement that awakens and renews our life force.

For Pollinator, the muscles to develop are all about intimate belonging—to your body, sensuality, community and friends, land or lineage, and our collective garden. Perhaps consider the following four questions, to help brainstorm the small doable actions that might focus your Star Chart for Pleasurable Connection.

1. What small doable things create a feeling of pleasurable connection to my body?
2. What small doable things create a feeling of pleasurable connection to my spirit or soul?
3. What small doable things create a feeling of pleasurable connection to community or friends?
4. What small doable things create a feeling of pleasurable connection to land or lineage?

Which of your answers excite and inspire you right now? Which answers jump off the page as things you realllllyyy need to do? Which answers feel grounding and stabilizing? Which feel a little edgy, but also deeply desirable?

Choose four that you'd love to devote to over the next two weeks. Then, let yourself begin!

As you move through the weeks, notice how you feel on the days when you've done more things on your Star Chart. Are there certain moves that are easier for you to do, others that are more difficult? Could the difficult moves be made a bit easier, so you can win at them? Doability is key. Again, the point isn't perfection—it's momentum.

Some of the small doable moves I've done while growing my Pollinator muscles have been:

- One dance a day
- Sleep by 10 PM (nothing like good sleep to feel great in your body)
- Daily coconut oil
- Daily breast massage
- Daily bath with candlelight
- Quick morning walk in nature
- Coherence practice
- Sing the Sh'ma at sunrise and sunset
- Five minutes meditating or laying on the floor listening to singing bowls
- Make a plan or keep a plan with a friend who feels really nourishing
- Smile at a stranger
- 30-second hug
- Eat a meal slowly and ecstatically
- Kiss the earth
- Listen to one song from my lineage
- Ask for advice from my ancestors
- Hug a tree

☆ PLEASURABLE CONNECTION star chart

1				
2				
3				
4				
5				
6				
7				
8				
9				
10				
11				
12				
13				
14				

Lineage Remembrance Practice

One way we can create a divine and embodied feeling of safe, intimate belonging is by reclaiming the music, language, dance, rituals, and prayers of our ancestors.[24]

Where on earth has your bloodline spent significant time? What are some of the ancient practices of interbeing that have historically amplified the health of your ancestors? You might feel longing or loss reading those questions. Perhaps you're so far removed from your lineage that you don't know the answers, or what's more challenging, you tell yourself there are no healthy ancestors to draw on.

Maybe you're ashamed of the deeds done by the people in your family line.[25]

On the flipside, you might have great pride in the place and people you come from. You might love the land, the language and the traditions of your kin.

Wherever you fall in the spread, the invitation with this practice is to look for small doable delights that connect you to a feeling of belonging with something bigger than you, that's also of you.

In my life, I've taken to a deep reconnection with Judaism, and more specifically, the ritual of Shabbat. Every Friday night I light two candles and sing the Sabbath prayers. Many Fridays, I gather and feast with my closest friends, inviting them into the sacred ceremony of rest, receptivity and communion with the divine. Over time, I've added the joy of playing Hebrew music all Friday afternoon and through the night.

A good friend of mine used to go to church every Sunday growing up, but was quite traumatized by certain components of the religious institution she was a part of. For her, Sunday church didn't feel safe, so instead she went to Sunday morning dance. She found a way to keep the rhythm of the rituals of her past, but replace

[24] *If you're seeking greater sense of belonging—to yourself, your lineage and community—my friend and colleague Becca Piastrelli does awesome work around that, as well as hosts a beautiful podcast called* Belonging. *Learn more at https://beccapiastrelli.com/*

[25] *If you struggle with your ancestral lines and are ready to do deep, profound work with your ancestors, I've done beautiful, loving ancestral imaginings with Tele Darden, who studied with my teacher Brigit, and is one of the most skilled practitioners I've worked with. Connect with her at nourishresilience.com.*

the action with something more nourishing. Interestingly, after years of going to Sunday morning dance, she moved to a new city where a radical lesbian was the pastor of a quirky, creative church. Curious, she began attending, reweaving the old with the new. She's loving it, like a familiar structure with a renewed soul.

My beloved friend and co-conspirator Elydé Arroyo hosts incredibly healing bajos (genital) steams in line with her Mesoamerican lineage. Through song, sweat, cacao, and circle, she invokes ancestors, receives from plant spirits, and reimagines embodied health—even after colonial forces tried to deny her people their practices.[26]

---

[26] *If you'd like to be a part of Elydé's magic, she also hosts online groups that facilitate a remembrance of your original medicine (no matter your people's lineage). You can find Elydé on Instagram at @groundedwombdoula or at groundedwomb.com.*

Chapter 10

SACRED GARDENER

FROM COLONIZATION to Co-CREATION

The Blueprint

Sacred Gardener is the visionary architect of the village. She sits in stillness, listening, with every sense available, to the entire ecosystem of plants, animals, humans and the divine so she can co-create with Life a cooperative design within, which all beings grow and thrive.

By taking space to merge with the natural world, Sacred Gardener becomes receptive to the wise way nature cooperates and regenerates. Sacred Gardener knows what she's creating and why. She's a spiritual permaculturist. A soulful scientist. A systems thinker and feeler. A sorceress and wizard. Receiver of Soul Seeds. Brave builder. Ultimate parent. Devoted pioneer. *She has divine will with human skills.*

She knows Soul Seed will always be a mystery that she's endowed to both guide and learn from. She knows Gatekeeper needs proper initiation in order to grow healthy protective powers. She knows Expressionista will never bloom if the soil isn't fertile, and the environment isn't accepting and encouraging. She knows Sage has things to say that no one else can even see, so lord, get the woman a microphone. She knows Groundskeeper is the unsung hero of stable rhythms and nourishing routines. She knows Pollinator holds the secret medicine of pleasure, togetherness, and remembrance, but that medicine will turn toxic when the garden is unwell. She knows it's her job to balance the ecosystem through radical listening and courageous, creative response.

While Sacred Gardener is infinitely wise, she is also consistently humbled by the unknown. Nevertheless, she's committed to showing up to the uncertainty, day after day, season after season, year after year…lifetime after lifetime. She has incredible successes and incredible failures and stays the course no matter.

Sacred Gardener finds solace in the divine and abundance in the earth. She calls in limitless faith and innovates with the limitations of matter. She never forces, but she does lead. She gives to and receives from the heavens and the land. She is the instrument: Great Mystery's hand.

Our collective Sacred Gardener is needed now. Our culture and earth, bodies and sexualities, have been trampled by the antithesis to the Sacred Gardener—the Corporate Colonizer.

Every move we make to cooperate with Life…every innovation of remembrance, every circular model of care, every conservation of precious resources, every collaboration with rather than extraction from that which we cherish, every honoring of the land and ancestors, every authentic falling apart and falling together into true interdependence cultivates the new and ancient Beloved Community[27] our humanity is longing for. This is the path and the prayer of Sacred Gardener. It doesn't come with guarantees, and no one has to walk it perfectly. Nature's messy, after all. Unpredictable and wild.

---

[27] *A phrase popularized by Dr. Martin Luther King, Jr., referencing a global vision in which all people can share in the wealth of the earth. (thekingcenter.org)*

To journey with your wholeness, your brokenness, your Blueprints and imprints—to say, "I'm here to wrestle with the divinity of my own life, every last inch of it, and see what miracles can grow out of the mud"—is to embrace the path of a Sacred Gardener. Embodying this call grows integrous power inside—power to build bridges from trauma to trust, fear to love, violence to care, exploitation to cooperation. Power to walk over those bridges, and guide and be guided by others as you journey together toward the vision of your wild hearts, the passion of your bravest bellies.

Sacred Gardener at a Glance

Body Connection: Crown, Spine, Bottoms of Feet

Your crown, the space just above the top of your head—where your halo would be if you were an angel—is the place through which you connect with the mystery of the unseen. The stars above and perhaps the ancestors. Divine wisdom and creative inspiration. Cosmic order and the dark portal of the unknown. Some call this source God, others call it the Universe, the Great Mystery or the Great Void. Naming the ineffable might be less meaningful than knowing that when your crown is ready, you can become receptive to celestial support and guidance. Eternal care can drip into you.

Your spine (and the corresponding nerves and neural pathways that run along it) are the superhighway that allows what has come in through the crown to travel down the midline of the body and branch off to your blood and muscles. Your spine is a superconductor that allows the formlessness of your Soul to sprout into the Seed of your body and eventually grow into all the other archetypes.

The bottoms of your feet root you to the earth, the home of your humanness. Through gravitational connection, you anchor into belonging. Inspiration from above lands into the matter of your body where the collective soil rises up to meet you, to resource your long walk home.

Natural Blueprint of Health: Co-Creation

You are in reverential relationship to all that is. You are here to listen for and respond to the call of co-creating a healthy ecosystem—one where medicine, miracles and raw existence can birth, grow, survive, thrive, struggle, die, and be reborn. You provide structure, vision, resources, care, and protection to all that grows in your garden. You are aware of outside threats and prepare and respond to them with martial power when need be. You know that what you do to your garden, you do to the whole: that you don't have to be any bigger than what deep coherence allows for. "Small is all," as adrienne maree brown writes in Emergent Strategy. You embrace right-sizeness, as cultural somatic therapist Tada Hozumi talks about. You meet the season's needs with presence and adaptability. You cultivate fertile abundance through prayerfully synching up with natural order and divine law.

Traumatic Imprint: Colonization

You are a participant in a colonial project (whether you yourself are a settler or a descendant of one, or an Indigenous person on unceded land), in which control was established over the Indigenous people of an area and land was stolen. As a result, you experience the stripping of the natural abundance of life. You experience the common practices of forcing, extracting, and capitalizing on the sacred resources of soul, body, culture, community, and land for the sake of gaining power over the wild. Systemic oppressions and divide and conquer strategies are employed to kill off anything in the way of the Colonizer's domination. Neglect, exploitation, shame, repression, manipulation, control, violence, isolation, and alienation are used to gain and keep control. You're subject to a culture that's at war with the laws of nature, the reverential capacity of humanity, and the love of the divine.

Hypo-Response to Colonization: Assimilation

- Pointing the violence of the system inward
- Safety by internalizing the forces of colonization
- Buying into false characterizations about the not-enoughness of your character

- Believing that if you contribute better to the toxicity of the system that's colonized you, you'll finally have enough, get free, win the game
- Disconnecting from or denying your roots—your body, soul, spirit, land, lineage, or original language
- Abiding to the hustle that erases your right-sizeness and right-relationship to Life
- Experiencing ongoing extraction of your natural gifts and resources
- Feeling deep shame, grief and regret around the loss of your indigeneity (and the way you've perhaps contributed to that loss in others, as well) that freezes your capacity to re-member right relations

When someone's in Assimilation, it can often feel threatening to remember the slower, more cooperative ways of nature and lineage. It can feel like danger (because it has been and might still be dangerous) to diverge from imperial or colonial power structures, and instead honor peaceful traditions, innovations, and embodiment.

Common fears and inner dialogues include:
- "This is just the way it is. I can't change the way it is, so I need to survive inside of it."
- "If you can't beat 'em, join 'em."
- "I feel so ashamed that I don't know my heritage…but it's gone now, so what can I do?"
- "What's wrong with me that I can't win at this stupid capitalist game? I'm doing all my personal practices, showing up daily, working super hard… One part of me knows this is a load of shit, but another part of me can't stop thinking I must not be good enough."
- "These people keep taking my magic, but I can't do anything about it. The momentum of extraction is so big that the only thing I can do is buddy up with the colonizer and hope they include me in their prosperity, even as they take from me."

Hyper-Response to Colonization: Supremacy

- Pointing the violence of the system downward or outward
- Safety by externalizing and using the force-energy of the system on others
- Embodying the energies of force, violence, power-over, extraction, or manipulation to try to keep or gain control
- Disrupting the natural abundance and sustainability of a people, place, environment, or culture for the sake of your own group's profit
- Proliferating ideologies and infrastructures that incarcerate or take from Indigenous bodies, land, and souls
- Denying of the sacred rights of all living things
- Appropriating (stealing) others' land, culture, language, or ways for your own profit or gain

When someone's in Supremacy, it can often feel like the world is designed as a game they have a chance at winning, so why would they not play full out—with all the weapons they can gather? It can feel threatening to look at the ways the game is inherently violent, destructive and toxic, because then they might have to consider not playing, not amassing power in unjust ways.

Common fears and inner dialogues include:

- "If I give them an inch, they'll take a yard. I've got to be hyper-protective and strict to stay safe."
- "I earned every advantage I have. Those people aren't working hard enough."
- "I'll show them who's boss!"
- "Amassing power and wealth are the only way I can belong, the only way I have value or matter."
- "If I start going down the road of justice, it'll never end. I've got a life / business / family to run."
- "We all have the same hours in a day as Beyoncé. It's all about the choices we make with the time we're given."

- "Aho!"—A white person, not in ceremony with a native person. Then after being called out, "What? We're all one!"
- "I'm not doing anything wrong. I didn't choose to be born with this privilege."

Special Acknowledgments

Special acknowledgments need to be made for this chapter before continuing on. My learning and sharing in these pages would not be possible without the many people from various walks of life that have informed me, both formally and informally.

People whose work I've read or studied over the last decade who have influenced my thinking and writing on decolonization in meaningful ways: Audre Lorde, bell hooks, adrienne maree browne, Bayo Akomolafe, Lyla June, Rabbi Tirza Firestone, Kim Tallbear, Resmaa Menakem, Charles Eisenstein, Dr. Joy DeGruy, Dallas Goldtooth, Leesa Renee Hall, the entire archives of the For the Wild podcast hosted by Ayana Young, and the humans at the Tamera Healing Biotope in Portugal, including founder Sabine Lichtenfels.

People who have shared their decolonial wisdom and stories over fires, meals, candlelight, sessions, ceremony, or chance encounter with me, who have left me forever changed from the transmission of their medicine: Cândido Gadaga, Elydé Arroyo, Darrell and Henry Red Cloud, Quincéy Xavier, Jen Lemen, Shawna Murray Brown, Jennifer Sterling, Dema Al-Kakhan, Elizabeth DiAlto, Ann Nguyen, Kelsey Gustafson, Assana Rae, Ev'Yan Whitney, Tada Hozumi, Shanda Catrice, and many, many more.

There are so many people who study, write about, live and breathe the work of decolonization far more than I do. Please know that I am a student here, not an expert, and share as a learner, to be of service to our collective healing. I bow humbly to the tireless work of those who devote their lives to this body of work.

Ask a too-big question
Wrestle with it
Make out with it
Take a nap inside of it
Dream irrational dreams inside the answer-less space
Break the boxes
of your mind
See what truth you
can't quite find
Bless the mystery—
The motherland of your becoming
and unbecoming
Dance your decolonization
There's nowhere to get but here
Timelessness is a revolutionary shape shifter

"Awakening to love can happen only as we let go of our obsession with power and domination… Living by a love ethic we learn to value loyalty and a commitment to sustained bonds over material advancement. While careers and making money remain important agendas, they never take precedence over valuing and nurturing human life and well-being. I know no one who has embraced a love ethic whose life has not become joyous and more fulfilling."
— bell hooks, *All About Love*

The Ocean Inside

For the last three years, I've spent my mornings at the ocean watching waves crash into rocks, clear deep blues in the winter, white caps glowing almost golden in the new-day sun. The Pacific has entered into my blood, bones, and soul. I write with, for, and from her, even though our relationship is new.

One thing the Pacific told me this morning as I prepared to work on this chapter was, *I'm not trying to make waves. I'm not trying to produce majestic power. I'm not trying to provide home and shelter for the sea turtles, starfish, yellowtail, or seals. I'm simply in relationship with the moon and the mystery, the reefs and the deep blue unseen, the icebergs and the stratosphere. These relationships make me the force of nature that I am. I am inseparable from them. We thrive or die together. We change and heal together.*

We are more akin to the ocean than we often remember. We are in an inextricable relationship with the land and air, the water and animals, the lavender bush and the honeybees. As one thing changes, suffers, heals, or shifts, so too do we. Adaptation to one piece of the web necessarily begets adaptation to all. And we are not separate from the web of nature. We are an essential part of the larger story.

While we as humans are inextricably interdependent with all things—human and non-human alike—we are also a vast, magnificent, sovereign body, unique with our own collective purpose, mission, and perhaps destiny. We are resilient and flowing with a strong, momentous life force that seeks survival and evolution in miraculous, unknowable-to-us ways. We adapt in micro-movements as the world around us changes. We change the world around us with every move we make.

Oppressive systems, structures and cultural norms—colonization, capitalism, racism, white supremacy, consumerism, fascism, and any -ism that denies the sacredness of all living things—are molding our collective human body. They are changing us in invisible, cellular ways. But every time we strip off the confines of these structures and realign to the vastness of our elemental nature, we also affect these systems, in invisible, unknowable, and perhaps magical ways.

It feels important to address the energetic possibilities of change at the onset of this chapter: a chapter about the very charged and challenging topic of colonization. With a difficulty as big as this—structural, infrastructural, cultural and ever-pressing—it can feel impossible to heal, transform or rearrange such toxic dynamics.

The truth is, I don't have answers, and answers are not my goal. My hope with this chapter is to anchor myself into questions that lead to revelation in their own time.

Who do I want to be in the face of such grave difficulty?
How do I want to embody?
Where do I wish to put my listening ears, my attentive heart?
What ways of relating might open me to the essence of the miracle of life?
What modes of operating serve to perpetuate systems I don't wish to participate in?
How can I have compassion and make space for the ugly, messy, wrong and raw in me?

The more harshly or aggressively a trauma spell lands in us, the more extreme we tend to become in our reaction to it. The more sensitive, empathic and emotionally attuned we are, the more we feel the weight of our collective trauma. In relation to colonization, it's common to become obsessed with either changing ourselves (hyper self-responsibility) or changing the system (hyper political). It's also common to become addicted to winning a zero-sum game (hyper capitalist). On the other hand, we can feel disparaging and hopeless that any change is possible at all, so why bother? (Hypo passionate.)

Over the years, I have found myself in double binds between competing hyper and hypo reactions. Hyper personal improvement (I must become better, smarter, healthier in order to survive) and hypo empowerment (nothing I do will ever be enough). Or hyper saviorship (I have to save people with less privilege than I have in order to feel okay about the world) and hypo compassion (trying to save others is destroying, deflating, and exhausting me, not to mention insulting them and putting a strain between us). When the opposing forces of a double bind pull at us at the same time, it paralyzes our agility, muffles our breath and stifles our creativity.

Zooming out on the idea that I am one of many, one wave in the vast ocean relating to all the other living things, changing, and being changed, shaping and being shaped,[28] has helped me unwind the tension of the double bind and reinvigorate my right-sizeness.

In relation to my place in the larger family of things, I open to the possibilities of both/and instead of closing down under the constriction of either/or. I can sense my personal path of healing as well as my call to collective contribution. I can come to know, deep in my bones, that what I do to myself, I do to the whole—and what I do to the whole, I do to myself. I can remember the rhythm of enoughness.

A prayer in response to the questions in my heart

Dear Life,

Make me a witch.

A sorceress.

A mystic.

A lover.

---

[28] *adrienne maree brown writes and talks a lot about the fractal nature of change, which I've been alluding to throughout this section, in her book Emergent Strategy and other works.*

An innovator.

A possibility-creator.

A griever.

A believer in children and new life and change and letting go.

A friend.

A listener.

A heart-cracked-open-story-witnesser.

A sanctuary of care.

A refuge.

A resting place.

An incubation cauldron.

An honest poem.

A safe home.

A mischievous trickster.

A pleasure-devotee.

A nature-communer.

A question-worshipper.

A mess-ups-permission-giver.

A radical warrioress for all that's meant to be remembered in these times.

Turn me into the stars looking down on our feral Earth.

Turn me into the ant carrying bread across the sidewalk.

Shapeshift my soul into a holy kind of wholeness,

where all the wrongness and all the fear,

all the mess ups and all the tears,

all the lust and all the fervor

can tumble through time, wild and wilder still.

Do not tame or domesticate me.

Rearrange me

into my most natural and supernatural,

sublime and sensuous self.

Is trauma a "me" problem or a "we" problem?

"Where we are born into privilege, we are charged with dismantling any myth of supremacy. Where we are born into struggle, we are charged with claiming our dignity, joy and liberation. Possibility: From that deep place of belonging to ourselves, we can understand that we are inherently worthy of each other."
— adrienne maree brown, *Emergent Strategy*

Some of us are more apt to experience trauma as a personal problem, something we ought to heal on our own in the company of a qualified professional. Often, this embodied perspective originates from people who are trapped in the illusion of the world of individualism, cut off from the circular relationship to community, spirit, and Earth. Perhaps people who are more positioned to get ahead in a culture of competition. Perhaps people who are white-bodied or white-passing, people with male bodies, people with skinny or pretty bodies, people with normative sexual orientations and gender identities, people with perfect English, people with able bodies, people with higher IQs.

Others are more apt to experience trauma as existing within a fabric of conditions—cultural, ancestral, political, and societal conditions—and therefore experience the possibility of healing as a group endeavor, a collective effort. Perhaps people who have been systematically oppressed, experienced war, been torn from their Indigenous land, persecuted for their religious beliefs, enslaved, or imprisoned due to the color of their skin.[29]

I fall into a strange land between the two. I'm a white woman, whose matrilineal line is Jewish. I was raised on stories of the systemic persecution of my people and felt a bone-deep fear around being born in my own bloodline.

At the same time, I'm a pretty, able-bodied, smart white woman whose family was upper-middle class in great school districts with safe neighborhoods and full pantries. I have white-body supremacy on stolen and colonized land.

---

[29] *I highly recommend Resmaa Menakem's seminal book, My Grandmother's Hands, that explores the embodiment of racialized trauma in the US, as well as body-based practices for racialized post-traumatic growth and somatic abolitionism.*

Am I privileged? Absolutely. Do I understand oppression in my bones? That, too. Has my bloodline been colonized? Yes. Has my bloodline colonized other lands and people? Yes.

There are great gifts and grave costs inside of the complexity of my human story. I'm sure that's true for you, too.

The Cost of Colonization

"Healing involves discomfort, but so does refusing to heal. And, over time, refusing to heal is always more painful."
— Resmaa Menakem, *My Grandmother's Hands*

I was lying on my living room floor, heart beating out of my chest, barely able to breathe. Where's my community? Where's my village? How many more days and nights am I going to have to eat alone? How many more false solutions am I going to have to buy and sell? How many more newsreels of environmental destruction or police brutality am I going to have to watch?

And then, the grand finale—

Will I die here in a cage I didn't create? A cage of hyper-individualism? A cage of capitalism and aloneness? A cage of Whiteness and self-contempt for where I am, for where I'm not?

Or will I ever be resourced enough to innovate my way out? Is it resource that's needed in the way we think of it—having a backup plan, security stocked in the cabinet? Or is it a different kind of resource? The resource of trust and rebellion, relationship and curiosity, radically devoted community ready to birth a new world together?

I saw myself looking to my friends and wondering, *What are we doing? What are we doing? What are we doing? This is so stupid. We should be together. We should pool our potential. We should collaborate. We should share the weight. We should win and lose together. We shouldn't be so alone.*

The Sacred Gardener psyche was screaming at me from the crown of my head to the soles of my feet:

Feel free to take a trauma-informed pause, if you'd like. Look around the room. Feel your feet. Exhale real loud. That's what I did. Then, frazzled and overwhelmed with the bigness of it all, I reached out to Tada Hozumi, a cultural somatic practitioner, and asked if we could work together on the topics of ancestry, colonization and trauma resolution. They gladly obliged.

In our second conversation I told Tada in a sort of embarrassed way the story I never tell anyone, about that time in my mid-twenties when I went to Pine Ridge, South Dakota—a Lakota reservation—and Darrell Red Cloud sang a song at the top of a hill where his great-great-grandfather was buried, and it felt like the song came from the soul of the earth itself, and I couldn't stop weeping, couldn't even catch my breath, and he came up to me a few minutes later and told me, "this land has stories to tell you, songs to sing you, ceremonies to share with you. Come back, Rachael. Come learn from this land." And I went back five times, deepening into the place and the people, the sagebrush and the sky, letting the Red Clouds welcome me into a world of original medicine.

Tada had me pause to notice what was happening in my body as I talked. I wept, felt a strange sensation in the bottoms of my feet, which didn't want to land, wanted rather to leap. I went on to share about that one time when the Red Clouds even invited me to sing in the sweat lodge—me, a white girl in an inipi of mostly Lakota men. Embarrassed and uncomfortable, I tried to get out of it.

"But what will I sing? This isn't my place. It doesn't feel right."

Ten men booed my response, a shared sound of disapproval that I'd tried to deny the honor I was just given.

"Just open your mouth and you'll know what to sing," Darrell's brother Henry said. "You're a spiritual leader, Rachael. You need initiating."

So I did, and he was right. But it wasn't Lakota that I sang. It was some long-lost sound of my own mother tongue. Perhaps a mixture of Hebrew and Gaelic. Perhaps the song of nature herself trumpeting from my soul.

I told Tada how I've never quite known how to integrate this experience, and they told me it's a common practice of Indigenous peoples to adopt colonizers into their culture. It's one-part collective hyper-socialization—a way to fawn off threat—another, clear recognition that something is missing in the individual who's displaced from her own land, her own traditions, her own language, her own song.

And I remembered how that opening with the Lakota, that invitation back to Earth and spirit, made me more curious again about my own kin: the way we pray, the way we sing and gather and dance. I wept from the deepest place in me, knowing that I could fully integrate this experience of Indigenous adoption by re-adopting my own lineage. I don't have to lead sweat lodges; I don't have to sing others' Indigenous songs in ceremonies with white people. I can rediscover and share my own lineages' practices. I can come home to my very own bloodline. I can find solace in my own ancient song and dance. I can be re-entranced by the timelessness of my very own indigeneity.

Ancestral Revival

When I was a kid, I didn't want to be Jewish. My mom insisted that I go to Hebrew School twice a week, but I'd protest regularly with hysterical shouts.

"I'm not Jewish! I'm not Jewish!"

We learned about the Holocaust from the time we were kids. We went to the museums, saw the shoes of thousands of kids stacked in piles, read the *Autobiography of Anne Frank*, watched *Schindler's List*.[30] Sometimes, it felt more like being initiated into a historical horror story than belonging to a rich lineage of traditions and spiritual practices. Of course, it was both. But the little-me felt overwhelmed by the history, the lineage, the legacy of loss my people experienced, and so she dissociated from that connection.

The truth is, I've studied North American Indigenous trauma and post-traumatic slave syndrome more than Holocaust trauma. A part of me still doesn't want to go there. A part of me would rather just be white.

Who wants to sing the songs that got them killed? Who wants to light the candles that led to their incineration? Who wants to dance the rituals of their people's demise?

---

[30] *A super intense three-hour Holocaust film produced and directed by Steven Spielberg.*

On the other hand, who wants to remember their lineage and revive their ancient, medicinal roots if that lineage was also corrupted into a colonizing force? Who wants to go back through the bloodline and make intergenerational repairs when they could just face forward and pretend that all is fair in love and war?

The resilient ones. That's who. The alchemists. The ones who throw their hands to the stars and say, "I know you made me this way for a reason. I know you put me in this place with this skin, this lineage, this legacy for a reason. And I know that reason wasn't death, enslavement, colonization or persecution, not power-over or power-under, but power-with, deep and vast connection to the rhythms and rituals that make souls strong, give life meaning, give community cohesion, give back to a place with prayer."

A few years ago, when I moved to San Diego, missing a feeling of home, I finally began sinking into my Jewish roots. I devoured books on Kabbalah, Earth-based Judaism, and the newest denomination, Renewal. I remembered how so much of Judaism's original practice was land-based, in harmony with the seasons, in celebration of the earth. I took refuge in these rituals, most especially Shabbat, becoming religious about keeping tech-free, work-free sabbaths with friends almost every Friday night.

Now I feel immense nourishment in keeping with the many-thousand-year-old traditions of my bloodline. I know that for much of time, Jewish people have been a diaspora, fleeing persecution from place to place. I know they often found their home in songs and language, traditions and togetherness, more than in specific bodies of land.

At the same time, while I know that after the Holocaust, a search for safe home was ever-pressing, I feel heartbroken that the state of Israel exists on the premise of displacing and oppressing Palestinian people.

I think white people in the U.S. secretly feel this way about the oppression of the native people, as well. We know in our bones this land was stolen. We know a genocide happened on our behalf. We know a language—many languages—were eradicated. Songs and rituals and ceremonies were suppressed.

We also know that for two hundred and forty-six years, Africans were enslaved on this land, and for another century, segregation was the law. We know that, both in the case of genocide and slavery, rape was used as a weapon of domination. We know the prison industrial complex still exists, that one in three black men will be incarcerated for crimes white men often get minimal fines for, and a black American is two and a half times more likely to be murdered by the police than a white one.

We know these things in our bones even if we don't know them in our minds. We can feel the truth even if we don't want to look at it. It haunts the wind; it cries through the creeks. It hurts us all—to different degrees, in different ways. It's not the end of the story, but it's where we've come from, and to do better moving forward, we have to look at where we've been.

The Resilience of the Colonized

The first time I flew into Rapid City, the closest airport to the Pine Ridge Lakota Reservation, I got a sinking feeling in my gut and a harrowing grief took over me. At the moment, I didn't know why. But it was the same feeling I had when I was a kid sitting in front of that big screen, watching the black-and-white tragedy of the Holocaust through *Schindler's List*.

It wasn't until I was invited to do a traditional Sweat Lodge Ceremony that I finally understood the origins of that mysterious grief. There, with the Red Cloud family, in the far-out hills of the Rez, my body returned to a dark, hot womb on top of the earth—a fully-encased, steaming, singing, drumming prayer of resilience. I crawled out of the two-hour sweat as the sun set peach and lavender behind rolling hills of speckled pine trees, and in that moment, felt the essence of eternity. An everlasting spiritual strength breathed through me.

Then, almost immediately, my heart dropped to my gut. The gravity of what had been stolen, murdered, repressed, and almost erased hit me like a ton of bricks. An immeasurable sacredness. A visceral transcendence. A steaming, singing, drumming resilience. An interconnected aliveness and reverence for all of life's relations.

I stood there humbled with both heartache and amazement that one of the strongest colonizing forces in human history tried to destroy the Lakota peoples' devout bond to the Great Mystery. That even they couldn't kill it off completely. That practices this strong lived on—defiantly—with quiet love and an immortal heartbeat of devotion.

The Lakota are warriors in this way. And they're not the only ones.

The Jews, so devoted to their practices, still light the candles, still sing the morning and evening Sh'ma, still gather for Shabbat, still lift the thirteen-year-old in a chair during their Bar or Bat Mitzvah celebration, a sacred coming of age ritual…even after a six-million-person Holocaust, even after diaspora and mass fleeing from persecution.

The Palestinians, a people of deep community and home, still find each other all over the world at street markets selling olive oil and za'atar, listening for each other's city of origin in their subtle accents and phrases. No matter that their villages no longer exist, got wiped out from maps. Despite the fact that their history and archives were burned, that the creation of Israel attempts to gaslight away the existence of Palestine to begin with. Despite displacement and the occupation of their homes, their mother tongue can still be placed. The foods from the land are still served around big tables with animated stories, traditional jokes, nostalgic hearts and resilient laughter. [31]

The Irish, a devoutly spiritual people who have been colonized again and again, still hid their ancient Druid practices within Catholicism so their descendants would be practicing the old ways even without knowing it. They held mass in the sheep fields, using rocks as altars, keeping traditions alive even when practicing their religion was punishable by death. [32]

The Vietnamese, an industrious, celebratory and resourceful people, still nourish bellies and souls with their pho and banh mi shops, still open restaurants that feed the whole family, still light the fireworks in the streets for Lunar New

---

[31] *Thank you Dema Al-Kakhan for being my forever Semite Sister across borders and bloodlines, and for sharing stories of your Palestinian lineage with such tender love and devotion. I will stand with you and your people for all of time.*

[32] *Thank you Kelsey Gustafson for traveling to your homeland and recollecting your people's songs, dances, laments, and wild poetic joys. Feeling the Celtic traditions rebloom in you melts something frozen in my heart. Kelsey teaches and guides post-traumatic growth through embodiment, myth, art and coaching at kelseygustafson.com/. She's a certified ReBloom Coach and an incredibly powerful space holder if you're seeking your own embodied homecoming.*

Year as a celebration of the new and a prayer for abundance, even after the U.S. killed two million in attempts to dominate and control a country that wasn't their own. The Vietnamese still pride themselves on a rapidly growing economy, still gather in the streets, still light incense and create altars in their homes in honor of loved ones passed, still find it in their hearts to practice forgiveness toward the Americans.[33]

The Puerto Ricans, a sensual, joyous people of many backgrounds—Indigenous, African, European and Caribbean—still dance into the night, feast with family and embody their freedom in the most celebratory ways, despite ongoing hardship and oppression. They still protest in the streets with clamorous pots and pans, demanding justice for their people on their occupied land.[34]

The African Americans still practiced Indigenous African religions to the best of their ability during the time of enslavement and birthed Hoodoo—a spiritual practice created from the fusion of various traditional African religions combined with regional, cultural, and other religious influences for protection and liberation. Regionally, they used nature and encoded the most dominant religion's hymns, saints, texts, and practices with ancient African wisdom to maintain their spirituality and traditions while also flying under the radar of the wrath of slaveholders. Today, so many African Americans still draw on ancestral practices to heal, connect to joy, and bring together community.[35]

The Cherokee, still hunt deer, turtle, alligator, using every part of the animal to nourish and resource their bodies and homes. Still sing and dance their powwow

[33] *Thank you Ann Nguyen for sharing your radiant lineage stories with me, for inviting me into your powerful and brave decolonial journey, and for being an ever-present pillar of love and togetherness in my life. Ann teaches and guides sexual and sensual healing, awakening and empowerment for women of color at theannnguyen.com. She's a certified ReBloom Coach who emanates joy, pleasure and the possibility of being fueled by your most orgasmic superpowers for the sake of our collective liberation.*

[34] *Thank you Elizabeth DiAlto for being a queen of cultivating safe spaces to learn, grow, heal and embody. And for being such a key learning-friend to me over the years. Witnessing your reconnection to your Puerto Rican lineage has been life-giving. If you're seeking a place to move your body in sensual, healing, invigorating ways, check out Elizabeth's online movement studio at wildsoulmovement.com.*

[35] *Thank you, Brittany Pollard, for sharing the depths of the journey you're on to remember and reclaim your roots. I'm honored to witness your process. You can learn more about Brittany's work holding healing space for the Black community at https://brittanypollard.com/.*

songs, even if, even when, the powwow is far away. Still make fry bread and laugh together in circles of community care.[36]

The witches of European descent—ever wise and connected to the medicine of the earth—still practice herbal medicine, women's health, abortion and midwifery after being burned, hung, buried alive, and demonized for their healing ways.

The queers still love deeply and extravagantly and contribute great beauty and fashion to culture, despite the demonization, criminalization, and colonization of their love. They still gather together to remember their holy wholeness even after being murdered, beaten, abandoned, disowned, hyper-sexualized, and violated for who and how they love.

The women still gather in circles under the moon to celebrate the cycles of life, to sync with the moon and their bleeding time, to share secrets, cry together, and uplift each other even amidst a sexist rape culture. After generations of patriarchy and oppression against female-bodied people, after modern politics have told them that their bodies are dirty and their stories don't matter, their reclamation persists.

And the men, even the men, after being told their masculinity need never include sensitivity, after their emotionality has been stripped and their complexity narrowed into small boxes of dominate and provide—still circle as brothers to feel, heal, and challenge each other. Still commune with nature and explore their spiritual purposes. Despite collective dissociation and shame, they're awakening, remembering, and re-occupying their range to be both peaceful and powerful, dignified and devotional.

Whoever you are, whatever your group, it's not too late for you. The parts of your ancient heart you long for are also longing for you. Because Spirit lives within the heart, and Spirit never dies, no matter the attempts or even partial successes at domination or colonization.

Just a few days ago, my neighbor and dear soul friend Syd Franklin passed away. He was 91 years old and had lived a long life full of love and contribution.

---

[36] *Thank you Jennifer Sterling for sharing the beauty and depth of your lineage with me, for being a steady source of authentic healing for Black and Indigenous women, for providing such powerful care inside the ReBloom community. If you are a BIWOC seeking gentle, embodied support around systemic trauma, Jennifer offers powerful dance/movement psychotherapy and holistic nutrition support at thebodyfullhealingproject. com.*

He had no children or grandchildren, so I stepped in as a surrogate of sorts. I was there for nearly every important threshold he crossed back into the other world, including walking into his home the moment after he died.

That morning, while he was still alive, I gathered wildflowers from around the neighborhood—rosemary, lavender, coastal sage scrub, all with wonderful fragrances—and placed them on his chest as he rested there in his final hours. In the afternoon, I went home for a bit to catch my breath, and when I walked back into his home at 6:26 PM, I found out that he had passed the moment just before.

In the hours after death, before they took away his body, his aide and I both saw something miraculous happen many times. The flowers atop his chest—without a heartbeat, without living lungs—moved up and down with the subtlest pulse of life. His spirit danced on.

Soon enough, the men from the mortuary came and wrapped his body in sheets in a sacred, silent, synchronized ceremony, then placed him in a thick, black bag. Before they wheeled Syd out of his home of fifty years, I kissed his body through the bag, and felt his spirit shoot out from the top of his head. It was bright white and immortal, cheerful and flirtatious. It was a visceral reminder of the eternal nature of Spirit.

It is my belief that lineages have a collective body. Even after holocaust or genocide, slavery, or colonization, even after languages are lost and traditions forgotten, even after entire species experience extinction—the collective Spirit of every lineage lives on. We can call these spirits home to our bodies, invoke them from the heavens, evoke them from our everlasting souls. We can remember our origins, even if we've been displaced or orphaned from them. There is an ancient heart we long for that also longs for us. If you've forgotten its language, no matter. It doesn't speak in words, so much as it speaks in rhythms. If you place your hand on your chest, you can still feel it dancing.

There is an ancienT heArT we long for that aLso longs foR us.

♡ ♡

And what about Whiteness?

In my conversations with Tada, we talked a lot about the nature of whiteness. They referred to whiteness as a dissociative response to diaspora. A way of coping with being so lost from home. A lostness from your own Indigenous culture: from the ancient part of you that knows how to grieve and repair, make medicines from the earth, call in councils of elders, sing songs from the valleys and oceans, rivers and trees, dance atop tables or in circles with family.

This lostness creates contempt for others and contempt for self:[37] a grumpy

---

[37] *I first heard this phrase from Andréa Renae Johnson in an interview we did for one of my courses. Check out their work at andrearenae.com.*

and grievous, invisible "offness" pervasive on both personal and cultural levels. A hyper-arousal of agitation that, when unresolved, collapses down into a deep freeze of disconnection.

As a white woman, it feels important for me to look into the conditioning that disconnects me from my ancient heart, to see with clarity the collective trauma spell that wants to be broken. Not to shame myself, but to liberate myself and others.

It feels important to face the things my ancestors gave up in order to assimilate to the colonial project and gain a sense of root security on a new land, in a new culture. The foods, dances, songs, languages, accents, body gestures or unique phrases that were lost. The traditions, mannerisms or beliefs that were forced out of us or that we willingly relinquished in order to experience levels of safety and sustenance in a new place with new people. It feels important to both grieve these losses and connect to the everlasting spirit of these ways, even if they're less embodied these days.

It feels important to name that my family's trading of our Indigenous ways for the sake of perceived power or well-being—our assimilation—was a trauma response.

When humans are given the choice between authenticity and belonging, we will always choose belonging, because belonging means survival.[38] This is the trap of hegemony—negotiations of power that sell out what's sacred for the sake of earning more perceived material advantages.

A Sacred Gardener makes powerful negotiations on the premise that everything is interconnected and affects everything else, so how can we cultivate the most wins across the board? How can the whole ecosystem of people, animals, land, and ancestors experience maximal collective benefit? Of course, things are never perfectly balanced—not in nature, not in humanity. Perfection isn't the point. But, as Rilke says, living the question is.

Unhealthy power exchanges—the colonial perspective—are built on the

---

[38] This is something Bear Hébert and I have talked about extensively, both informed by a collection of decolonial thinkers and feelers.

notions of supremacy and subordination, and therefore winning and losing, being in, or being out.

What do you do when you're so lost from your own original medicine, far away and settled now on another's land? How do you cope with the metastasized shame in your heart that hardens into denial? That strikes unconscious attacks on the patience of Earth-based pacing, the tediousness of togetherness? That insists on dividing and conquering all reminders of your ancient harmony?

I know it can be hard to look at, uncomfortable to see. That's part of the make-up of whiteness: it is barely cognizant of itself as a form of denial. A collective freeze over the reality of building a nation on genocide and slavery. It goes so deep that whiteness splits from its heart and develops a persona that can win approval, status and "safety." A sort of collective narcissism that feeds the capitalist machine and the individual ego. Assimilation to secret dominance.

This survival mechanism has been utilized by white people for centuries, passed down generationally. We learned it from our parents. They learned it from theirs. And it will continue down the lines of white lineage until someone is willing to stay with the pain of colonization, feel it, see the way it hurts and harms them, too. The way it allows dehumanization of self and others. Until the blessing of co-creation and healthy negotiation is received again as sacred remembrance in the soul.

But why? Why did this happen?

In episode 126 of the podcast *For the Wild*, Ayana Young interviews Lyla June, an Indigenous environmental scientist, doctoral student, educator, community organizer, and musician of Diné (Navajo), Tsétsêhéstâhese (Cheyenne), and European lineages. In their powerful conversation called "On Resistance and Forgiveness in the Final Years of Patriarchy," Lyla stopped me in my tracks with this systemic context:

Around the year 1000, up to about 1500, you see a lot of major shifts [in European culture from its Earth-based, Goddess-worshipping origins]. The most important shift that I always bring up is the destruction of European Indigenous women. They estimate in the burning times that six to nine million European women were buried alive, drowned alive, burned alive, raped, beaten or tortured, or multiple of those at once.

It's really important to understand that just like they tried to destroy the women of our communities in America as a war tactic, so too did they try to destroy the women of Europe as a war tactic, because when you destroy the women, you destroy the whole thing.

It's very important to understand that capitalism is an expression of the pain of the destruction of Indigenous European women...and that these Indigenous European women were so brutally treated—worse than Native Americans were by far, believe it or not—that the men who loved them went insane. And the only way to try to relieve that insanity was to try and compensate in other ways. To find meaning in the accumulation of wealth. To find meaning in becoming a high reputation. To find meaning in domination.

We have to understand that capitalism and colonialism are a direct outgrowth of the abuse of the women of Europe. And once you understand that, it's much easier to forgive. It's much easier to honor the fact that Europeans didn't just wake up one day and say, *Hey, I think I want to commit genocide on a whole continent of people.* That didn't happen. People didn't just say, *Oh, I would love to destroy millions of people today.* That is a form of psychosis that comes from deep intergenerational trauma, a deep painful wound in the side of Europe, which is the destruction of the women.

Sometimes, as humans, I see us looking around the world thinking, *My God, what have we done? We are poisoning this planet; we are cancer on this earth.* Maybe you can relate? June also said this at the end of her interview:

We can be a gift to the land. What if we could become a people where the presence of humanity is actually what helps everything go around, helps the world turn?

This matches with what a Yoruba elder told all of us at the Parliament of World Religions in Toronto last year…he said, *In the Yoruba language, the word for human being is "chosen one."* And at first, I was like, *that sounds kinda weird.* But then he started explaining it more. He said, *We were chosen to be the stewards of the land.* And that really sparked something in me for some reason. I was like, *wow…maybe, just maybe, the earth doesn't just like humans—maybe she actually needs us.*

Maybe this brain we were given by Creator is supposed to be used to groom the land, to maintain the land, to make sure the deer have grass to eat, to make sure the buffalo have grass to eat by burning patches on the plains. Making sure that the desert is taken care of. My people, we eat yucca fruit, we eat sumac berry, we eat wolfberry, we eat rice grass. Making sure all the other animals have berries to eat, too. Planting berries along the desert scape. Reseeding the land. Burning the land in low intensity fires where necessary. Pruning the land. Taking care of the beavers.

Everything has a purpose here. Every single thing. You know, would Creator just make humans like an accident? My people would say, *no. Humans are not an accident. We are supposed to be here. We belong here.* It's just that when Coyote infiltrates us and tries to turn us into his vibe—which is all about enslaving and power and hierarchy—that's when we lose touch with our true purpose on the land.

And so how do we come back to becoming medicine on the land? I think one way you can do that is to plant a pollinator garden. You know? That's one simple thing. Human beings can plant seeds. We have these hands, we have soil, we have water. If you plant a whole bunch of flowers that pollinators like, you are being medicine to the land. It's not that hard.

In the *For the Wild* podcast episode 115, "On Pleasure as Birthright,"[39] adrienne maree brown said, "Our bodies right now at this moment are both colonizers on this planet and colonized spaces on this planet. Getting in a right relationship with our bodies is key to getting in right relationship with the planet."

What if you could begin revering your body as beloved? What if you could soften into your own flesh enough to thaw the deep freeze, feel the unfelt feels? What if you could start observing the ways you try to dominate, win or force, then pattern interrupt those impulses with patience, allowing or sharing? What if you could listen to the wisdom-keepers of our world—maybe once or twice a month on a podcast, tuning into their timeless knowledge around interdependence and inter-sovereignty?

What if these small, doable steps can be done season after season, year after year, decade after decade, until a new, more untamed and interrelated way reblooms in you? What if remembering co-creation is a long game, not a short one? What if it's a wild one, not a tidy one? What if you're allowed to experiment, get it wrong, fail, learn and make magic from the whole long journey?

They say every seven generations an alchemist is born in the family line, to heal things both forwards and backwards for the next seven generations. May ours be a generation of collective Sacred Gardeners that renew the role of humans in the larger family of things.

It's okay to feel uncomfortable inside these pages

For white people, especially, this can be hard stuff to look at. (For everyone, really.) I've been studying racism, systemic oppression, and privilege for almost fifteen years. I grew up in diverse communities and have relationships with lots of people not like me. I did at least one hundred hours of intimate in-person privilege

---

[39] *Episode 115 of For The Wild: On Pleasure as Birthright with adrienne maree brown.*

and oppression workshops in college with mixed-race, mixed-class, mixed-religion groups. Even so, I'm just now getting more comfortable in this conversation. Even now, I'm constantly humbled by this work.

It's okay to take a moment to feel however you feel reading this. It's okay to pause and check in. It's okay if a hot heat of shame is melting something frozen inside. It's okay if you want to run or hide. It's okay if you want to object. It's okay if you don't feel ready yet. It's okay if you're fuming with rage. It's okay if you wish it was another way. It's okay if you feel broken hearted beyond belief. It's okay if you feel tender relief. It's okay if you feel numb and nothing at all. Be honest with yourself about wherever you are in this private moment between you and these words.

One part of the process of breaking our collective trauma spell is being able to tell how entranced you are by it, where you sit in relationship to it, how you want to protect or dismantle it, release or uphold it. Another part is engaging the dance of decolonization and reblooming co-creation in a way that's doable for your system.

Remember in the last chapter when you read about the concept of me-development pendulating with we-development? The more rooted you are in a safe sense of "me," the more available you become to co-creating a healthy "we." And—the safer the "we" space feels, the more open your "me" becomes to deeper individual healing. It's okay to start where it feels simpler for you. But just remember, the "me" and the "we" are forever interconnected. You can't bypass the "we-space" and expect to experience deep liberation in the "me-space"—no matter how privileged you are. Similarly, it's hard to be a healthy member of the "we" if your "me" challenges are running your emotions, physiology or mind.

Give yourself the chance to digest these ideas. And if your heart cracked open a bit, plant a seed inside the empty space: a seed of devotion to regrowing right-relationship—to the land, each other and the ancestors. Tend the seed with regular care. It could flower fast or grow really slow. Just keep showing up to it. Do your best to keep the seed alive.

Cultivating Your Sacred Gardener

In the mornings, back at the Pacific, I pray with my sit bones planted firmly atop the seven-million-year-old rocks of Windansea Beach, a land originally inhabited by the Kumeyaay people for 12,000 years before the common era. I do the coherence practice for the Sacred Gardener with my hands raised to the sky, thrown to the stars of the ancestors.

Use me, move me, make me an instrument—for the highest expression of love, the deepest resonating truth, and the greatest good for all, myself included. Feed me, fill me, make me a vessel—for the highest expression of love, the deepest resonating truth and the greatest good for all, myself included. I am listening. I am willing. I am devoted. Thank you, thank you, thank you.

I thank the seagulls and the rocks, the waves and the sand, the original peoples of the land and the ones living here now. I sing the Sh'ma, an ancient Hebrew prayer praising the ineffable mystery of Creation. I kiss the earth, then walk home and start my day.

Say prayers to the land and the heavens enough times and you'll find yourself in holy energetic coherence with Life: in a co-creative dance with that divine mystery that made you. You'll start remembering your Old Ways, even if you've lost their names—even if you can't remember your own Indigenous language and aren't quite sure about your traditions. You'll start feeling the pain of being divorced from the circular and inclusive, cohesive and holistic, wild and unapologetic parts of your nature. You'll start sensing that a new and ancient way is possible. A marriage of innovation and tradition, self-expression and belonging, predictable rhythms and raw, fluctuating moods.

These days, I pray a lot about divesting from winner-takes-all economic models. I'm studying and researching circular wealth and intend on founding a worker-owned coaching cooperative called the ReBloom Collective. I'd like for part of our economic plan to be rooted in redistribution of wealth to Indigenous and Black women+ of color doing trauma resolution work in their communities.

It's a particular kind of challenge to give up a game you've been reared and steered to win, but the cost of "winning" alone is a dangerous loss to the soul. It's a special kind of task to ask yourself, to ask your people: how can we unwind from toxic individualism, re-learn how to share, remember the magic of togetherness at the root?

It won't happen fast—togetherness requires trust—and the truth is, capitalism pits us against one another. It diminishes right-relationship—to our own bodies, one another, the earth, and the messages of the ancestors—so that we just keep buying and denying our inherent enoughness. But it's not too late. The more we pray, the more we get quiet and listen, the more we can grow and learn and change together. We can remember a better way forward.

The Sacred Gardener is an archetype of miracles, creativity, endless abundance, and reverent relationship with Life. While humans have a pretty gnarly history of colonization, patriarchy, and oppression, we also have a glorious and ever-growing legacy of human rights, social innovations, peace movements, and restorative justice processes. The suffragists, the abolitionists, the climate activists, the lineage-keepers, the righteous rebels, the ones who refused to play by broken rules, the ones who hid my ancestors in attics.

We can become good ancestors, as Layla Saad calls it. We can be the ones at our great-great-grandchildren's backs, cheering them on from the stars above, sending them insights, innovations, stories, songs, and remembrances. We can do our part. We can.

Growing into Co-Creators

When you or your clients have done enough "me-healing" but still feel the aches and limitations of individualizing the challenges that are bigger than you alone, often an innovative urge will grab you from the gut, keep you up at night and whisper to you in the dreamtime.

Tell me if this sounds familiar: You've shown up as a client to the trauma specialist for the last few years. You've established healthy "me-practices" that keep you mostly regulated and resilient. You've grown a life that's working in a very personalized, individual way. But still—there's a void. You look out at the world with worry and disappointment. You feel trapped inside hyper-individualized boxes. You're isolated, lonely, or can't escape systemic biases or oppressions. You're longing to live in a new world, a new collective garden, but no one's growing it for you. You're ashamed you haven't been able to figure this shit out on your own, and also resent yourself for thinking you were supposed to do it all alone. So you sit there asking yourself, *what the hell do I do?*

Assana came to me after a few years as a successful sex, trauma, and spirituality coach. She was brilliant, trauma-informed, articulate, and had a hefty following. But still, she kept finding herself frozen inside of her business and unable to pinpoint why.

After a thorough intake process, we realized there were compounding trauma spells double-binding her creative energy. Her Soul Seed needed both emotional and financial resources—fast. Her Expressionista felt swallowed with shame that she didn't have what she needed already. Her Sacred Gardener didn't want to succumb to the cultural trauma spell of utilizing hyper-capitalist marketing schemes to earn herself what she needed, but she didn't yet know another way. And her body? It was still stuck in habits of speed, over-performing, over-sharing, and pressuring herself to be the best.

Assana would show up to sessions with hot tears shedding through frozen fear. "Is it stupid, so, so stupid that I don't want you to know that I'm in this spot? That I want to keep it a secret that I need so much help right now? That I just want to maintain the appearance of having it all together?"

I knew Assana to be a woman of radical cultural critique, so I sensed that speaking to that part of her would help to unshame the struggle. "Assana, we all need support from time-to-time. Only a culture of hyper-individualism tells you otherwise." She exhaled deep relief. Then we took some time to anchor into the Blueprints of each archetype that was showing up for her: to unshame their hyper or hypo expressions and name the underlying health of their needs.

We sat with her Soul Seed and her need to receive money, support, and encouragement. Her Expressionista and her need to be fully accepted in her unique medicine. Her Sage and her need to trust her own inner-guidance and inner-authority. Her Sacred Gardener and her need to show up with prayerful creativity to build healthy containers within which both her personhood and business could thrive.

As the Blueprints anchored, Assana's awareness around what was out of alignment became clearer. The ways her business was running on levels of manipulation and scarcity stared her in the face. *This isn't who I really am,* her soul whispered. The way she'd been shortchanging her genius and expertise, undercharging for her life-changing gifts, illuminated. *I'm allowed to need and receive more,* her power insisted. The oversharing and under-nesting she'd done in an attempt to be seen and loved for all of who she is. *I can process some things in private,* her wisest self told her. *I can be witnessed and acknowledged where I really need and want it most—close in, right at the center.*

By naming the various trauma spells that were double-binding Assana's Blueprints, she was able to shed the shame of her individual struggles, then surrender into a vulnerable process of actually receiving what she needed in our coaching container. She needed care. She needed reassurance. She needed recognition. She needed celebration. She needed encouragement to follow her radical knowing. She needed to transform old nervous system dynamics that were continually triggering her and diminishing her capacity to be present to herself, to meet and tend to her deepest hungers. By working together to help her receive those individual needs, more space grew within her to show up to her outer world of work in an inspired, innovative and regulated way.

Assana eventually created a successful group called Rooted: a mastermind and coaching program for nurturing right relationship to soul, body, Earth, lineage, and sex. In her own words, "Rooted is a transformative container that guides you into coming back to yourself and soul by healing your wounds and connecting to your roots, while realigning yourself and life in a way that deconstructs and heals the European, colonized mindset we carry built on scarcity and oppression."[40] Creating this kind of container was a bold move for Assana, only made possible by the overlap of enough "me"- *and* "we"-healing.

---

[40] *You can learn more about Assana Rae Halder and her powerful work at instagram.com/erotic.earth. embodiment/ or assanarae.com.*

In my own business, for many years I struggled as an archetypal Savior Atlas.[41] I tried to hold up the weight of the world alone all alone. Take on every problem as my own. Feel personally responsible to mother *alllll* the Secret Bad Girls on Earth. Rigid Self Reliance, the hyper response to Neglect, as well as the hypo response of Self-Denial, seeped into my career at every corner. I gave, past the point of my capacity, nearly everything I had in me. Talk about hypo-Gatekeeping.

But these things weren't just responses to my personal trauma spells of Neglect and Exploitation; they were also responses to collective trauma spells.

I was responding to a culture that didn't seem to care about sexual violence or its aftermath. I was responding to a culture that, at the time, was rarely educating or talking about trauma. I was responding to a culture that trained me to do my best to fix challenging symptoms all by myself, rather than collaborate on regrowing better conditions together. I was responding to a culture that reinforced personal brands with individual success. I was trying my best to make it in our dog-eat-dog world—and do good at the same time. An uncomfortable but common combination of hyper and hypo responses to Colonization.

I will save the world, at any cost to me!
I will even buy into the extractive conditioning that's colonized me!
I will use the master's tools to try to dismantle the master's house![42]
I will get ahead as far and fast as I can… thennnn I'll figure this collective healing
shit out.

But there were limits to my approach. At times, I was running multiple groups at once, with upwards of 30 women in my care and little-to-no assistance or support. I'd grow increasingly overwhelmed by the volume of trauma in my energetic space, then get sick, stoned, or into an unfulfilling relational dynamic to escape. Hyper to hypo. Overwork to collapse. The shortcomings of our collective

---

[41] *A a metaphor master Integral Coach Chela Davison came up with for me in our life-changing and long-term work together.*

[42] *Hat tip: Audre Lorde's famous essay and book,* The Master's Tools Will Never Dismantle the Master's House.

garden running through my nervous system. My individual self so entranced by the struggle to survive that I couldn't quite innovate or collaborate for a new and ancient way forward. My inner-Sage knowing all along that something was wrong. *This isn't natural,* she'd whisper incessantly. *This isn't the way of true wisdom.*

In some ways, I needed the hyper to hypo fluctuating. It was my bootcamp of becoming. Through contrast and grief, through horrific anxiety, I learned to lean on nature more, to cultivate deep devotion to meditation, movement, and prayer. I learned to take on fewer clients at a time, and ones who were in greater alignment with my capacities and passions. I learned to grow contempt for the systems that were never meant to help us thrive as a human family. I struggled and wrestled and wept over reality. I lost hope so many times, and each bottoming out brought me to my knees in deeper devotion to finding a way out of our polluted ocean—this time together.

I began having more and more conversations about the topic of hyper-individualism with clients, students, mentors and friends. Everyone I talked to was struggling inside the same tenuous bubble. And it was pissing me off. Something needed to change in a titrated, doable way. Something circular and collective, cooperative, and communal, needed to be remembered at a pace digestible to my nervous system and our shared soma.

After years of reading books, listening to podcasts, talking with peers, dreaming with friends, receiving support from mentors, attuning to the ways of the natural world, and doing the ReBloom Coherence Practice for guidance—it finally felt like time to take the baby steps my soul had been calling for.

If the bigger goal is to be able to have a worker-owned coaching cooperative, what would be a small, first step toward that kind of intimate collaboration? I wondered. What I came up with was a more decentralized power structure to the ReBloom Coach Training, based on the assets of the people I've known longest who'd be qualified and interested in joining forces. We call ourselves the Hive, and among us is a Community Auntie, a Program Manager, a Hostess with the Mostess, a Nervous System Expert, a bunch of really qualified coaches and mentors, a Tech Wizard, and more.

While, for now, this isn't radically different from running a company with various employees or contractors, the *way* that people came into their roles was not conventional to current business standards. It was based on relational understandings of one another's strengths. It was based on observing the assets of our community and seeing what we could grow with those assets, rather than deciding who or what we needed to create ahead of time, then extracting unnatural capacities from ourselves or others. It was a permaculture-like approach.

In the future, this approach will be taken even more cooperatively. We'll share more initial sweat equity as well as profits. We'll do more creative collaboration on joint offerings. There will be full economic transparency. But for now, we've begun with a relational, strength-based approach to having meaningful roles within the circle. Titration. Little by little.

To an extent, healthy Sacred Gardening *does* require healing our individual traumas. I've done a shit ton of personal healing to be able to honor my role as a powerful leader without shrinking in shame or fear of retribution. To be able to sense, name, ask for and receive the support I need. To sense the value of what I offer and allow my soil to be deeply replenished for what I give. Regenerative collaborations are born from the collectivization of those who can both self-regulate and co-regulate.

But there are major cultural gaps that will always make the "me" sick, no matter how much healing we do on our own. And for those gaps, we need the courage and wildness to leap into the space between stars, the vastness of the void, the mysterious future and ancient Indigenous past of true Beloved Community. We need a radical kind of faith so that we can catch each other's arms across the sky or underground, in serendipitous stranger-meetings at coffee shops around town. We need to reach out, leap out, trust in the miracle of finding and being found—even if, even when, we're not quite sure how.

We need to remember and return to the ancestors of our callings, the ones who've mythically stood where we're standing now, the ones from which we've inherited our passion to move forward with greater truth and truer love. We need to ask them, *When culture and systems and power-over tried to divide your belonging— to each other, to the land, to a righteous path of interdependence, what did you do? What did you choose? How did you stay woven together?*

We can learn from the people who've been asking these questions for many, many generations. The ones who've had to hold onto their ancestors for guidance, because the state would offer them no breaks nor true parentage. The Lakota. The Kumeyaay. The Palestinians. The African Americans. The Vietnamese. The Kayapo. The Sicani. The Maasai.

We can learn from the land. We can learn from nature. We can learn from our own cyclical bodies that resonate with the cycles of Earth and stars.

The Sacred Gardener's wisdom is rooted in the interdependence of all things. It's the symphonic conductor of the harmony of interbeing. It's in you, it's in me, it's in us. And I believe, like a prayer, a plea, and a dance, that there is wild beauty we create when we awaken our ancient inner-song.

Decolonizing Your Sexuality

No matter who you are, or what land you live on, your sexuality has an indigeneity. A way in which you might most naturally inhabit and express your eroticism. A sexual song and dance that's inspired by the original landscape of your heart, soul, shadows and hungers, rather than culturally prescribed or conditioned norms. Your most true sexual song and dance could express itself in a variety of ways. From how you groom your pubic hair (or don't), to how you like to sound. From the power dynamics you most crave, to the number of people you want to love and fuck at once. From your gender identity, to your sexual orientation. From sex meaning something deep and sacred to you, to sex meaning something light and playful to you.

Your decolonized sexuality is the most authentic, true-to-the-bone expression of how you love to feel or share your sexuality. (Including if you're asexual or tend to not feel or share your sexuality as much.)

Like land, our sexuality can be colonized, stripped of its Indigenous song and dance, sacred sites and original tongue. It can be packaged to sell without our consent and shipped far from the homeland where its value is lost, unseen and unfelt. It can be forced into limiting confines of gendered boxes and sanitized sensuality, easier to buy and sell. Less complex. Less wild. Less divine. Less messy.

Indigeneity is a source of dignity and honor. To uphold a sacred bond between the innermost nature of a being and the outer expression of reality is a deep form of loving integrity. To uphold a sacred bond between your most natural sexual preferences and truths, and the way you live your sex life is one of the most powerful things you can do to restore order to your world and ours. Whether your sexual preferences are mushy gushy, romantic and PG, or XXX raunchy kink.

Of course, our sexuality is not static. It is a living, ever-changing expression of where we are in our lives. We are forever being pressed into new positions of steamy, surprising truth.

We can't stop change. But we can honor the truth of the way our eroticism wants to emerge or rest, in every moment. We can open our hearts and connect from that place. Wholehearted communion with Life is the signature of co-creation. The more you decolonize your sexuality, the more your heart will show up inside of it. To co-create with your truest nature is to decolonize your sexuality. To see and honor your true self, to let your true self be seen and honored by others. To invite someone into the song and dance of your authentic desire. To love the sacredness of your unique erotic inclination. To fill your eroticism with reverence.

If my Wholeness is at the edges, then that is where I want to go.

If my Wholeness is at the edges, then that is where I want to go.
You do not have to follow me there or approve of my character.
You do not have to like my shape, my crooked lines, my wild smile, the sound of my shout in ecstasy or anger.
If my Wholeness is at the edges, I want to color outside my own lines.
I want to find the name that no one gave me but myself.
I wanna tell you, I walked all the way here only to discover I was wearing the wrong size shoes.
They're all too small for me.
The only thing that fits is Love.
And it turns out Love is made up of Truth.

And it turns out, if you walk long enough, having kicked off the too-small
shoes…
You find out that Truth at first blisters the hell out of you…
until it makes you raw…
and then, until it makes you soft…
and finally, until it makes you strong.

If my Wholeness is at the edges, then that is where I want to go.

Blistered.
Raw.
Soft.
Strong.

Strong enough to know the deep exhale of occupying all my senses, fences,
growls, cackles, moans.
Soft enough to know even the strong need a home made of care.
Raw enough to follow the fire of my desire—fuck it, take my shoes, I'll crawl
if I have to.
Blistered enough to be fed up with all the ways, all the names, all the
signatures and false characters I let domesticate me, like a too-tight shoe—
You can't enjoy yourself in those cages.
You can't dance like that!

There is no contract that can contain the Wild me.
You cannot shame me, burn me or holocaust me.

I am eternity, edgeless, infinite sovereignty and I have blessed all the land of
me—the barren and the bountiful—with kisses and cleansing
and joyful soul tending.

If my Wholeness is at the edges, then that is where I want to go.

I am not afraid to find Love.

I am not afraid to find Sorrow.

Essential Sacred Gardener Practices

Sacred Gardener Coherence Practice

This coherence practice is designed to connect you to the Blueprint of co-creation. You might wish to do it outside or in a place that feels sacred to you, like in front of your altar.

With your feet planted firmly on the ground and your arms raised up above your head (or at any level that's comfortable for you), imagine yourself as a channel, a vessel, an instrument of care that receives insight, abundance, and nourishment from both the stars above and the earth below. Perhaps, with an inhale, imagine drawing energy down from the cosmos, through your spine or central channel, then exhaling it into the earth. Then on your next inhale, imagine drawing energy up from the earth, through your spine or central channel, then exhaling it into the cosmos.[43]

Say inwardly or outwardly the following affirmations over and over again, pausing in between lines to allow your body time to integrate, until you feel complete.

---

[43] *I first learned this Tree of Life breath from Rabbi Tirzah Firestone's audiobook,* The Woman's Kabbalah.

Use me, move me, make me an instrument
For the highest expression of love
The deepest resonating truth
And the greatest good for all, myself included
Feed me, fill me, make me a vessel
For the highest expression of love
The deepest resonating truth
And the greatest good for all, myself included

I am listening
I am willing
I am devoted
Thank you

What do you hear as you tune in and listen to guidance from above and below? What energetic, spiritual, felt-sense, or visual clues are you offered as your next best co-creative steps? How does it feel to receive this possible wisdom?

Read one book, listen to one podcast

When it comes to breaking the tremendous collective trauma spell of colonization, baby steps are key. Like all things, if we go too far, too fast, too furious, we'll burn out and shy away. Instead, let's practice seeing and sensing just how big of an undertaking it is to go against the cultural grain of colonization to become a Co-Creator. Then let's ask ourselves, what's the smallest doable step?

I love to let myself receive insight and wisdom from elders and teachers in a titrated way. One podcast episode a month, two books a year, saying yes to that one class or mentor I know would really help. I love to follow the curiosity of my breaking heart. I love to ask, "What's wrecking me, and who knows a thing or two about it?"

Sometimes that question leads me back to my own lineage to learn more about it. Sometimes it leads me to understanding the history and economic context of our current systems.

Where would that question lead you? What baby step of deepening awareness or understanding might you feel called to take?

Be the Sacred Gardener of Your Business

Business is one of the big places the core wound of Colonization shows up. Consider journaling on one or many of the following questions as a way of beginning to shift home to the Blueprint of Co-Creation in your business:

- Am I fracking my own resources for profit? If so, what might self-honor do instead?
- Am I overworking my body in a way that doesn't honor its natural rhythms? If so, how might I plan for not only expansion, but also contraction? Not only growth, but also rest?
- Am I extracting my soul's wisdom for every ounce and morsel of insight? Are there some lessons or learnings that want to be kept private, personal, or sacred?
- Am I appropriating someone else's culture, heritage, or traditions, making money off of another's lineage? If so, what might greater reverence and right-relationship do?
- Am I producing things or running offerings that harm the land and leave a negative environmental impact? If so, how might I shift or offset these impacts?
- Am I embodying top-down infrastructures in my business that don't allow for true collaboration, shared intelligence, shared risk and shared gain? If so, what small steps toward more circular ways of creating might I take?
- What prices would reflect win-for-all situations, wherein I receive the compensation I need, and others are also able to afford my work?
- What's my biggest prayer for humanity and the planet? What are the secret prayers that live in my ancient heart? Does my business mission reflect those prayers?
- What guidance around my business has been wanting to get my attention?
- If I were to raise my hand to the divine—asking to be used for a sacred call—what would I declare that I'm available for?

Move from Individualism to Togetherness

Where in your life are you struggling to do it all alone? Where are you feeling overwhelmed or ashamed that you can't hold it together? If you gave yourself the grace of viewing your struggle as a mechanism of capitalism, white supremacy, ableism, etc.—oppressive forces that insist you should always be able to tough it out and get by—could that free up some space for you to be a bit more human and *humane* with yourself? Might you feel more encouraged or inspired to lean into the vulnerable possibility of togetherness, where aloneness was once the only way?

Moving from individualism to togetherness can't just happen conceptually. It requires a radical kind of practice that often pushes up against the ways we've been trained to secure safety, status and belonging.

Individualism hoards for itself and its smallest inner-circle.
Togetherness shares across boundaries of "you" and "me," nourishing the "we" field that simultaneously nourishes it back.

Individualism rushes to get ahead.
Togetherness leaves no one behind.

Individualism hides out when things are feeling off or hard—tries to save face.
Togetherness leans into the tender mess and cleans it up side-by-side—or bares sacred witness to that which can't be fixed.

What areas of your life are you stuck under the trauma spell of hyper-individualism? What small moves toward genuine, vulnerable togetherness might truly change your life, if practiced regularly, if leaned into as a new form of "social security"?

Plant Collective Dream Seeds

Big systemic change can feel overwhelming to pursue alone—and for good reason. We're not meant to. We're meant to flock together, change the shapes of our systems with movements of mass remembering.

If you run a group coaching program, a training, or are part of a community of friends devoted to upending systemic oppression, begin by bringing the following questions about a specific topic of great concern (antiracism, economic justice, environmental regeneration, etc.) to your shared space:

- If anything and everything were possible, and we could co-create a new reality around this topic of great concern, what would we let ourselves dream for our specific, local community?
- If anything and everything were possible, and we could co-create a new reality around this topic of great concern, what would we let ourselves dream for the wider world?
- How do we dream of making this change, and with whom, again if anything and everything were possible?

Invite each person present to break the boxes of their normal logical confines and dream bigger and more wild than they would usually let themselves.

To start, set a 10-minute timer and have everyone dream with their pens to paper privately. Then, break people into pairs to read their Collective Dream Seeds to one another. Once partners have heard each other's dreams, set another 10-minute timer and have them write another set of even more audacious dreams—this time, together. Finally, regroup with the wider circle and see what's emerged from your collective field.

Don't try to force plans or actions quite yet. Instead, take all of your sacred Dream Seeds and ceremonially "plant" them—into the actual earth, or into some sort of treasure chest that you'll return to later.

At your next meeting, sit in a circle and process what comes up for people, what stands in the way of pursuing their most devotional dreams together. It's important to address challenges, doubts, fears, and insecurities, and to do so together, rather than in private. After all, remember—systemic change doesn't happen alone, it happens through community movements. As you address challenges, people will feel safer to bring forward their gifts, devotion, and assets without fear or reservation.

As a group, you can regularly return to your Collective Field of Dreams to see how they're doing. Have you given up on them, let them go to seed? Do some feel more abundant and co-nourishing than others? Does it feel clear that you and your community could sustain something incredible if you decided to commit to it together?

People often need time and a process to commit to big ideas. Give your community the chance to continually circle up around the possibility of co-creating a miracle where there was once only hopelessness, and you'll be surprised what can emerge if there's no rush and no force, just open hearts that are earnest and in it together.

Chapter 11

TRAUMA-INFORMED
COACHING
SKILLS

Hello, dear. You've been on quite the journey with this book so far, yeah? You've read the ReBloom Allegory, learned about the inner-workings of the nervous system, and gone on a deep dive into all seven ReBloom archetypes. We're about to explore dozens of essential tools for working with trauma, but before we continue on, check in with yourself. How's your body feeling? Your energy levels? Your heart? Are you ready for this next phase of applied learning? If so, let's roll. If not, is there some way your body is seeking to digest, process or move with what you've taken in thus far? Remember: you get to honor yourself, even while reading this book.

While there are endless modalities, philosophies, and principles around how to work with trauma, in this chapter, I'll share fundamental starting points. After all, the fundamentals are everything. Often, we think that we need more and more complex knowledge in order to facilitate phenomenal transformation. But I've found that getting great at the basics creates a powerful foundation upon which more complex care can be offered.

The ABCs of Trauma-Informed Care

The ABCs of Trauma-Informed Care are five simple coaching skills that can be strung together to help your client harmonize with the pace and needs of their nervous system. As you embrace the foundation of these ABC's with your clients, safe and effective somatic transformation will take place more and more.

Many coaching approaches include fast-paced questioning or in-session practices that call on the cognitive reasoning of the client in order to make change. Big risks and bold moves can be the encouraged industry-standard to a new reality. On the other hand, many therapeutic approaches spend a lot of time talking about the past, decades perhaps. While these approaches aren't bad or wrong, they're also not the most effective path to long-lasting nervous system transformation.

The ABCs of Trauma-Informed Care are a bottom-up, present-tense, deeply reverential skill set that work with the natural intelligence of the body and soul to heal and regenerate in its own time and pace.

Our culture is dominated by energies of force, extraction, pushing, and pressuring. But nature—both outside us and within us—has a different way. Nature knows how to feel and experience itself, and slowly rearrange so that Life continues to renew, even after difficulty, trauma, illness, death, or destruction.

The ABCs will help you help your clients listen to the wisest nature of their physiology, nervous system, heart, and soul in the moment, allowing for the intelligence of their wildness to come back online, heal and thrive in a way that's organic, sustaining, deep, and grounded.

As I've taught my clients how to work with and embrace the ABCs, they've reported experiencing profound levels of embodied trust, leading to more confidence, feelings of safety, relational healing and thriving, as well as greater physical wellness and energy.

The ABCs of Trauma-Informed Care are:

Attunement

Body-First

Consent and Cooperation

Doability

Trust

Attunement

Attunement, most importantly, is about presence. Being with whatever's happening in this very moment—this place, this time. It's about turning toward the here and now with attention, compassion, and care.

When we experience something challenging or traumatic that overwhelms our capacity to cope, one of the first things that can happen is a loss of attunement, sensitization and orientation to present-tense place and time. Disorientation and disorganization can flood the mind and body, leaving us out of sorts and with a growing sense of dysregulation inside. Because the body stores difficulties from the past at the level of the nervous system, when our clients process their trauma in sessions, the same disorientation, disorganization, or dysregulation associated with that past trauma will often emerge as they share.[44]

This is where helping our clients attune to present time and place becomes critically supportive. If at least some part of your client (their witness self, their "adult" self, their "higher" self, parts of their body...) can maintain access to the here and now throughout your sessions, you can support them in bringing the power and regulation of their present-tense regulation into the difficulty of the past. If, on the other hand, your client feels swallowed up by the somatics of a traumatic moment or dynamic as they're sharing, they'll be less able to meet those difficult conditions with a new sense of empowered choice. The whole point of trauma resolution is to be able to encounter an old difficulty but with new conditions in

---

[44] *Peter Levine,* Waking the Tiger

order to co-create a new internal relationship to that past experience. In order to do this, our clients must maintain levels of presence that we can help facilitate by inviting them to be aware of what's happening here and now, even as parts of them get pulled into the allure of an overwhelming past.

Cognitive attunement is about being able to turn with presence toward the current reality, narrative, experiences, age, and options of the moment.

Felt-sense attunement is about being able to turn with presence toward the current experience of the body, energy, or emotions.

How to use attunement in a session

It's normal for our clients to bring things from other times or places into their sessions. As a coach, it's important to meet our clients where they are with compassion, curiosity, and mirroring. And—when adding the skill of attunement to a session, we would practice shifting our client's attention from the story they're sharing, to the experience they're having in the here-and-now as they share.

"Wow, I hear you talking about your experience at 7 years old. That sounds like that was hard. As you hear yourself sharing that just right now, I wonder what there is to notice in this moment, this place and time?"

"Mmm, it sounds like you're experiencing similar sensations now in this moment as you did back then in that moment. Does that land as true for you? If so, what are you noticing just right here and now?"

Present-tense attunement helps slow the nervous system from the potential of looping in an old emergency response. By bringing awareness to the experience of the moment, your client's regulation, choice, and agency can grow.

To amplify the power of attunement even more, as you invite your client to attune to their present-tense thoughts and experiences, you might also attune to your own. As a coach, specifically attuning to the *health, stability, or predictability* in the moment—in yourself, your client, your relational field, and/or the space you're sharing—can help regulate a session. Additionally, when you can energetically attune to the vital nature around your office while your clients are in process, you can amplify the field of health, making greater alchemy possible.

Body-Based

We take a body-based (also known as somatic) approach to coaching around trauma because trauma operates from the less-cognitive parts of our being. As we tune into and sync up with our sensations, physical cues, instincts, impulses, and embodied energetics (the language of the nervous system), we can begin to allow old, unconscious nervous system patterns to slowly move, heal, and transform.

Interoception is your perceptive capacity to sense the experiences of your body; your ability to notice temperature, pain, hunger, thirst, neutrality, expansion, contraction, comfort, pleasure, weightedness, speed, buoyancy, gravity, energy, fluidity, texture, and more.

Leading trauma specialists and neurobiologists agree that the development of interoceptive awareness is the foundation of emotional well-being and regulation. The more we grow our interoceptive capacities, the more we can link specific embodied cues to correlated emotions, needs, limits and desires.[45] The more presence and connection we have to these embodied cues and their corresponding feelings and needs, the more we can creatively act to ensure our needs get met or employ resilient strategies when they're unable to be. This responsiveness to and resourcefulness around one's internal state can create a profound sense of safety and empowerment, where previously a swirl of sensations might have left one feeling anxious, overwhelmed, or panicked, without a clear sense of what the sensations were pointing to.

"Being responsive to interoceptive information allows an individual to be aware of an emotion cue early, and therefore to process, interpret and strategize

---

[45] Nurturing Reslience *by Kathy Kain and Stephen Terrel.*

at the onset of stressful events," writes Cynthia Price, a body therapy research specialist. To help our clients interocept their experience, we might ask them questions that gently guide them into the experience of their physiology, in a way that's also attuned to the present moment. For example, perhaps your client is talking about an intense situation for her. You might notice she seems upset but is still up in her head about it. She hasn't quite dropped down into her felt-sense experience of the moment.

You might say:

"Mmm, yes. I hear everything you're saying about this! I'm wondering what might be happening below the story, perhaps in your body just right here and now, as your body hears you share about this? Maybe in terms of temperature, speed, expansion, constriction, pain, neutrality... maybe even color, image or energy... Anything to notice? It's okay if not."

- Notice the invitation is to drop *below the mind*, to stay in this moment, and to look for felt-sense experiences.
- Notice that there are examples of potential felt-sense experiences, in case the client is less familiar with interocepting their experience.
- Notice there's permission to *not* be feeling anything, sensation-wise.
- Notice this is not asking, "Where do you feel that in your body?"

I've noticed that the question, "Where do you feel that in your body?" doesn't always land. Especially for clients who are less comfortable with interoception. It can come across as pressure to sense their physical experience with specificity, when in fact, sometimes trauma desensitizes and shuts down our capacity to interocept.

When our questions are more open-ended...

"I wonder if there's anything to notice below the story, perhaps in your body...?"

And also offered with a bit of guidance…

"Maybe in terms of temperature, speed, expansion, constriction, pain, neutrality…perhaps even color, image, or energy…?"

Your client has a chance to wonder, as opposed to feeling forced to perform some kind of knowing.

If your client struggles with interoception, reassure them that that's totally okay. Instead, you might offer that they notice their body language or posture.

"Maybe just noticing how you're positioned right now, how your body language is feeling. No need to change anything. Just perhaps noticing if you can."

Or if someone is experiencing bigger levels of freeze or numbness, you might ask:

"If you could *imagine* connecting to sensations in your body, what do you think that might feel like? You don't have to actually know. But if you let yourself imagine…I wonder what, if anything, shows up…?"

Interoception and body-based awareness is especially helpful for rebuilding self-trust in one's capacity to feel and respond to danger with awakened power. Because of this, it's supportive to help our clients recognize what physical cues match to certain emotions.

For example, if a client reports that they feel safe in the moment, I might follow up by saying:

"Oh, how lovely that you're feeling safe. I wonder…tuning into your physiology just right now, what sensations are you experiencing that let you know you feel safe?"

Then, once the client identifies the sensations ("my breath feels slow, my mind feels clear, I feel gentle warmth all over…") we might hang out with the dual awareness of the *emotional* feeling of "safety" and *felt-sense* experience of "safety," giving time for body and mind to sync up via bi-directional communication. In the future, when your client is out in the world and experiences sensations that are not grounded, clear, and warm, they might have a better capacity to notice that they don't feel safe, then act accordingly.

The same approach can be applied to emotional and physiological states of arousal. A client might mention that they're feeling super unsafe as they talk about a traumatic experience from the past. You might then ask,

"I'm curious if you might tune into your body right now. Are there physical cues in this moment that let you know you're feeling unsafe?"

They might notice knots in their stomach and a clenched jaw, for example. From there you might affirm that stomach knots and a clenched jaw seem like healthy responses to the trauma they're speaking of, affirming the accuracy of the bi-directional communication between body and mind.

Another body-based question you might ask your client is if they notice any instincts or impulses.

"I hear you saying you feel really angry about this. I'm wondering if you drop below the mental, human components of anger, and move a bit more into the simple animal self, are there any instincts or impulses that arise?"

"Mmmm…I hear the sadness in your voice as you share about this. I'm curious what there is to notice in a felt-sense way just right now? Perhaps any impulses, instincts, needs or desires at the body level?"

Consent & Cooperation

Informed Consent

We begin with informed consent to help grow interpersonal trust between coach and client, and also to empower our client's choices every step of the way. Informed consent is about explaining what you might explore together and how you might explore it, both in terms of the bigger context and the smaller context.

Bigger context:

"I wonder if we might check out what's going on below the story, in your body, in our sessions together? As we work at the level of the body and allow your emotions and mind to sync with your physiology, feelings of self-trust and safety tend to grow. That said, the body is where we store a lot of unfelt emotions, sensations, and even memories. Sometimes, when we work at that level, deep things can come up and it can be a lot. We'll always go slow and you can always opt out. I'm curious what you think or feel about connecting more to your body?"

Smaller context:

"It feels like we're going into somewhat intense territory right now. I'm sensing it might be great to move through an experience of allowing this fight energy to be felt and released a bit. That might look like inviting in some animal instincts, allowing them to express themselves (energetically, visually or in micro-movements) and really making sure you land on the other side feeling more connected to your Blueprint, stable and grounded. We'll go slow and you can always pause or shift the direction. Afterward, you might feel more energized, or a bit emotional and tired. I'll do my best to help you land in a contained place. How does that land? Does it feel doable to explore at the body-level with this?

Notice in both of these examples, the coach is sharing with the client...

- Where they think it might be helpful to go
- How they might go there
- That there's always a choice to stop, pause or slow things down
- What that experience might feel like in the moment
- What it might be like afterward
- The opportunity to reflect on the offer, interocept their experience, and choose their path forward

Cooperation

As your client learns to attune to the moment and interocept the experience in their body more and more... and as they grow their sense of interpersonal trust through informed consent... there's an opportunity for them to have an experience that might be very new to them: *honoring their physiological cues in the presence of another human.*

It's one thing to notice our physiology. It's another thing to trust it long enough, and with enough compassionate permission, that we can release stored traumatic imprints and come back into alignment with our Natural Blueprint of Health. It's even more powerful to do this in relationship—because relationship is where we get hurt, so relationship is where we have the most potential to heal.

Cooperation is about working with the physiology in a way that affirms its inherent wisdom and inner path to healing; allowing, harmonizing with, and honoring the sensations, instincts, impulses, feelings, limits and needs of the moment. Cooperation works on the premise that we have self-correcting physiologies and are absolutely wired for re-regulation. When there's enough curiosity, compassion, presence, permission and attunement in the relational field between coach and client, miracles occur with no forced interventions needed.

In sessions, this can look like:

Allowing (working with) instincts, feelings, impulses, and sensations instead of resisting or changing them.

"I hear you saying you're feeling really tired right now. I wonder if we might *allow* a little bit of space and time for the tiredness to be here, instead of needing it to change. As your body hears me say that, I wonder what might want to happen?"

"I hear you saying there's a lot of heat and anger rising through your chest, out of your mouth. Perhaps we can *allow* a little bit of time for that energy to continue moving through you, without needing it to get smaller or go away…"

Inviting your client to **harmonize** with their needs, desires, sensations, or emotions, instead of judging, shaming, or denying them.

"I hear you saying it feels embarrassing for you to let yourself feel the grief. You don't *have* to grieve right now, but I do also wonder if there's a small way you might *harmonize with* that part of your body that's aching and wanting to release that ache…?"

"I hear you saying you want to hide right now because you feel so ashamed. I wonder if you might let yourself hide for a few moments… work *with* that feeling instead of pushing yourself to feel something else… maybe for however long you need?"

Respecting limits (embodied, energetic or emotional "no"s), rather than calling limits "resistance" or trying to "positive-think" someone into a "yes."

"It sounds like talking about this is really not something you want to do. I wonder what there is to notice if we take it off the table—if we say *you don't have to go here until you're ready*?"

"I hear you saying you feel really resistant to noticing what's happening in your body. Great. I totally honor and respect that. Sometimes it can feel like a whole can of worms is living in the body. So *we don't have to go there right now*—or ever. What if your resistance to feeling your body is supporting you in some way…?"

Noticing and allowing the **tidal nature of existence**. Energy (both in the body and in nature) moves in a tidal rhythm of up and then down, in and then out, fast and then slow, birth and then death. When you're attuned to the tide of experience happening for your client, you can encourage the allowance and completion of one tide of experience at a time, rather than rushing to the next.[46]

"I wonder what might happen if the exhaustion you're describing had the opportunity to move through a *full wave of experience*? What if, given enough space to rest, the tidal nature of your body would return to an awakeness in *its own right timing*? Perhaps notice what happens in your embodied reality as you hear me say those words…"

Notice how in all of these examples, there's a **working with** rather than against the natural flow of the current physiology. As we work *with* what's happening—especially if what's happening in the body is a rigid or fixed nervous system pattern—we give old physiological experiences a chance to express themselves with more consciousness and awareness. This conscious, gentle expression to previously unconscious patterns makes space for those patterns to transform and complete (especially when the expression happens in a shared relational space).

But if we work *against* those old embodied patterns, trying to force them to change, they don't get to live their purpose (which almost always is about keeping the client safe), and threatened, the pattern often holds on tighter.

[46] *This is a core concept of cranial sacral therapy, again taught to me by Brigit Viksnins in Alchemical Alignment.*

Doability & Titration

A lot of the personal development industry harps on fast and furious transformation. Big leaps. Going 110%. All or nothing, bitches.

But the truth is, our nervous systems are wired for homeostasis. They don't like big dramatic change. So when it comes to re-aligning the nervous system from trauma to health and resiliency, it's more efficient, sustainable, and long-lasting to take small, doable steps in harmony with the natural instincts of the current momentum, with micro adjustments toward greater coherence. Both in terms of in-session experiences and out-of-session practices.

Here's a fun, nerdy science term for ya: *titration.*

Remember in high school chemistry when you were learning to mix baking powder and vinegar together, and before you knew it—POOF!—a bubbling magical explosion was before you?

Titration is the process of adding one substance to another—a little bit at a time—to see how the two substances interact. The goal is to be careful enough that you avoid explosions or implosions but daring enough that you inspire transformation.

In terms of trauma resolution, there are various couplings of "substances" that could be added together in a titrated way to inspire transformation.

Client **plus** coach in a vulnerable, revealing, interpersonal dynamic.

Client **plus** the re-telling of a traumatic experience.

Client **plus** interocepting something that's challenging for them, like anger or pleasure.

Client **plus** any practice that involves moving through a highly charged emotional or physical experience.

As coach, it's critical that you *dose the intensity lightly*, instead of dramatically.

There's a minimum effective dosage that activates the system just enough to invoke arousal and inspire transformation, but not too much that it would send your client into dysregulation, dissociation, or panic. Especially when it comes to sensitive nervous systems, too much, too soon, too fast can activate old triggers beyond the capacity for your client to maintain witness consciousness, and before you know it, send them looping into hyper or hypo arousal.

However, if you can encourage and support your clients in...

- Focusing on experiencing only *doable amounts of intensity at a time* (and unshaming this need)
- Doing smaller movements, micro-movements, or even just imagining movement when it comes to following physiological, emotional, or energetic instincts (as opposed to big, cathartic movements)
- Taking one baby step at a time, seeing how it lands in the system, then taking another if there's more capacity
- Asking what the smallest doable step would be in terms of integrating the shifts they've had in session into a practice, homework or out-of-session integration (as opposed to encouraging gigantic leaps that might overextend their current physiology)

...then you can help facilitate deep but gentle, sustaining transformation.

Titration Practice

Nervous systems that have smaller capacities for intensity tend to revert to all-or-nothing decision making. To a compromised nervous system, it can often feel safer to secure a quick impulsive stance of defense or attack than to weigh complexity. Complex decision making requires time, space and higher-level cognition—all things that can become scarce when we're physiologically triggered or operating within a smaller range of resilience.

Whether your clients are activated with hyper or hypo energies, it can help if you remind them that small hinges swing big doors. This question can change the game:

"What's the SMALLEST doable step?"

- If you client is moving too fast, looping in hyper energies, it can help them anchor back into baby steps and the power of less-is-more
- If your client is having a hard time motivating themselves, collapsed in hypo energies, it can give them permission to lower their standards and do just one tiny piece at a time, thus increasing their chances of success

In sessions, this might look like inviting your client to engage an intense topic in the smallest doable way, rather than feeling as though they're supposed to dive in headlong and never come up for air.

It might sound something like:

"If you had permission to only do what felt truly doable here, what might that be?"

Or...

"If there was no need for big cathartic movements, but perhaps just small subtle ones, what might you let yourself do, or even just imagine doing?"

Minimum Effective Dosage with In-Session Exercises and Post-Session Practices

Another important component of "doability" is in relationship to in-session exercises and post-session practices.

If you're too goal-oriented with coaching exercises inside sessions, you might lose contact with the experience your client is having in the moment, perpetuating patterns of force rather than presence.

Similarly, if post-session practices are too big for your client's current capacity, they may pressure themselves to perform or shame themselves for failing.

In both cases, we want to find the sweet spot of the "minimum effective dosage."

What's the smallest doable—but also potent enough—exercise or practice for your client to experience that allows for both stretching *and* digesting?

Working with your clients in this way is one of the most honoring and efficient forms of facilitating healing. It teaches the essential skill of noticing and honoring limits—fundamental for a life of healthy self-consent and consent with others.

Trust

The ABCs are a medicine of natural regeneration. The more your clients begin feeling the embodied coherence of attuned, body-based, consensual, cooperative doability, the more they'll begin trusting their own inherent wisdom. And the more they trust themselves to be in an aware and consensual relationship with themselves, the more they'll trust themselves to be in aware and consensual relationships with others.

This trust, though, is hinged a bit on you, as coach, trusting the medicine as well.

How much do *you* trust that your client has an inherent treatment plan hidden within the ups and downs of their physiological and emotional expressions? How much do you trust their Natural Blueprint of Health to come back online, given enough time, presence, compassion, and permission? How much do you trust these things for *yourself*?

Ultimately, the more you live and embody the regeneration of the ABCs in your own life, the more you'll be able to hold a field of trust for your clients to come into attuned, body-based, consensual, and cooperative doability in their lives.

An old friend of mine used to be a doula. I remember her telling me once about an elderly mentor of hers. She would read the newspaper while the mother was in labor. Because she'd seen the process of birth so many times—the ups and downs, the ebbs and flows—she knew when a real emergency was happening versus usual birthing intensity. She was so incredibly trusting in the natural process of birth that she'd just hang out and wait until it was really time to do something.

Trust during sessions can be experienced as:

- Non-biased witnessing, with compassion and presence
- No need to fix intensity
- Allowing the moment to be difficult sometimes—so long as it's not so difficult that it's dangerous
- Letting the wave of experience take however long it takes
- Not needing to talk it all out all the time, so much as breathe and witness it all move through
- A deep knowing that rearranging happens through the heating up of what was once stuck frozen, and that this heating can sometimes be hard, but hard doesn't necessarily mean bad
- Slow, quiet knowing that things are changing under the surface

Trust is not indifference or apathy. It's an ability to meet your client's intensity without getting on their emergency train with them. It's knowing where that train is going, or when it's gotten off track and needs a bit of redirecting. Your capacity to trust increases the more fluent you become in the natural order of embodied and emotional alchemy.

Pause, Space, Witness, Wow

On the subject of trust, one way to embody trust in sessions with clients is by employing what I like to call "Pause, Space, Witness, Wow."

Cognition moves eight times faster than the body's capacity to sync up with it. When our clients experience a wave of embodied information (lots of tears, a big swell of heat, synching up with their Natural Blueprint Essence, increased tension somewhere, a miraculous feeling of their grandmother holding their baby-self, etc.) it's important to offer reverence and space to the experience in order to fully integrate it at the nervous-system level.

Our physiology develops, grows and heals with a tidal rhythm. After things expand, they want to contract and integrate before expanding again. After things are loud, they want to be quiet and reflective before adding more volume. After things are hard, they want to be easy for a little while before moving toward difficulty again.

When your client moves through a big experience, it's often supportive to cocoon that experience with a gentle, present pause:

"Wow, this feels big. How about we pause for a few moments to give room to what's showing itself?"

"Would you be up for hanging out with this experience a bit longer, without needing to change or alter it?"

"What if we pause to notice what happens in the body when we give a bit more time and space for this wave of experience?"

When the coach calls a "pause" in the session, this is an incredible opportunity to amplify the field of health. Find your center as coach, connect to your Blueprint Essence or the health of nature outside of your office. Embody mindful compassion and centered presence as much as possible. You are creating a powerful field of co-regulation, and this non-invasive, health-filled space gives your client's body the opportunity to experience new levels of self-correction and Blueprint remembrance.

During your pause, it might also be supportive to call in or be receptive to any earthly, celestial or angelic support that wants to assist in the alchemy of the session.

Finally, allow the client to be the one to determine when the pause is complete. Look for cues such as them looking up at you, moving in a way that seems ready to move on, or speaking.

Educating Your Client

The land of trauma resolution can be confusing and disorienting to traverse. One of the most important skills you can develop as a trauma-informed coach is that of orienting your client to the process they're amidst, educating them about their nervous system and how it works, and helping them locate themselves on a map of healing.

While there's no definitive beginning, middle, or end to trauma resolution, there are core competencies our clients can grow and develop. We can help them see what those core competencies are—from relational to embodied coherence—and illuminate where they're already thriving and where you hope to help them grow.

When we employ this critical orientation skill, we provide the guidance, context, and mental framework needed for our client to ease into the process. Knowing where you are on the map and why—plus how to get to where you want to go—offers a salve that soothes confusion, shame, and overwhelm. Educational orientation breaks the nebulous, intimidating process of trauma resolution down into a doable journey.

I recommend teaching your clients little by little, in bite-size bits over time, based on what naturally emerges in your sessions. For instance, if your client brings to you the topic of their chronic fear in bed with their partner, that might be the perfect moment to teach the nature of incomplete traumatic emergency responses, or how having experiences of boundary repairs can help improve felt-sense safety and choice.

Invitational Language

When people have histories of trauma and boundary violations, the development of self-consent—knowing and honoring their embodied *yeses* or *nos*—can often be stunted. As coaches, we can help our clients connect with their empowered capacity to make self-honoring choices by giving them options every step of the way. While this might, at first to some, seem passive or weak, the truth is that few things are more powerful than non-attached invitational language. It calls on another's highest self to choose. It honors every person's capacity to know what's best for them. It's reverence, in language. It's a version of love.

How to use invitational language

As you begin a session:

- "Perhaps notice if you'd like to connect with an intention for this session. If so, what might it be?"
- "Would it be okay if I guided us through a bit of grounding to get things started here? If so, is there a type you would prefer?"
- "Perhaps connecting a bit to your legs, sit bones or the earth beneath you, maybe noticing anything that feels possibly grounded, neutral, stable, or predictable…."

As a session deepens into more tender or intense content, and you sense a certain direction would be helpful:

- "I'm getting the sense that a certain direction might be helpful here. How about I tell you my hunch, and you can let me know how it lands?"

As you're working somatically:

- "Perhaps notice if there's a sound your body might want to make right now. If so, what wants to happen as you hear that you have permission to make it?"
- "Is there a movement you might want to make right now? If so, is there a way that feels doable for you to make it?"
- "If you were in charge of this session and it could deepen or lighten according to your true needs right now, what would you let yourself do?"
- "Would you be up for allowing the intensity for a few moments, instead of trying to change it?"

As you complete your session:

- "What might feel good to say or do to close out this session for yourself?"
- "There are some practices I'd love to invite you into if they resonate. Perhaps tune in. Do they land? If so, how often would you like to do them?"

Notice that with each of these examples, there's lots of permission to opt in or opt out, go deeper or lighter, and the open-endedness allows your client the room to co-create their experience according to their true feelings and needs.

Invitational language is not about "asking for permission" every step of the way. It's about making room for your client to choose the level and way in which they engage with the direction you offer.

You can be DIRECT
without being
FORCEFUL.
You can be
open-ended
without being
passive.
This is the ART of
invitational language.

Direct invitational language:

"My sense is that if we tune into the dark energy in your heart, it might show us where it wants to go. What's your sense?"

Non-invitational language:

"I'm going to remove the dark entity in your heart now. Take a deep breath while I pull it out."

Note: some modalities use a less invitational approach, for instance, many forms of shamanism that I've encountered. It's not that less invitational language is bad or wrong (it can be deeply effective), it's just that it's not the same as a trauma-informed approach.

Invitational language honors the inner-authority, wisdom, and capacity of the client's Natural Blueprint of Health as well as inherent pace, process and intrinsic healing plan.

Non-invitational language assumes the practitioner is the one who can see and sense better than the client themself, and under that assumption, directs the client without collaboration.

Orienting

Orientation is the natural capacity that animals have for scanning the environment and assessing levels of safety.[47] The body engages with the environment to register and map, is it safe? Can I settle here to eat, sleep or hang out? Or will I need to run? Our human animal bodies have this same safety instinct, however, with unresolved trauma, this instinct can become hyper or hypo—over-active (hypervigilant) or under-active (unaware of threat).

---

[47] *Peter Levine,* Waking the Tiger

Benefits of orienting:

- When we help our clients re-regulate their "orientation muscles" in sessions, their nervous system receives support returning to a more responsive rather than reactive state.
- Orienting can help your client's body come more into present time and place, amplifying the moment's relative neutrality, stability, or safety.
- Orienting in moments of overwhelm can help slow activation spikes of fight, flight, or freeze, giving your client more access to choice before symptoms begin looping.

To help your client orient, you might suggest something like this:

"Before we dive into today's session, I might invite you to notice your back against the chair, your spine, the backs of your legs. Perhaps turning your head very slowly, look around your space, and let yourself notice what shapes and colors stand out to you, perhaps also the sounds and smells. Let your senses connect with what's around you, without anything needing to happen. Allow your eyes to rest back and your senses to receive. Maybe noticing the sensations in your body as you simply let your attention linger on the objects in the room that stand out—without needing to change anything. What happens inside as you softly and slowly orient to the present time and place?"

Often, as clients begin to reawaken more regulated orientation skills, they experience levels of safety, security, openness, quietude, softness, centeredness, or fullness. As such, this is a great skill to use at the beginning of sessions, or during times when a bit of soothing, distracting or stabilizing may be supportive.

Resourcing and Amplifying Health

When working with clients in the territory of trauma, orienting, synchronizing and attuning to health, stability, predictability, comfort, or vitality before, during and after engaging difficulty, helps create a wide base of support for weathering intensity.

Health can come in many shapes, sizes and forms:

- The parts of the body or soul that feel most luscious, supple, resilient, and eternal.
- The stability and predictability of the floor below and the earth beneath the floor.
- The great-grandmother who had a legacy of wild love and creativity.
- The powerful, wide tree trunks and roots all around the home.
- The team of angels that feel ever-present and available.
- The crystals that ground and soothe.
- The delightful essential oil blend.
- The music that transports you to a place of peace.
- The essence of your favorite spot on Earth.
- The predictability of the four cardinal directions, the constellations above, the journey of the sun across the sky from east to west.
- The morning birdsong.
- The feeling of your fingers strumming the guitar.
- The sound of your best friend's voice on the other end of the phone.
- The ease you have when you slide paint across a canvas.
- The deep sigh in your bones when you turn your phone off at 8 PM.
- The soft fur of your beloved pet.
- The steady chest of partnership you can fall into at the end of the day.

While your clients may not connect to all of these examples, the pieces of health they *do* connect to are what we might call their "resources" or "layers of support;" the things they can turn toward—either tangibly or in their imagination—for embodied and psychic support before, during and between sessions.

When our clients first come to us, one of the most supportive practices we can do is invite them to write what I like to call a Whole Body Exhale List. A list of all of the resources and layers of support they have available to them, if and when they need them.

Practice: Whole Body Exhale List

To help your clients feel safer and more supported throughout your time working together, invite them to create a "Whole Body Exhale List." This is a list of their very specific resources and layers of support that help them feel more safe, stable, cared for, vital, and well. The things that give their body, heart, and soul solace, ease, or support when they're under stress or difficulty. The things they never regret doing. The things, big or small, that have a soothing effect on them and create an experience of deep exhale in their bodies. It's important that your clients have easy-enough access to the things that they write on their list, as opposed to writing things that might feel desirable but out of reach.

I encourage my clients to write this list by hand, and then put it on their refrigerator or somewhere else equally visible and accessible, so it's there as a constant reminder of resources and layers of support they can turn to in need. I also encourage my clients to begin connecting with more of their "Whole Body Exhales"—even if nothing's wrong or overwhelming. I share with them how this will help increase their Window of Tolerance and cultivate a wider base of support for our work together.

Discover and Attune to Your Client's Natural Blueprint Essence

Another thing that's wonderful to do at the beginning of a relationship with a new client is a practice for discovering their Natural Blueprint Essence. The unbreakable source of beauty, love, health and unique personality that's intrinsic to their heart and soul. The energy of pure and total radiance that is the fullest expression of both their body's wellness and their soul's fulfillment.

You could do a visualization with your client at the beginning of your work together as an intimate process of co-discovery. Or you could use your intuitive sight to sense into their greatest gifts, then check in with them for accuracy.

"My sense is your essence is gentle but strong and wildly creative. Does that land when you hear me say it? If so, are there textures, colors, sensations, or images that might show up as you hear me speaking into your Blueprint a bit?"

So often, with new clients we begin with all that's difficult and hard, listening and looking for the patterns of the broken bits. But what if, as guides, we were to familiarize ourselves with our clients' greatest gifts first? We could return to those gifts when things become more tender or challenging in future sessions? We could go to greater depths, knowing we have access to the unbreakable light, that we can invite it back for support whenever needed?

Side note: it's so helpful to know your own Natural Blueprint Essence as a coach! Often, before a session, I'll take a little walk outside and imagine my Natural Blueprint Essence meeting with my client's Natural Blueprint Essence. I'll see my client in their greatest wellness—both physically and energetically—then see if there are any messages their Blueprint wants to share with mine about the session. Wild insights come through in these little five-minute drop-ins that often support the session in a big way.

Once you've established a baseline relationship to safety resources, health, and Natural Blueprint Essence, you can draw on those things throughout your sessions with clients to help ground at the beginning of a session or to help soothe or stabilize during intensity.

Connecting with your Client's Natural Blueprint Essence in Sessions

At the beginning of a session, you might invite your client to connect with their Natural Blueprint Essence for a few moments, paying particular attention to its colors, textures, embodiment, and temperatures. During the session, if moments of overwhelm or difficulty arise while processing something traumatic, you might invite your client to pendulate back to their Natural Blueprint Essence, if it feels doable or accessible for them.

"I wonder what happens in your system as I invite the possibility that your Natural Blueprint Essence is also here, even as you sit amidst this difficulty. Does that essence feel accessible to you in this moment, without having to erase what's hard right now?"

Resource and Amplify Your Own Health as a Coach

Oftentimes, our clients are anticipating their session with us all day, for multiple days or maybe even weeks before arriving at our door, which can mean their bodies have been subconsciously preparing to process old trauma for an equal amount of time. I've had countless sessions where a client showed up in a total tizzy, revealing that some big traumatic occurrence (similar to their usual pattern) happened earlier that day. This is no accident.

The momentum of difficulty or emergency in a client's life will sometimes amplify when they begin the process of trauma resolution. Things that have been long-buried often surface, alongside feelings of old grief, panic, anger, or fear.

For this reason, it's important that whenever possible, you begin with your clients in their health, dip into their difficulty, then spiral back to their health. Begin in the Blueprint, dip into the imprint, then spiral back to the Blueprint.

But how do you do that if your client is coming into a session with a speed or momentum of difficulty, stress, trauma, shut down, or emergency? How do you honor what your client is bringing to you without succumbing to the momentum of it?

"The momentum of emergency is fast and contagious," Brigit once shared in a training. "Growing your own momentum of health is the best way to not catch the bug. Because whichever momentum is bigger—your health or their emergency— will energetically dominate the session."

When your clients bring their intensity to you, it's very helpful to have a wide base of health in your own physiology, so you're not offering care from a "faux window of tolerance," as Kathy Kain describes it. Working from a super-savior self is a position that often leads to physical or emotional burnout.

Amplifying your own health and resilience, on the other hand, as well as inviting the power of nature and the divine into your sessions, will create a powerful foundational healing space for your client (and you!).

- What's *your* Whole Body Exhale List?
- What's *your* Natural Blueprint Essence?
- What are the ways *you* love to connect to joy, aliveness, wellness, Source, or sweetness?
- Can you take time each day at the start of your day or perhaps before sessions to connect to your resources and layers of support?

Momentum shifts little by little over time, not in one fell swoop. Our bodies prefer homeostasis to change. When you're growing new habits, new momentums of health, it's okay to start small, gradually increasing your capacity for wellness and aliveness over time. (It's great to remind your clients of this gradual momentum shift as well!) It's okay to commit to whatever feels easiest or simplest, instead of pressuring yourself to perform self-care perfection.

What's the SMALLEST
DOABLE STEP
in the DIRECTION
of your DESIRE?
DO THAT.
That's the key
to SUSTAINABLE
Change.

Speaking of sustainability, one way you can amplify your own health as a trauma resolution guide is by tip-toeing into the field of trauma resolution, rather than rushing in. Overloading your nervous system and heart with a full roster of clients who have heavy trauma while you're still getting your footing with this body of work might cause energetic or emotional injury—in you or them. When my students are beginning to branch into the field of trauma resolution, I recommend that they start small with perhaps one or two trauma resolution clients, then increase those numbers according to capacity, desire, and joy for the work.

There have been times when I was working with a lot of clients who had intense trauma without as much nurturance in my personal life, and it was very hard on my system. Through difficulty, I've learned the importance of titrating my load, working with a diversity of clients (some perhaps in deep trauma, others in more health), prioritizing my personal joys and healthy relationships, as well as allowing for a tidal relationship to this body of work—incorporating breaks, pauses, and sabbaticals for total-system replenishment into my annual calendar, if and when possible.

- Where are you in your relationship to working with trauma?
- Can you titrate your way in, and pendulate to health whenever possible, honoring your energy and simultaneously providing healthy (rather than harmful) stretches into this territory?

Last, it's important—critical!—that as a coach or guide working with trauma, you have someone you can turn to for extra support or to work with your own physiology and emotional body. Some seasons of my life, I opt for wordless embodied support like regular acupuncture or body work. Even a really great embodiment class can be enough. Other times, I opt for a season or two with a trusted trauma resolution practitioner. Other times still, I seek out an older mentor or guide who might offer wise counsel or perspective. Different eras of our lives call for different kinds of care, but I do believe it's important if we're giving a lot to others to also have sources from which we receive, nourish and replenish.

- What regular practices do you have for coming into regulated aliveness, in both body and soul?
- Are you getting the support you need as deeper pieces of your own work show themselves?

Cocooning

When we're fetuses in the womb, we grow in patterns of expansion and contraction. It's our most natural evolutionary rhythm.[48] Yet, as we're acculturated into the powerful forces of colonization and capitalism—systems that perpetuate unnatural rhythms of mass accumulation and unsustainable growth, followed by collapse—we forget our essential rhythm.

Part of breaking our personal trauma spell is breaking our collective trauma spell, as well. Part of remembering our personal Natural Blueprint of Health is remembering our collective Natural Blueprint of Health, as well. The more our businesses and coaching practices mirror both personal and collective Natural Blueprints of Health, the more powerful and regenerative our services will be—for both our clients and ourselves. As such, the notion of "cocooning" is an essential component to running a healthy business and undergoing sustainable healing, growth, and transformation processes.

Cocooning is about giving as much time, energy, and attention to contraction as you give to expansion. For our clients, it's about reminding them that even if we're moving slowly or gently in session, working at the layer of the nervous system is still a big expansion.

- Can they give themselves more time and space both before and after sessions to prepare, rest, digest, and integrate?
- Can they add more nurturance, sleep, down time, and easeful, joyful activities to their weekly rhythms during the time that we're doing trauma resolution processes together?

---

[48] Brigit Viksnins, *Alchemical Alignment* via her pre- and perinatal trauma resolution studies.

I always encourage my clients to double or triple their "whole body exhales" throughout the duration of our work together, to support the cocooning and integrating of what we're doing.

If we move too quickly through the sensitivity of nervous system healing, we mirror the forceful and unsustainable rhythms of our culture, and shortchange ourselves of the natural pace of restoration—slow, efficient, and miraculous.

For ourselves as coaches, it's about embodying the principle of cocooning in relationship to our client work, our program launches, our creative output, and our own personal lives.

- Can you plan time before and after your sessions, or at the beginning and end of your workday, to contract into prayer, restorative movement, connection to your resources, rest, digestion, co-regulation or play?
- Can you plan extra time and space before and after hosting retreats or events—"cocoon days"—where you do no work, but instead totally fill or refill your well with things that bring you joy, nurture and aliveness?
- Can you map your work to the seasons a bit, whenever possible? Planning extra time for rest and reflection in the winter, extra time for play and connection in the summer, extra time for focusing and creating in the fall and extra time for professional emergence and creativity in the spring...?
- Can you plan extra time before and after business launches to fill your tank, receive for you?
- Can you give yourself extra emotional support before doing something hard (not only after you're in an emergency or overwhelmed...)?

Energetic Hygiene

So often, in the world of the healing arts, there's a strong focus on putting up shields of protection or cord-cutting in order to maintain energetic hygiene. While those can be tremendously helpful (and I do them from time-to-time), there's another way that I like to teach energetic hygiene, which has more to do with amplifying health and less to do with external protection.

In the world of trauma resolution, you can come in contact with a lot of intensity. The momentum of health you bring to your sessions is an important component of energetic hygiene. As such, before every session with clients, I like to do one or all of the following things, depending on my current state as well as the client who's coming:

- Take a short walk and meditate on my Blueprint Essence as well as my client's
- Imagine myself and my client both inside our own fully robust toruses, cocoons of light and energetic wellness…embodied sovereignty that exudes health and illuminates possibility, as well as offers protection from anything unwanted or unhelpful
- Imagine the felt-sense experience and emotions of the highest possible energetic outcome for the session, as though they are already occurring

During sessions, I do the same thing in moments of intensity. As coaches, we'll often attempt to talk our clients down off a ledge or into a different perspective. But simply holding an energetic field that's attuned to *your own* Natural Blueprint Essence and torus, as well as theirs, can create a potent field of health within which our clients can alchemize their imprints and re-regulate to their Blueprint, without either of you feeling overwhelmed.

After sessions, I reconnect once more to my own and my client's Blueprints. It's also helpful to imagine your client back in their own space, their own torus and their own self-regulated nervous system, as a way of creating healthy separation.

Developing Sovereign Clients

The body and soul have their own inherent treatment plan for healing—their own natural intelligences and divine timelines. As coaches, can we let go of our need to control our client's experience, and instead, invite their sovereign wisdom, choice and desire to come forth?

Sometimes, the body will say, *No, I'm not ready to go there—to that big intense thing that's coming up—in this space, place or time.* While it's true that we occasionally need encouragement to move toward difficulty, I think, generally speaking, our culture is way too pushy. We tend to label our client's (or our own) embodied wisdom about moving at a slower pace as "resistance," instead of listening and cooperating with the natural desire inside.

I like to think that every nervous system secretly knows just how much intensity it's ready to process, and where, and with whom. What if instead of pushing our clients where *we* think they need to go, we honored their sovereign capacity to sense and self-direct their next best move? On the other hand, what if instead of turning into passive bystanders of our client's inner-wisdom, only ever taking a back seat to their process, we learned to tango with their waves of sensation and authentic emergent direction in a co-creative dance of doable activation and resolution? What if by encouraging our clients to say *no* to our invitations, to go slower or change routes at any time, they could feel more empowered to enter choicefully into heated territory—with their own volition, at their own speed, in their own way?

Is it resistance or is it trauma?

This is a question I'm asked all the time by facilitators who have been schooled in the world of *no pain, no gain.* As a coach, you have no way of knowing whether your client's *no* is resistance or trauma. Luckily, it's not your job to determine that. It's your job to help someone safely decide for themselves what they're ready to move into and through.

From my experience leading hundreds of students and clients through the territory of trauma resolution, I've learned that most people have been socialized and entrained to force themselves past their limits. Most people think pushing is the way to get where they want to go. Who cares if they're in consent with themselves, or not? In fact, most people aren't even sure what it means or how it feels to be in consent with themselves—to feel, honor and embrace their limits.

Ever hear the phrase, "we slow down, to get aligned, to speed back up?" As we help our clients develop sovereignty, help them know what *yes, no,* and *maybe* feel like in their bodies—then encourage them to honor what they sense—they come into super-alignment with their natural healing timeline. This super-alignment with right-pace is *far more efficient in the long run* than the all-too-common experience of pushing through, getting retraumatized, and being left with deeper grooves of difficulty and nervous system dysregulation, as a result.

As such, I encourage making lots of space for your clients' *no* to emerge, be heard and respected for two big reasons. One: reclaiming choice is a critical piece of healing, especially when so many violations are rooted in nonconsensual, forceful experiences. Two: if you encourage your student to push their body past its instinct to pause or lean back, that's when retraumatizing experiences like dissociation, hyper-socializing to the coach, or over-performing followed by collapse can happen.

Practice for Developing Sovereign Clients

Part 1

At the beginning of a coaching relationship with a new client, invite them to think of a time when they said *yes* to something they didn't really want to do, something that was in truth, a *no* for them. Then invite them to notice what it feels like in their body as they bring this memory to mind. Invite them to look for the images, sensations, or body language that emerges. Then invite them to share, perhaps both in words and with a body gesture or posture.

Part 2

Next, invite your client to think of a time when they said *yes* to something that they were scared to do, but that was ultimately aligned and good for them. Again, invite them to notice what it feels like in their body as they bring this memory to mind. Invite them to attune to any images, sensations or body language that appears. Invite them to share again in words or gestures.

Emphasize that the first experience is what it feels and looks like to force yourself into something. The second experience is what it feels and looks like to consensually move toward something that you're scared to do but aligned with.

Part 3

Invite your client to revisit their example of self-force. Give them the chance to say aloud to you, as if you were the one they had said *yes* to when they meant *no*:

"I need to pause." Or, "I change my mind." Or, "I'm a *no*, thank you."

Part 4

Thank your client for pausing, changing their mind, or saying *no*.

Part 5

Take some time to allow your client to notice how it feels in their body to practice pausing, changing their mind or saying *no* to you, as well as how it feels to receive respect and honor in return.

Clients will often find this practice uncomfortable or emotional. I like to emphasize that a lot of our work together will be growing their capacity to pause, change their mind, and say *no*—and then be met with care and reverence for their choice. I tell them how tender this can be if it's not something they have experienced much historically.

This practice alone could literally change your client's life, especially if they tend toward hyper-socialization for safety. Creating a positive imprint, where they are allowed to say *no* to you and be met with respect, appreciation and honor, is irreplaceable.

Pendulation

Pendulation is the process of allowing your client to move between two differing states; in the context of trauma resolution, this usually means moving between a state of arousal and a state of neutrality. As a coach, pendulation involves guiding your client to weave back and forth between challenge and resource, activation and calm, difficulty and ease.

The dance between charged and simple states builds capacity for your client to be able to witness, be present to, work with and contain more intense physiological or emotional experiences. With a greater capacity for intensity, your client can bring more presence to old traumatic imprints (or new pleasurable experiences!) that were previously too overwhelming to witness, touch, or stay with. Presence creates fluidity where the physiology was once rigid—and with fluidity, the nervous system has the opportunity to transform. There's a felt-sense experience of choice that re-emerges. With more nourishment in the nervous system, the body begins to remember how to self-correct and renew.

You can guide pendulation between any of the following things (and more):

Body and mind

"Wow, it seems like tuning into your body is a bit overwhelming right now. I'm curious what you're *thinking* about this process?"

Story and felt-sense experience

"I'm hearing a lot of speed in your voice as you tell this story. I wonder if you drop below the story, what is there to notice in your body?"

Fast and slow physiology

"Ah, yes. I hear you that your heart is racing. Without having to ignore or erase the heart-race, I wonder if there are any parts of your body that feel a bit more *slow or neutral* just right now?"

Internal experience and external experience

"As your body begins to feel a bit formless and floaty, I wonder if you might tune into the temperature and solidity of the chair beneath you? Can you sense your legs or sit bones in contact with the chair? The material of the chair?"

Deep topic and shallow topic

"I'm sensing it might be a bit overwhelming to be talking about this subject right now. Does that land? We can always transition to something a bit less intense momentarily. In fact, we don't ever have to go there if you don't want to."

Sometimes, giving the option for a client to "never" have to do something creates a liberatory experience of choice if they've been pressuring themselves or experiencing pressure from others.

In these pendulation examples,[49] the goal is to support the client in feeling more resourced, stable or neutral, in the moments when overwhelm could send them looping or spinning outside their range of resilience.

Once your client's system is a bit more resourced, you might then wait to see if a green light comes to titrate a bit of intensity again. Sometimes your client has capacity for another wave of titrated experience, and sometimes instead, a nice, long integration and digestion of the one experience is more supportive.

As a recap:

- **Pendulation** can be thought of as the turn signal back to safety, accompanied by gentle brakes on the intensity.
- **Titration** can be thought of as a slow and sensitive gas pedal toward intensity.

---

[49] *developed from teachings by Brigit Viksnins.*

Everyone has a different capacity for depth of intensity, and that capacity differs based on topic, time of the month, and current life conditions of stress or ease. Feeling for your client's capacity *in this moment, on this day,* and working compassionately with both their drive toward and pull away from charged states, is the safest, most trauma-informed, and sustainable way of facilitating deep, lasting change.

Note: when you facilitate pendulation, it's helpful to bring awareness to the reality that two things can be happening at the same time in your client's experience. For example, there can be fast and slow, overwhelming and neutral, what's happening inside their body and what's happening outside their body, what's happening with themselves and what's happening between the two of you, what's happening in their mind and what's happening in their felt-sense experience, etc.

With less access to higher level cognition, the trauma-mind often gets fixated in either-or, all-or-nothing perspectives.

"My WHOLE BODY is freaking out."

As you facilitate pendulation, it's a wonderful opportunity to help your client widen their view to include a both-and perspective.

"Even as your body is freaking out, I wonder if there's anything you notice, anything at all—perhaps the trees outside, the chair beneath you—that *isn't* freaking out. We don't have to erase the whole body freak out. But perhaps we can widen our view to include something that's a bit more stable right now, and hang out with both things for a moment...?"

The idea of pendulation isn't to force your client into a neutral place, but rather to *expand their awareness to include more than just what's big, intense or overwhelming.* By allowing both neutral *and* charged experiences to co-exist, the intensity of what's charged often softens, without feeling bypassed or threatened.

Celebrating and Amplifying Natural Blueprints of Health without Bypassing Difficulty

When our clients are struggling (in life or in sessions) the less-regulated physiology, operating within a smaller window of tolerance, tends to move into hyper and hypo states more quickly. In these states, it's harder to have accurate self-perception and self-esteem.

As coaches, we can help our clients learn to appreciate what's working inside of them and on their behalf—even when they're struggling—as a way of amplifying and allowing those instincts, and also as a way of pendulating difficulty and resourcing wellness.

Any impulse, instinct or expression that is authentic and true—even if it's uncomfortable, vulnerable, or difficult for your client—can be seen and celebrated as an asset in sessions. That said, it's important that when we're celebrating and amplifying Natural Blueprints of Health, we're also acknowledging difficulty—allowing for the both/and of resource and challenge to exist together, instead of forcing positivity, which would be another way of buying into either/or thinking.

Examples of celebrating and amplifying Natural Blueprints of Health without bypassing difficulty:

"I really hear how angry you are about this. I'm appreciating your capacity to sense your anger and stay present to it. That feels powerful to me. How does it feel for you?"

"I hear how big this grief is for you. I'm appreciating your vulnerability, the way you're letting your emotions move through you. I'm also appreciating your capacity to let me sit with you in this. It feels sacred to me. How does it feel for you?"

"Wow, even though there's a lot of confusion and subsequent frustration here, I'm also hearing your clarity about what you need. I'm appreciating your capacity to be in touch with your needs. How does that part of things feel for you?"

Notice that in each of these examples, there's:

- An acknowledgment of difficulty (instead of any attempt to change it, make it better, or act like it's not that bad).
- An appreciation of some display of capacity on the client's part, expressed as an "I statement" (even if they're displaying something that might be uncomfortable for them).
- An admission of how it feels to be present with them as the coach (optional, but often powerful).
- A question about how they're experiencing themselves in relationship to the Blueprint you just pointed out.

Practice: Appreciate the wisdom of your client's instincts and impulses

Oftentimes, our clients have received the messaging that their instincts are bad, shameful or wrong. Instincts to run, be annoyed, hide, push away, put up a boundary, check out, cry, ask for reassurance, employ skepticism, sigh, make a loud noise, move their body, moan with pleasure, eat when they're hungry, or pee when they need to are often repressed, ignored, or overridden.

Our instincts and impulses are part of our natural intelligence, impeccably designed to nourish and protect us. Helping our clients re-grow right-relationships with their instincts and impulses—hearing and heeding them whenever possible— is a key component to post-traumatic growth.

Additionally, humans tend to have a pretty strong negativity bias as part of their reptilian-brain defense mechanisms. We look for what's wrong, off, unsafe, dangerous, or not working more often than we look for what's right, on, safe or well, as a form of preemptive protection. Especially when people have histories of developmental trauma, their reptilian brains can become overactive, therefore increasing the negativity bias.

As coaches, we don't want to disarm, soothe or bypass our clients' protective instincts or even their negativity bias. Attempts at disarming a protection mechanism will likely only create more defense. So how do we work with someone who's tending toward perhaps over-protection? Rather than *disarming* a negativity bias or protective instinct, highlight the health inside of it, and encourage it to express fully and to completion. Often, this invitation alone leads to an emerging desire inside your client for a *break* from this over-used part of them.

With trauma, our instincts can become fixed, rigid, repressed, frozen, or overactive in our bodies. With gentle appreciation of the wisdom of our instincts, those dysregulated impulses can animate, embody, and finally complete in doable bits at a time.

The effects of embodying our dysregulated physiology in the company of a safe, nonjudgmental, compassionate other can be profound. Our rigidity can loosen. Our fixations can soften. Our negativity can open into possibility. And our bodies can get the message that it's safe to be whole in relationship to another.

For example, let's say your client is feeling depressed about her friend group, in grief that most of the people around her are struggling with addiction. She's expressing a level of hopelessness and feels as if nothing will ever change. This is a great chance to appreciate the wisdom of her sadness, without bypassing the difficulty she's in.

"I hear that it's hard. That's so valid. And—I'm really appreciating your grief. I perceive that as the healthiest, wisest part of you, crying for something better. I wonder what happens for you as I acknowledge your grief as wise?"

In a moment when a client may feel embarrassed that she feels an instinct to hide, this might be a wonderful opportunity to destigmatize and rather appreciate her instinct as wise.

"While it might feel awkward to want to hide, I want you to know I honor your body's instinctual wisdom. Maybe it never got to hide in a moment when it really needed to. Maybe now it could have that chance. You are totally welcome to hide here. I wonder, as your body registers that permission, what happens inside?"

In a moment when a client is feeling shame about her tears or grief, you might appreciate her capacity to feel, when before she was only numb.

"Oof, this is hard. I'm really appreciating your capacity to feel it even though it's challenging."

In these moments of appreciation, it's best to use "I" statements, as opposed to "you" statements.

"I'm really appreciating your capacity to feel..."

Versus –

"You're doing such a good job feeling..."

Curiosity (as Opposed to Forced Intervention)

The Whole Holy Point of trauma resolution is to renew our client's connection with their intrinsic embodied wisdom, genius, presence, and resiliency. We do this specifically in the places where they've become most disconnected or fractured, with one part of their awareness in the present and another part still surviving through a past threat. When you employ genuine curiosity with your client, as opposed to steering their healing, you make space for your client's Natural Blueprint or inherent treatment plan to reveal itself.

Sometimes, we fear that if we don't discover and "fix" our client's problems immediately, they won't get any value. But I've found the opposite to be true. Curiosity allows for our clients' next-most-emergent layer of information that's wanting attention to *reveal itself in its own right-timing*—without any force needed.

While in a successful trauma-resolution dance, the coach sometimes leads and other times follows, erring on the side of curiosity *first* can help you discover the right lead-follow dynamic between you and your client. Some clients feel most safe being led, others feel most safe doing the leading. Even with the clients who feel most safe being led, curiously allowing room for them to discover their own preferred direction can help inspire more self-trust.

Great curious questions you can ask include:

"If the wisest part of you were in charge of your trauma resolution, how do you think it would do this?"

"What's it like to be you right now?"

"If your body were in charge right now, where would it have you or our session go next?"

"What's it like for you to be experiencing those sensations?"

"What are you noticing now after we just moved through that?"

"What's it like for you to be exploring this?"

"What are you sensing, on any level…body, emotions, energy, mind?"

"Where do you sense we should go with this?"

Brief and frequent eye contact

After decades of working with people with trauma, Ray Castillino, a pre- and perinatal healing pioneer, found that the pendulation between gentle, connected eye contact, and an averted gaze gives clients the experience of safe attachment—inspiring both intimacy and privacy, rather than overwhelm or anxiety.

When working with a client or even around friends or family, you might practice the tempo of looking toward them, looking down, or gently away, then looking toward them again. This brief and frequent eye contact creates optimal conditions for exploring both intensity and intimacy.

Sometimes I like to share with a new client:

"You might notice I'm not staring at you during our whole session. I sometimes avert my gaze to offer respect and privacy to your system, to allow space and time for you to have your own experience without needing to also be attending to mine. But my presence is always here."

Compassion without Caretaking[50]

No one is helpless. Not even people spiraling under trauma spells. However, it's not always easy to have ongoing compassion for someone who's in a hard spot without becoming impatient and moving toward caretaking in order to "solve the problem" of their difficulty. I've learned that the more a coach takes on their client's trauma as their burden to bear, the weaker everyone becomes.

For extra empathic coaches, this can be a big challenge. You want to help! You want to make things easier! But when your care is taking a toll on you, it can leave you burnt out and wanting to quit the whole gig altogether.

Here's what I recommend, instead of over-holding and burning out. Offer compassion for the spot your client is in, then follow that compassion with curiosity about your client's *own inherent wisdom, knowing, and next-best-response.* In my experience, for those of us with big hearts and a propensity to over-hold, this is the strongest kind of care possible: inter-sovereign support.

---

[50]*This concept and the corresponding way of working with it was taught to me by Chris Dierkes, a very talented soul reader and guide. Learn more about working with Chris at chrisdierkes.com/.*

- Inter-sovereign support maintains your own sovereignty while also invoking theirs.
- Inter-sovereign support is wholeness helping wholeness.
- Inter-sovereign support is life-giving, co-nourishing, and regenerative.

The opposite? Saviorship. Thinking that unless you swoop in and offer salvation, your client will fall apart. That very dynamic disempowers the rise of your client's inner-adult. While there *are* moments in which our client's need our immediate help (redirecting toward safety when they're way off track, seeing something clearly when there's been instances of gaslighting, or calling in higher wisdom when they feel a bit hijacked, for instance), in many cases, swooping in to save someone doesn't empower their sovereign strength. Additionally, while interdependence is a key part of a post-traumatic society, even in those cultures and communities, growing our individual resiliency and self-regulation is essential.

I believe that trusting in someone's capacity to access and resource their own inner wisdom, creativity and wholeness is often one of the most loving things we can do...even if it's not what our clients want us to do.

So...here's how you can do that:

Trust your client's unbreakable core—undoubtedly and without waiver. Attune to their health in the moment. Revere them "naturally creative, resourceful and whole," as Karen and Henry Kimsey-House of the Coaches Training Institute term it. Then...*acknowledge the difference between them and you, their* pain, and *your* sovereignty.

"I hear that you're hurting with ____. That sounds challenging."

"I'm really sorry for your [pain, challenge, struggle]. That sounds hard."

Just naming that the pain or hurt is *theirs* (not yours) can go a long way to unwind from toxic caretaking where you may unconsciously take on their hurt or pain as your own. Even though you have empathy for your client, remember: your client is the one hurting, not you. Allow them to keep their experience, their pain, their feelings as their own.

Finally, ask a follow-up question that empowers and invokes their creative capacity.

"Have you thought about what you want to do about it?"

"Do you have a sense about what you need in order to move through it?"

These follow-up questions put the ball back into your client's court and assumes their creative capacity to respond to challenges. Let them offer their own ideas and instincts before adding bits of your own.

Can you offer RADICAL CARE Without taking on the position of SAVIOR?

Inviting Valiant Resources

Trauma lives in the body as stored imprints of unresolved difficulty that bring along with them incomplete protective emergency responses. As layers of defensive physiology shift and return to Blueprint, higher-level cognition comes back online, along with new perspectives, hope, possibilities, creativity, and trust.

So often, we try to *reason* our way into new inner realities. While this may work from time-to-time, when our body security system at an animal level is reminded of something that was threatening to us in our past, it needs to experience resolution around that threat at the level of the body in order to shift back into regulation. Try as we may to convince ourselves that *that was then and this is now*, our nervous system and its unresolved imprints tend to rule our reality.

When we're working with clients to help them resolve these secret patterns, it can be helpful to invite them to drop below the cognitive story and into the potential simplicity of sensations, instincts, and impulses. Furthermore, we can "prime the pump" for our client's "success" around topics where they once suffered only pain, loss, or inescapable violation, by helping them call on a "valiant resource." A resource that can prove empowering, protective, fierce, supportive, or essential to the specific resolution or completion they need.[51]

Valiant resources can come in a variety of forms, sizes, and shapes. They can be animal, celestial, cosmic, ancestral, soulful, earthly, or archetypal. They can be a past, future, or parallel version of yourself. They can be a form of divine parentage or even an environment so supportive to the difficulty at hand that the challenged part of you can finally feel safe and protected. Even if it doesn't make "rational sense" to you or your client right away, almost anything that offers an embodied sense of empowerment or relief to your client in the moment could be called on as a valiant resource.

For example, your client could have a long-held freeze that they're processing with you. When you ask them if there's some kind of resource or layer of support

---

[51] *Valiant resources is another tool I learned from Brigit Viksnins in Alchemical Alignment.*

that you might call into their experience, they get a flash of angels. As you hang out with the angelic light that your client senses is emanating into her, the deep freeze begins to gently and softly thaw, grief moves through and out of her body, and new insights begin developing.

On the other hand, let's say your client is experiencing a syndromal fight energy. When you prime the pump for a valiant resource to support them, they sense the presence of a cheetah. As you work with the cheetah, it begins to enter into your client, awakening their jaw and muscles, and sharpening their vision. A mobilization is happening that gives way to waves of heat releasing from your client's body.

With the help of valiant resources, your client can experience permission to access and awaken parts of their physiology, energetic frequency and inner-landscape that was perhaps rigid, stuck or fixed in a more hyper or hypo state. With more range of motion and vitality online, old nervous system patterns can finally resolve and complete themselves, and your client's Natural Blueprint of Health can plump back up inside their bodies—sometimes even more than ever before.

What are examples of valiant resources?

After having countless sessions myself, as well as working with hundreds of clients, I've noticed some patterns around the moments in which certain types of valiant resources tend to show up. Every person is different, and this list is in no way meant to be prescriptive or limiting. The most important thing is to help your client listen for any resource that wants to reveal itself in the moment. But I'm including some trends I've noticed in case they are helpful to you.

- **Animals** – Animals often arrive to help connect to specific instincts (to fight, run, hide, burrow, sleep, huddle together, shake, attack).
- **Earth elements** – Earth elements can emerge when connecting to a certain speed or energy would be supportive (slow, stable, and grounded…fast, rushing, and destructive…calm or quiet…).
- **Places in nature, the universe or an alternative location** – A change in

scenery can present itself when physical protection, rest, rejuvenation, or nourishment is the medicine the body needs in order to have a break from prolonged difficulty or violation. Systemic trauma, inescapable environmental conditions, and chronic pain or chronic illness often inspire a need for a change in scenery.

- **Celestial beings, angels or archangels** – Celestial beings, angels, or archangels often show up to support death, birth, pregnancy, grief, dissociation, deep freeze, or religious trauma, as well as specific prayers associated with that being.

- **Cosmic beings or life from other realms** – Cosmic beings or life from other realms (possibly aliens) often show up when working with life callings, big messages, creativity, or when breaking long-held soul-contracts or patterns.

- **Ancestors** – When traumas and gifts run deep in the ancestral line, ancestors may reveal themselves to support a related healing process, or ask for support themselves.

- **Certain ages of self** – When healing developmental trauma, a Blueprint version of a younger self often emerges. Similarly, a Blueprint version of your own inner-parent may arise to re-parent your younger self. Sometimes your current-aged Highest or Wisest self shows up for this same cause.

- **Divine parent** – When healing deep abandonment, neglect, or banishment wounds, sometimes a "more than human" parent can show up to help hold how big the pain is, relieving pressure from humans to do the job.

- **Soul family** – Often, when we're working with topics of belonging, secure community attachment, or the need to be seen and known, kept safe and loved by the group...entire families or villages of support—those who've loved you unconditionally in this lifetime, on this plane, and in others—will come around to aid the process.

- **Archetypes** – When we're trying to access a more dormant part of ourselves, an archetypal character can sometimes show up to support us (either as an under-accessed version of us, or as a separate entity that we relate to).

Sometimes, these more "specific" resources don't show up—but rather, a simple impulse or instinct takes hold. Perhaps a color, energy, texture, or object shows up. It all counts.

When do you invite valiant resources?

- When "activation," "trigger," or "charge" are present
- When things feel stuck or overwhelming for your client
- When any of the "hyper" trauma responses emerge—fight, flight, hypervigilance, hypersocialization
- When any of the "hypo" trauma responses emerge—freeze, grief, dissociation, shame, chronic pain, or illness

If these conditions arise, and your client also has enough capacity to attune to the moment and call in a layer of support, a valiant resource usually proves medicinal. If your client is less able to access presence, invite them to pendulate to something more stable and predictable before moving toward a valiant resource.

How do you invite your client to possibly access a valiant resource?

When you notice your client is experiencing activation, trigger, or charge, you can simply ask them:

"I wonder if you drop below the story right now, perhaps to the simpler *instincts, impulses, needs, or sensations* in your body…what's there to notice?"

"Below the story, if we keep things very simple at the level of the animal body, which includes awareness of energy and emotion, but is less concerned with story…what *instincts, impulses, or subtle movements and energies* are there to notice?"

As your client begins to describe more symptoms of physiological trauma responses, then you might get curious:

"Sometimes, in these moments of activation, valiant resources like to reveal themselves to support us in our healing…animals, ancestors, celestial beings, archetypes…I wonder as you hear me mentioning that possibility if there's anything you can sense might want to support you in this moment…?"

"As your body hears the possibility that the more animal-you is welcome here, what, if anything, shows up?"

"Is there an animal-energy that might want to support you in this moment?"

It's often helpful for our clients when we list a few general possibilities of valiant resources, then quietly allow them to see what emerges in their own inner-landscape. If nothing emerges, let the possibility go and just keep things simple by focusing on sensations.

If your client identifies a valiant resource to work with, help your client relate to it in a felt-sense way:

"Wow…as that animal reveals itself, perhaps notice where and how it's showing up. Is it inside your body? Outside your body? Just an image? As an energy, weight or feeling? There's no right or wrong way."

Allow your client time and space to be with this resource, letting the resource relate to your client in whatever way is naturally emergent.

Perhaps after some time, prime the pump again…

"As you allow yourself to relate to this resource, notice what naturally begins to happen…

Does it want to merge with you?
Does it want to protect you?
Does it want to move through you?

Does it want to move you somewhere?

Let's give some space and time to see what wants to happen…"

If your client's instinct becomes one of movement (perhaps because an animal merged with their body…) encourage those movements to be "micro" or even just energetic. Bigger movements are also welcome, but the goal is for your client to be able to observe the sensations happening inside of them as they experience them, as a way of harmonizing with any subtle completions happening at the nervous system level.

If your client senses an image or scene, allow time for that scene to happen and unfold by embodying a quiet presence and curiosity while your client has their experience.

If your client is feeling intense sensations, return to the ABCs…helping them tune into how they might collaborate with those sensations and energies, allowing them to move through the body.

As things begin to shift and change, check back in about the original valiant resource. Where is it now? How is it doing? What's happening in relationship to that resource? Sometimes the scenery changes, sometimes your client will rest with their resource, sometimes they'll feel a surge of energy and become enlivened, sometimes they'll cry, and their resource will support them, sometimes other celestial beings show up, and sometimes a renewed sense of perspective will arise.

Invite Witness Consciousness

"Witness consciousness" is a term originally derived from the Buddhist lineage of mindfulness, wherein you bring attention to your experience in the present moment without judgment.[52] This attention is offered through an internal "neutral observer" that's attuned to the other parts of you (your mind, emotions, sensations, ego, etc.).

---

[52] *If you or a client is wanting to learn more about mindfulness, I highly recommend the work of Vietnamese Zen Master Thich Nhat Hanh. He has a free Plum Village app with ample meditations and talks. His renowned book Peace is Every Step is also a powerful place to begin.*

In the case of working with clients, we want to help them develop their capacity to observe themselves in sessions, because self-observation tends to increase one's window of tolerance for intensity and allow for more spaciousness and choice where there was once only reactivity, speed or syndromal responses. When clients are especially caught up in a lot of "story," it can be helpful to titrate witness consciousness into the experience, which can lead to more interoception and body-based processing.

How to facilitate witness consciousness with a client

Demonstrating your own witness consciousness:

"Wow, I notice that as you say that my mind speeds up with a bit of curiosity, but my body is still fairly grounded and neutral. I wonder what happens for you as you say that?"

Inviting them to observe their experience while it's happening, as opposed to only being swept up in it:

"Maybe simply observe what it's like for you to be in this moment right now…"

"I'm hearing a lot of fixation on the story right now. That's totally cool. And I also wonder…if you took a neutral observer position right now, and witnessed what it's like to be you in this moment…what would you see, sense or notice?"

"Wow, you've shared a lot. I'm wondering what it's like to be you right now."

Notice these examples all invite a neutral observation of the present moment.

Nurture Doable Aliveness and Connection

What do we do when our clients are in parasympathetic shut down (hypo), and nothing seems to be supporting their process? When toxic shame, unresolved grief, chronic pain, chronic illness, or avoidant attachment patterns are overwhelming our client's capacity to lean into connection, life, and aliveness?

Valiant resources can often support our clients under these conditions, especially celestial, ancestral, divine parentage or nature resources. But often, in these moments, our clients need an emphasis on no forced intervention. Rather, offering gentle, doable affirmation that they can be in the hypo state they're in, and still be cared about, loved, and connected to—without pressure to reciprocate those gestures—is just the medicine that's needed.

Nurturing doable aliveness and connection looks and sounds like:

Meeting the hypo without needing it to change:

"If we allow this pain/grief/shame to be here right now, without needing it to change…perhaps turning toward it with patience and care…what arises?"

Relating to the hypo with compassion, and inviting your client to do the same:

"I'm relating to your hypo right now with lots of care and patience, trust, and compassion. If you imagined your most compassionate self in relationship to the hypo part of you, what would you notice? How might that look, sense, sound, or feel just right here and now?"

Giving the hypo lots of time and space to exist, without any pressure for it to change sooner than it's ready:

"What if you had permission to sleep for 10,000 years, with no pressure to perform? And what if we offer present care to the super-tired part of you the whole time?"

Inviting in layers of support to help make the hypo feel a bit safer, held, seen, or warmed:

> "I hear you that you feel stuck in this depressive state. I wonder if instead of feeling like you have to shift out of it, we could invite something to show up to support you while you're in it. Does that feel doable? If so, what might show up?"

The trick with hypo is to allow it enough space, time, compassion, patience, and care for a natural thawing or melting to occur. Once thawing or melting naturally happen in their own time, some form of life-force often awakens. At times, that life-force is the next layer of emergency response: fight, flight, hypersocialization, hypervigilance. If that happens, it's often appropriate to gently invite valiant resources. Other times, renewal, hope, compassion, or a feeling of gratitude emerge after layers of hypo have resolved.

Contextualize systemic, historical, ancestral, or cultural trauma

Often, our clients will individualize their collective trauma spells. They'll blame and shame themselves for feeling Othered. They'll think it's their fault that they can't win the losing game of capitalism or cultivate security in a culture stripped of true "social security" (a term my dear friend Cândido Gadaga often uses to describe beloved community). They'll forget the larger systemic, historical, ancestral, or cultural story that they are a byproduct of, and in a very colonized way, internalize their every challenge as a personal flaw.

Resmaa Menakem developed a term called "HIPP Theory," which stands for four layers of trauma we can experience: historical, intergenerational, persistent institutional, and personal.[53] With this wider lens in mind, he says that "trauma decontextualized in a person looks like personality. Trauma decontextualized in

---

[53] *I highly recommend Resmaa Menakem's book,* My Grandmother's Hands, *for more in-depth guidance on working with collective trauma, specifically as it relates to race.*

a family looks like family traits. Trauma decontextualized in a people looks like culture." As such, it can be phenomenally healing for our clients to experience the re-contextualization of their collective traumas and the appropriate naming of their sources.

How you might speak to collective trauma in a session:

"I hear you saying you feel anxious whenever you're in a space of all cis- het-women; that it brings up a fear that you're not good enough and will never belong. I also hear you also saying that it feels like a personal confidence issue to you; that something's wrong with your self-esteem. It sounds a bit to me like you're feeling like this is all your fault, like you've done something wrong. But what if it's the *culture*, not you? What if it makes total sense how isolating that feels? Can we start with that possibility first?"

"I understand that you feel like if only you could improve your mindset your business would be in better shape. It makes sense that you feel frustrated with how easily you freeze in this arena, how overwhelmed and paralyzed you get. That's gotta be scary when you depend on the success of your business in order to pay your bills. And—I wonder if we might explore the possibility that you're trying to survive a culture that asks you to be disembodied and self-extracting, to always push and never rest…when you're still a human being with needs for seasons of creative production and seasons of rest and reflection. I wonder as I say that, what do you notice inside?"

Here's the thing that often happens in sessions when the focus moves from internalizing to externalizing the cost collective trauma spells: embodied resonance matched with cognitive dissonance. The body cries or sighs with great relief. Then the mind objects in fear. Because we are taught in capitalist white supremacy culture that without the ability to compete, dominate and win, we will be very, very unsafe. We have been wildly indoctrinated into a myth of individualism, so much so that even as it harms us, we stay loyal to it. Even as it starves us, we run back for crumbs.

Most of us in colonized culture, especially white people, have atrophied togetherness muscles. We think collaboration and pulling our resources means losing our individuality, creativity, or voice. We can hardly imagine a symphony of various instruments playing the same song in harmonic beauty. And so, in sessions with clients, this becomes the question. "But how? But with whom? But it's so scary, vulnerable, far out of reach."

My clients wail to me about this. I mean *wail*. And I nod. I get it. The imprint of extractive supremacy culture is strong. The momentum is roaring. The road home to the Blueprint is humbling, confusing, and disorienting. I've been on it for a decade. I still get lost in the world of "me."

I tell people to stay with the questions. To stay in the ache. To pray about it. To reach out and talk about how hard it is with friends of similar affinity groups. To do these things again and again as spells of re-sensitization. And then, to look for and say yes to small, doable ways they can begin inviting more embodiment, community, togetherness, and collaboration into their lives. How they can co-create spaces with others who belong to similar groups, bringing their gifts, and powers together for the greater good.

Chapter 12

The Four Cornerstones of Embodied Ethics

Call me naive, but this is what I believe: there is a Blueprint of ethics that is rooted in our *human desire to do right by one another*. We want to help, not harm each other; love, not hurt each other. We want to make decisions that are in service to the greatest good for all, both in short- and long-term ways. Plain and simple: we care about each other.

When you read those words, what comes up for you? Does your body exhale with relief? Do you cringe in disagreement or feel hypervigilant with doubt? All feelings are welcome.

Just because a Blueprint of ethics exists, doesn't mean it's always embodied—personally, professionally, culturally, or systemically.

However, it's important to begin the conversation of ethics anchored in the Blueprint, or else we run the risk of assuming that without rigid rules and regulations, our natural impulse is to do wrong by one another. I don't believe that's true.

While safety precautions and codes of ethics are helpful, important and necessary in the field of trauma resolution, I've found that the all-too-common reality is this: the rule books don't dictate behavior. Evolutionary development does.

The coach who has a funky relationship to money based on family of origin traumas (rooted in capitalism and patriarchy), might over-price and over-hype her offerings, then use shady sales techniques to enroll prospective clients, all without having a safe or effective offer. Whereas, the coach who's done a lot of healing work around exploitation and colonization, both personal and collective—who's come into her healthy Gatekeeper and Sacred Gardener—might offer things she's more qualified to offer with more right-fit prices and appropriate marketing techniques.

The coach who has his own unresolved need for emotional approval or validation might blur lines with clients and have unhealthy expressions of codependent dual relationships. Whereas, the coach who has a more secure Soul Seed and nuanced Gatekeeper, might be able to navigate an inter-sovereign dual relationship where mutual care is ever present, but during sessions, the focus remains on the client.

The guide who is still recovering from a harmful rupture with one of her own teachers might accidentally go on to employ the very hurt that was done to her. Or, paranoid about potentially causing harm, she might over-correct her behaviors, being too lenient with boundaries when and where they're needed. Whereas, the guide who is actively in a process of healing and growing from a past rupture will be able to discern, with Sage clarity, appropriate, mutually empowering relational dynamics with her students and clients.

The bad news is, whether we like it or not, even if we care a ton about our ethical impact on others, we all have blindspots, imprints, and edges that can lead to harmful behavior. The good news is, as we evolve, so too do our ethics. As we heal, our ethics heal with us.

As we evolve, so too do our ethics.

As we heal, our ethics heal with us.

I've heard of or known many teachers, healers, or practitioners who, upon being confronted for inappropriate or unethical behavior, turned to gaslighting, manipulation, and denial as self-defense. Those responses tell us more about that person's emotional and spiritual development, as well as their lacking nervous system resiliency around feedback and feelings of shame, than they do about their intention to cause harm to their student or client. Sadly, that doesn't excuse the added salt of dismissal to the wound they already caused. It worsens it.

With self-compassion as coaches and guides, as well as self-responsibility, we can feel remorse for our ethical ruptures or missteps, then let those mistakes become opportunities for maturation, growth, healing, and change.

My fundamental perspective that ethics and healing are a co-evolving dance is the basis of the Four Cornerstones of Embodied Ethics:

1. Personal and collective healing
2. Ongoing education and feedback
3. ConSensual Sales and Marketing
4. Intersovereign Interpersonal Agreements

Cornerstone 1: Personal and Collective Healing

One of the most important components of being a safe trauma resolution coach is continuing to do your own healing work. Remember the concept of resourcing? As a practitioner, how wide is your base of support—in terms of physiology, energy, spirituality, psychology, community, communion with land, elders, ancestors? How healthy is the field that your clients step into? The more robust your own field of health, the more you can navigate and even dance amidst complex situations with power, creativity and possibility.

Earlier in my career as a coach and guide, I had to be very strict with the rule of no dual relationships (as most ethical guides will suggest). I didn't have a wide enough base of sovereignty to make grounded negotiations with clients or be able to discern who was ready for those negotiations and who wasn't. Now, I still very rarely have dual relationships when it comes to long-term one-on-one trauma resolution containers. But, in some special cases I'll take extra time to do a thorough "feeler process" with people who I've known for a while, who have very developed self-awareness, self-responsibility, and interpersonal skills. We'll usually "couch" our personal relationship for the time of our professional work together and return to a more casual dynamic through a ritual process of completion around our professional dynamic. It's only through my own extensive Gatekeeper and Sage healing that I'm able to move through those tricky relational territories with grace, carefulness, and confidence.

Opinion: we don't have to embody some illusory standard of perfection as coaches, healers, or guides. Are you kidding? We got into this line of work because we were sensitive to pain and suffering. We will hurt, harm, mess up, and be a mess, even as professionals. Expecting perfection of ourselves only perpetuates extra shame and fear, elements that block true growth and change.

As we release expectations of perfection, we can commit with humility to our personal healing. We can face ourselves and our shortcomings in earnest and decide to keep growing anyway. We can remember that when we heal, we regenerate everything around us. So commit to yourself. Commit to your embodied and relational coherence. Commit to healing the deep stuff you've been too afraid to touch. Commit to healing internalized colonization, white supremacy, patriarchy, racism, homophobia, transphobia, ableism, classism, and more. Find others who want to do this healing, too, and stick together. Go into the mud until the miracle finds you. Your healing will become the good ground upon which you, your beloveds and your clients can rebloom.

Remember, your ethical capacities only stretch as far as your evolutionary development. As such, I thought I'd share a few examples of common mishaps I see or hear about in coach-client dynamics, and how development on the part of the coach could create greater safety for all.

Unsafe Speed

The coach doesn't give proper informed consent about the bigness or intensity of the work they facilitate, and the client is ill-prepared in their life outside of sessions to support the process they're about to dive into. The client perhaps isn't very resourced financially or relationally, and the depth they go into ends up posing a threat to their mental health, stability and capacity to function in their daily lives. The coach continues to insist that if they just keep pushing through, it will all get better. The client breaks down and ends up leaving the coaching container.

As the coach continues to do their own personal healing, they realize they have a tendency to push themselves past their own limits and beyond their true embodied and emotional capacity. The better the coach gets at honoring the natural rhythms, requirements and needs of their body, heart, and soul, the healthier their coaching containers become.

Romantic Rupture

The coach and client develop romantic feelings for one another. Instead of the coach directly addressing the matter and seeking to negotiate to find a safe and responsible way forward (perhaps giving a minimum of a six-month communication pause to unravel the existing power dynamic, then seeing where they would both like to go from there), they continue forward in a hurry trying to adjust the contract to include sexual or romantic dynamics, all the while, the client is still paying the coach. Or they break the contract all together, the coach offers a refund to the client, and they move right into a sexual and romantic relationship without any pause.

There's a level of shame hanging over both of their heads because they fear they're doing something wrong. The coach might feel as though they're taking advantage of their client. The client might feel as though they have to remain a secret to protect the coach's reputation. But they're also both excited by the thrill of the connection. Things continue to speed along, until eventually, the dynamic implodes. The coach feels tired of playing the "helper" even though they're no longer in that professional role, and the client feels constantly demeaned by the coach.

As the coach continues to commit to their personal healing, they start to see that this situation was indicative of a common theme for them: only feeling safe in intimacy when they're in obvious positions of power. As they begin to grow awareness and do healing around this theme, they feel remorse and regret that their own invulnerability led to a rupture on someone else's journey. While that previous client isn't open to repair, the coach becomes devoted to the process of practicing vulnerability in more areas of their lives. Their personal healing and their ethical capacities are co-evolving.

Triangle of Drama

The coach, with a history of feeling safe over-holding, buys into an undue pressure placed on practitioners to be saviors rather than facilitators. Before the coach knows it, their client is demanding extensive extra support, and the coach feels violated and victimized by their own client. The coach then withdraws under their client's pressure, and the client feels unseen, untended, and neglected by the coach who's now in the seat of perpetrator.[54]

This same client comes into the coaching relationship without their adult-self present, expecting, hoping, or anticipating that the coach will save, fix, or heal them (consciously or unconsciously). The client fails to take responsibility for their own healing, giving undue power to the coach. When the weight of the situation is too heavy for the coach to magically fix, the client becomes attacking, or some sort of dramatic experience happens (an injury, illness, or relational emergency) that puts more pressure on the coach to show up bigger. The coach, exhausted by the dynamic, and frozen in their own fear of failure, stops showing up to sessions, ghosting the client all together.

As the coach stays on the path of their personal healing, they begin to realize they have a common difficulty with others expecting them to hold too much. Their own developmental history of codependency makes it hard for them to own and communicate boundaries around their needs, limits, and what clients can expect from them in terms of availability. However, as they begin to embody more sovereignty, they also begin differentiating between their clients' feelings of powerlessness and their own responsibility as coach. They see their role as creator, coach, or challenger, rather than victim, savior, or perpetrator.[55] When their client tries to put them into one of the latter roles, they see if their client might witness the dynamic at hand and instead invite in their wiser self into the relational field to take some self-responsibility. The coach is able to stay present amidst the intensity because they've grown through their codependency.

Trying to be the Best

The level of trauma a client is bringing into the coaching container is more than what they revealed during the feeler call process (or more than they themselves were aware of) and their needs end up being beyond the scope-of-practice for the

[54] *Google Karpman's Triangle of Drama to read all about this lovely arrangement.*

[55] *The reverse roles of Karpman's Triangle of Drama.*

coach. The coach feels in over her head and doesn't know how to show up for the client, so she dreads their sessions, offers care from a faux window of tolerance (beyond her capacity) and burns out. Or does a crappy job with the client.

As the coach continues her healing process, she realizes she has shame around not being the best at everything. The more she accepts her natural likes and dislikes, strengths, and weaknesses, the more she's able to honor who her right-fit clients are and are not. She's also better able to name, without feelings of shame, when a client's needs are beyond her qualification, then safely refer out to a more right-fit practitioner. She becomes aware that having and owning her limitations with humble transparency is actually a greater form of service than trying to serve those she doesn't have capacity or qualification to serve.

Cultural Incompetency

The coach, a white woman, desiring to be inclusive, says that her practice is open to people with various backgrounds and identities. She has a client with intersecting identities that are more systemically Othered, and unconsciously says things that are harmful, gaslighting, and belittling to this client.

The client feels misunderstood and unsafe around topics such as race, sexuality, gender expression, ability, age, religion, class, body size, or nationality. The client then begins to either hypersocialize, appeasing their coach's cultural ineptness, or freeze, slowly backing away from the healing container all together. Maybe they leave the container without saying anything, not wanting to do the emotional labor of explaining that they feel unsafe in a space that was supposed to be healing for them. The coach doesn't quite understand what happened or why, and just chocks it up to the client having boat loads of "resistance" and "unresolved anger," all the while badgering them to complete their payment plan.

As the coach continues unlearning around systems of oppression, she realizes she was an unsafe space for her previous client. Wracked with guilt, she writes a long apology email to said client asking for forgiveness. The client feels overwhelmed by the email that still centers the coach's experience, and replies sharing that the apology feels harmful. The coach gets defensive and offended.

Again, the coach continues her unlearning process and realizes the harm she caused in her apology email. She sends the previous client a refund for the work they did together, and lets them know she's continuing her unlearning process and needs no response in return. At this point, she starts to understand that she's not yet prepared to serve those with identities more systemically Othered than she. Instead, she has on her website a list of coaches and guides that work specifically with various affinity groups and passes business opportunities to those who would be a more safe fit for said prospective clients, while she continues to heal and unlearn around systems of oppression.

In time, she grows her cultural competency and increases her capacity to work with a diversity of clients. While she still has referrals on her website, she's also more transparent about where she is in her unlearning process, offering prospective clients an opportunity to opt in or out from her care with more information.

Phew. As you can see, there are many ways that interpersonal dynamics can get tricky—quick. And, as coaches, the more we are engaged in a holistic growth and healing process, the more likely we are to catch these dynamics before they go too far or prevent them from happening in the first place.

Perhaps take a pause and notice how your body's doing after reading those examples. It's possible that you've experienced one or more of those dynamics, as either coach or client. Maybe allow some time for a wave of experience to reveal itself and move through you. A level of self-forgiveness might be supportive in this moment, as well. Not to condone or bypass less-than-ideal decisions, but to offer some compassion toward your humanity. Compassion loosens the freeze of toxic shame and makes space for us to consider consequences level-headedly and change behavior accordingly.

Cornerstone 2: Ongoing Education and Feedback

In my experience, the healthiest relationships, professional or personal, are the ones in which all parties involved are devoted to learning and growing, as well as receiving feedback from their counterpart about how the relationship is going.

When we as coaches, teachers, and guides remain active and curious students, not only do we keep our tools up-to-date, but we also put ourselves into a state of receptivity for change, evolution, and progress. Learning is like an informal feedback loop, where we're evaluating what we already know next to new experiences, possibilities, and perspectives, and in turn, become fuller, vaster, and deeper. Our widened expanse becomes the fertile ground we cultivate for others.

When we neglect to learn new things or close to the process of being changed, our work can take on a stale rigidity. We can become creatures of habit more than creatures of discovery, and within our rote motions, lose the presence, passion, and suppleness of a truly great guide. But when we let new life enter us, every experience of showing up to our students or clients becomes animated with our own renewed zest for learning.

As you've gathered by now, so much of what works for post-traumatic growth is far different than cultural memes about pushing through or "no pain, no gain." The more you learn about and begin to embody nervous system transformation and regulation, the safer you'll become for your clients. The more you heal your relationship to systems of oppression, the more we can all get free together, as Desiree Adaway says.

Every year, I make an educational wish list. I write down at least 30 books I'd like to read, documentaries I'd like to watch, teachers I'd like to learn from, and topics I'd like to dive into. I never learn as much as I want to, but I give myself a big, giant permission slip to be insatiably curious about life, love, the earth, and others.

Feedback is an important form of education. When you take the pulse of how your service is landing for your students or clients, both part-way through the process as well as at the end, you get to learn about how your craft is being received, what's marvelous about your medicine, and what could become more refined.

The feedback I ask for varies, based on the container being held, but the questions generally include the following themes:

- What's going really well, blowing your mind or supporting you in super-powerful ways?

- What could be better organized, structured, or delivered so you can receive the medicine of this container more fully?
- What's not working or needs attention?
- What's cultivating a feeling of empowered safety, and what could help create a safer and braver space?
- How's the speed?
- How's the depth / intensity level?
- Anything that needs to be cleared or named on the interpersonal plane?
- What's feeling most valuable? What's your favorite part?
- What's your least favorite part?
- Would you like to leave a testimonial? If so, here are some guiding questions: What were you experiencing prior to this container that had you sign up? How have you changed inside this container? What about the container made those changes possible? Who would you recommend this container to? Anything else you'd love to share?

It's important to reassure people that your aim in asking for feedback is learning and growth, and you are welcoming of constructive suggestions or revelation of blindspots. If you're running a group or educational experience, you may wish to allow the feedback to be anonymous so that students or participants feel freer to share openly.

Cornerstone 3: ConSensual Sales and Marketing

If one of the main objectives in post-traumatic growth is reblooming sovereign choice, I want that energy present from the very first interactions I have with my prospective students and clients. Enter: ConSensual Sales and Marketing. Sales and marketing rooted in transparency, honest qualifications, authentic passion, and clear options.

Grievously, the coaching industry is not run this way. Things like withholding the prices of your services, changing someone's state in a sales call then making them offers they can only receive if they sign up with their credit card right then and there, and over-promising then under-delivering results, are all common practices.

We can do better. Here's how.

ConSensual Sales

My ConSensual Sales process is rooted in two primary ethos: harm reduction and authentic resonance. The Whole Holy Point of ConSensual Sales is for both coach and client to experience a sense of clear, empowered choice…and then to make a decision about working together, or not, in coherence with their whole-bodied, whole-hearted truth. This is the path that I've found offers the greatest chance for safe, enjoyable healing and transformation.

Scope-of-practice, resonance, time, energy, and money—all of these things are essential to explore and feel out before relationships of intense interpersonal healing should form. When you begin a healing relationship on the grounds of compassionate, safety-oriented transparency, that relationship can do what it's intended to do: empower the person who's come for healing to make informed choices about what's best for them. Empower the coach or guide to do the same.

Non-ConSensual Sales, on the other hand, is when either coach or client withholds information about what they need for the therapeutic relationship to be safe, ideal, and doable. When a coach begins a healing relationship on the grounds of scarcity, manipulation, coercion, or withholding of the full truth as a way to amplify graspy desire from the client, the container will always have those energetics coloring the space. The client will be more likely to feel disempowered and dependent on the coach's recognition, approval, or direction.

Going through a ConSensual Sales process is often healing in and of itself for both coach and client. Even if the coach and prospective client don't end up being a match to work together, you imprint each other with reverence and respect for the truth. Hallelujah.

As the coach, a prerequisite to the ConSensual Sales process is understanding and honoring your current scope-of-practice based on your training, experience, and passion. In order to make intersovereign negotiations, you as the sovereign

Gatekeeper of your business need to know your honest *yeses* and *nos*. So to begin, let's look at a list of topics that prospective clients might bring your way. I find it helpful to assess these topics through the lens of three questions that help reduce harm and amplify authentic resonance:

Is it *safe* for me to work with this topic?

Is it *ideal* for me to work with this topic?

Is it *doable* for me to work with this topic?

- **Safe** is about scope-of-practice. Do you have education or ample experience with this topic?
- **Ideal** is about resonance and joy. Do you like working with the topic? Does it excite you or fuel your passion?
- **Doable** is about resources. Can you sustain working with that topic? Does it regenerate and feed you? Is it within your window of tolerance to be with the topic?

It's critical to consider the following topics a client might be seeking support around, and ask yourself with conservative judgment: Can I safely work with this challenge? Have I been properly trained? Am I self-regulated enough around the topic? Would it be ideal and enjoyable for me to work with this challenge? Would it be sustainable for me to work with this topic over time?

I suggest putting a check mark next to each topic that feels "safe," "ideal," and "doable." The topics which have three check marks are the topics you're clear to promote, narrow in on, and advertise that you work with. The topics that have less than three check marks, are less ideal and potentially unethical for you.

Your scope-of-practice changes and develops as you do, so this isn't a set in stone litmus test. It flexes over time. Being honest about your capacities and desires as a practitioner is essential to running an ethical, safe practice for everyone—yourself included.

Scope of Practice List

Neglect / worthiness / mattering

Exploitation / boundaries / boundary repairs

Shame / repression / whole-self expression

Identity ownership

Sensual expression

Manipulation / control / self-trust

Devotional calling

Chronic pain

Genital pain

Pleasure

Orgasm

Couples support

Non-monogamy

Sex after trauma

Erotic blueprints

Kink

Co-dependence

Anxious attachment

Avoidant attachment

Depression

Childhood molestation

Rape

Financial abuse

Complex developmental trauma

Narcissistic abuse

Religious trauma

Cult abuse

Disability

Violence / Empowered safety

Isolation / intimate belonging

Birth trauma

Sexual orientation

Gender identity

Race-based trauma

Grief

Death

Sex Addiction

Love Addiction

Substance Addiction

Porn Addiction

Disordered eating

Body image

Chronic illness

Inherited trauma

Ancestral reconnection

Spirituality

Professional development

Business coaching

Life work, purpose, legacy

Money

Suicidality

Bipolar

OCD

Sex work

Anxiety

Community-building

Colonization / decolonization

Once you've done the internal work of getting clear around your safe, ideal, and doable scope-of-practice, you can use your internal coherence to fuel your marketing. Share, write about, teach on, and cater to the topics that regenerate you the most. When people show up to work with you, they'll know what drew them in and you'll be that much closer to working with right-fit clients.

ConSensual Sales Calls

Especially when working in long-term post-traumatic growth containers of any kind, one-on-one, educational, or group, I highly suggest having helpful barriers of entry like applications and "feeler calls." This, again, is for the sake of both harm-reduction and resonance amplification.

You might know what topics are most safe, ideal, and doable for *you* to work with, but for your healing containers to be most effective, you want to also check with prospective clients to see if the work you're offering is safe, ideal and doable for *them*.

During my feeler calls, I share with total transparency that the goal is for us to both feel into three big things:

Is it *safe* for us to work together?
Is it *ideal* for us to work together?
Is it *doable* for us to work together?

In the context of the feeler call…

- **Safe** is about scope-of-practice. Are their needs and my skills, education, and experience compatible?
- **Ideal** is about chemistry. Do we like each other? Vibe? Have an inherent feeling of trust, or a sense that trust can grow?
- **Doable** is about resources. Is this the right moment for them to dive into this deep work? Are they resourced with supportive friends or family, enough cash, enough time? If our finances aren't a perfect fit, is it doable for me to offer sliding scale services or a scholarship?

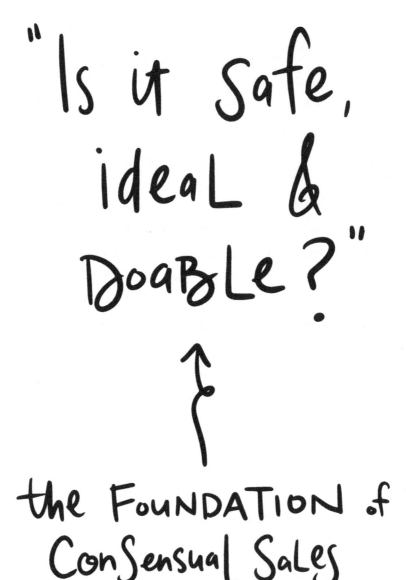

"Is it safe, ideaL & DoaBLe?"

the FoUNDATiON of ConSensual Sales

As a guide, encouraging our prospective clients to ask themselves these questions invites them to be more self-aware, personally responsible, and resourced in their decision. Asking ourselves these questions gives us the opportunity to feel into whether the prospective client is within our scope-of-practice, someone we feel like we can really enjoy showing up for, and someone we feel energized by the possibility of working with.

The deepest healing we can experience happens in the same place that we've experienced the deepest hurt—relationship. One way we can take a true stand for healing relationships is by only working with people who we feel confident we can support and are passionate about supporting. On the other hand, one way we can perpetuate relational hurt, is by being inauthentic and incoherent around who we work with—offering our services with half-heartedness. It's okay if you don't feel drawn to serve everyone. The greatest gift you can offer anyone is honesty. Have the courage to say *no*, to let some people go, to release them to others who can meet them with joy and passion.

If you'd like a free 2-hour class all about ConSensual Sales, head to rebloomtogether.com/sales. Learn the in-depth process and hear answers to questions about things like cost objections, pricing, and how to let a prospective client know if it's not a good fit to work together.

ConSensual Marketing

Although we complicate it with algorithms, ads, and fancy copy, the truth is, marketing is simple. Marketing is the art of revealing your best medicine to the world. That art can be crafted through the transmission of your embodiment, through teaching, through storytelling, through making direct invitations, through offering discounts or sales, through advertising or through word-of-mouth referrals. Each person's marketing style will differ. But regardless of your unique way, and contrary to popular practice, marketing can be both fun and ethical. It is absolutely possible to fold consent and honor into every facet of your marketing, enjoy yourself, and make great money.

Wanna know how? Here are some important questions to help you get to that place of abundant coherence:

- Is your marketing open, non-attached, clear, and transparent? Or is it sneaky, scarcity-creating, discreet, vague, or full of hype without depth of practice?
- If there are things that feel a bit masked in your marketing, what could you do to bring more transparency forward?
- Do you imagine that your prospective clients feel empowered or disempowered reading your sales page? Do you sense that they feel needy,

nervous, and desperate when scanning through your offers, or discerning and in-choice? Comfortable or uncomfortable?

- Do your sales pages and marketing efforts share all the information your prospective clients might need in order to feel rooted in their own capacity to choose what's best for them? If not, what needs to be added or taken out?

- Does your marketing imply that others need you and your work in order to be okay? Does it insinuate a level of brokenness on the part of the client, and all-knowingness on the part of you, the "expert?" If so, how might you update your language to reflect your prospective client's wholeness?

The energetics you create with your website, sales pages, social media, and marketing all trickle into your coaching relationships. What's the energy you want to infuse your coach-client relationships with? Does your marketing represent that energy? You get to be a stand for the relational energetics you want to see in the world. Even if you've been conditioned into extractive, manipulative, or transactional ways of earning and securing income, with a brave heart and willingness to self-examine and pivot, your conditioning can change.

Cornerstone 4: Intersovereign Interpersonal Agreements [56]

With the first three cornerstones in place, the fourth cornerstone of intersovereign interpersonal agreements stands a much better chance at success. Because you've done enough of your inner-work to know what you're awesome at and where your blindspots or triggers are. Because you've continued to grow and learn professionally, both in formal and interpersonal ways. Because you've accurately portrayed your capacities and limits in your marketing and sales. Because you've had honest conversations with prospective clients to ensure you're a good fit for each other. All of this inner-work creates healthy boundaries of entry into your professional sphere, making it so whoever passes through will most

---

[56] *This process was inspired by a similar process developed and shared with me by Tada Hozumi around relational community agreements.*

likely be thoroughly aligned. Now it's just about fulfilling on that alignment with professionalism and care.

The truth is every relationship is unique. I believe it's not only worth the time but actually a core healing experience in many cases to negotiate intersovereign interpersonal agreements with our one-on-one clients, as well as groups. This is a newer practice I've adopted, and I highly recommend it. I've found that many of my clients who've gone through interpersonal boundary violations or toxic ruptures in their past, experience profound healing by engaging this process. They feel it's almost worth the cost of admission off the bat. I've also found that in the relationships where we take the time to make intersovereign, interpersonal agreements, there's more depth and safety in the relational field.

Below are ten recommended intersovereign interpersonal agreements. Along with each, there are questions for you and your client to both consider, perhaps in a session, or perhaps over email (and then discussed or reviewed in a session). The combination of your shared answers to these inquiries become your nuanced and personalized code of ethics with one another.

I don't go through an in-depth process about each agreement with every client. That would take a very long time! Instead, I send the agreements and questions my client's way and ask which ones might feel sticky for them, and which they may wish to talk about. If, in our feeler call, some themes flagged for me as potential challenges for my client, I'll propose that we spend some time parsing through a few related agreements.

Finally, it feels important for you to know that these agreements are born from my mistakes, my heartaches, and my regrets, both as a coach and a client, a student and a teacher, an employer and an employee. It's okay to make mistakes. It's okay to have regrets. It's never too late to start over, try again, or do better.

Agreement 1: We are all naturally creative, resourceful, and whole.

In *Co-Active Coaching* by Karen and Henry Kimsey-House, the book that helped define the field of professional coaching, they describe co-active coaching as *a relationship between two equals for the purpose of meeting the client's needs.* They go on to write:

The primary building block for all co-active coaching is this: Clients have the answers or they can find the answers. From the co-active coach's point of view, nothing is wrong or broken, and there is no need to fix the client. The coach does not deliver answers; the coach asks questions and invites discovery.

Sometimes clients don't think they have the answers. They'd rather believe someone else–an expert–has the answers for them, which can lead to a natural desire to buy the answers in a packaged program rather than doing the work that needs to be done to find their own solutions.

In my experience, many ethical dilemmas occur between coach and client when this fundamental co-active principle that all humans are naturally resourceful, creative, and whole is violated, and games of saviorship, victim, and perpetrator play out.

Even if you're using the ReBloom model as a framework to help offer a map and context to your clients' post-traumatic growth journey, it's essential that foundationally, you trust their Blueprint, their soul's unique path and timeline, their wisdom and their intrinsic wellness, in order for the dynamic to remain rooted in empowering intersovereignty.

Questions to consider:

- When I'm embodying my best version of creativity, resourcefulness or wholeness, how does it look, sound, or feel? What do I tell myself? What do I believe about myself and the world?
- How does it look, sound, or feel when I fall out of trust with my creativity, resourcefulness, or wholeness? What do I tell myself, then? What do I believe about myself in that state? What helps me re-grow a sense of self-trust?
- Are there times when I don't trust in others creativity, resourcefulness, or wholeness? If so, when does that tend to show up? What moves,

mindsets or practices help me return to a state of holding others as creative, resourceful, and whole?

Agreement 2: We are all adults here.

For a coach-client relationship to be safe, in the realm of trauma resolution especially, both parties must show up with a full commitment to bringing their most adult-self to the dynamic.

It's, of course, expected that younger, triggered or traumatized parts will show up for the client. But toxic codependency can happen in healing relationships when the client expects that their coach will save, hold or fix their younger self for them, rather than help them to bring their own presence, love, and power to that hurting part.

Of course, the coach is present to help facilitate a return to Blueprint, but they are not solely responsible for that occurring. This is an important distinction for both coach and client to hold together in order to keep the healing container empowering for the client.

Questions to consider:

- What are some ways we might be able to tell if your inner-child or trauma response is taking over? (Taking over either your healing process, or our client-coach dynamic?)
- In the case that happens, what can you do to help call your inner-adult back into the space? What tried and true methods do you know for creating stabilization and resource in your body? How about ways you tend to best be able to access your inner-wisdom or most loving, powerful self?
- In the case that happens, what can I do to help you call your inner-adult back into the space? To invite your stabilization, resource, inner-wisdom, and presence?

Agreement 3: Coach honors the privacy, confidentiality and anonymity of the client.

Especially with the show-all, tell-all nature that the digital age often embodies, it's important that clients know they are coming to a safe, private, confidential space. I tell all my clients beginning on our feeler calls that our conversations are between us and us alone. I share that the only instance where I might talk about our work together is in the case that I'm seeking counsel or support from a mentor, in which case I'd keep their identity fully confidential.

Also, because I'm a teacher and writer, I let my clients know that if ever I were to want to share a piece of their story for educational purposes, I would do so in a way that completely shifts any identifying factors about them, so much so that they might not even know I was sharing or writing about them. In the case that I want to tell a less anonymous story, I would ask explicit permission, give them room to name any piece they don't want shared, show them what I've written before it's published, and invite lots of space for their *no*. (Both of these things, by the way, I've been very careful to do throughout this book.)

Just to be clear: confidential means that what someone shares with you in session, stays in session. Anonymous means you don't reveal who your clients are to others. Your clients can share that they're working with you if they'd like, but that's their discretion to share, not yours.

Questions to consider:

- What pieces of your privacy feel very important to you that I honor?
- May I share about things I learned as a coach while working with you (perhaps in writing via a newsletter, social media, or book, or perhaps verbally though my teaching to other coaches in training), if I keep your identity anonymous? If so, would you like for me to let you know beforehand?
- In the case of in-person workshops or trainings: Do you consent to having your photo taken? How about possibly being used in future marketing material?

- In the case that you reveal that you're considering harming yourself, are there people you'd like me to reach out to?
- If I'm concerned that you will hurt yourself or another, I retain the right to notify proper authorities. Do you consent to that?

Agreement 4: Coach and client seek to co-create clarity around the limits and bounds of the working relationship, then honor those agreements.

Container structure and predictability is an important part of a safe therapeutic relationship. When boundaries are murky, insecure attachment often forms in the relational field. Unclear expectations, standards, and norms can lead to fear, flakiness, or resentment for either coach or client. But when the lines of the relationship are clear, and the norms are firmly set, both parties can relax into the known container.

Questions to consider:

- How does the coach have clients schedule their sessions? All up front, or as they go? If the client prefers the opposite way, is the coach okay with flexing to their preference, or is the coach's scheduling process firmer?
- What kind of session cancellation or rescheduling process does the coach offer? What's okay and not okay?
- What's important to the coach about timeliness? Is there a certain grace-period for being late for a session before the session is canceled? (10 minutes, for example.)
- In the case of a client not showing up to a session without notice or communication, do they get to rebook that session, or are they charged for sessions they miss without notice?
- How does billing work? Before or after sessions? At the beginning of a month, prior to services offered, or at the end of a month, after services have been offered?
- What happens if invoices are unpaid?
- What turn-around time with emails or contact outside of sessions does

the coach offer? Is this supportive enough to the client? If the client needs more outside-of-session support, is that something the coach is open to negotiating? Does the coach need anything from the client in order for that increased care to be okay to them?

- More simply stated, what out-of-session communication is the coach available for or not available for?
- How does the coach handle refunds in the case of services paid for but not delivered?
- Under what circumstances are refunds offered and not offered?
- After our coaching container is over, can we be friends?
- Can we be friends *during* our coaching container?

Note: the coach can have non-negotiable standards around any of the above topics. In the case that you create standards for your practice (as many healing professionals will choose to do, myself included), it's best to have those standards communicated in writing from the beginning in an initial contract.

Agreement 5: In the case of entering into a dual relationship (where perhaps you are currently friends, family, or co-workers of some kind, and will now also be in a coaching container) coach and client agree to powerfully prepare for this new therapeutic context, check in about it as they go, and make and uphold shared agreements.

More traditional therapeutic models will steer you away from having any kind of dual personal-professional healing relationships. I, myself, tend toward that standard, especially with one-on-one trauma resolution support. However, as my work expands to include a lot of teaching and groups, I'm finding dual relationships to be more common.

The following questions can be helpful for navigating dual relationships regarding coach-client, student-teacher, as well as boss-employee. It's suggested that both parties answer all the questions and have a generally settled, positive, and stable feeling inside before deciding to move into the dual relationship.

Questions to consider:

- What fears or concerns might you have about entering into a dual relationship?
- What hopes and desires might you have about working together professionally?
- What feels important to protect or preserve in our personal relationship, and how might we work to do that?
- Power dynamics can often show up in coach-client, student-teacher, boss-employee relationships, even when both parties intend to focus on everyone's innate creativity, resourcefulness, and wholeness. What are your tendencies around power dynamics that it might help for us to be aware of? How do you want to check yourself if you find yourself falling into those dynamics?
- How often do you think we should check in about how the dual relationship is going? What questions feel important for us to check in around? Can we put those conversations on the calendar, so we don't lose track of them?

Agreement 6: Romance and sexuality are not part of this professional coach-client dynamic. In the case that romantic or sexual feelings begin developing on either or both sides, we will name the dynamic and take appropriate next-steps to work with what's arising.

Working in the incredibly intimate landscape of the soul and nervous system can sometimes bring up feelings of romantic love or sexual desire. This is a normal-enough occurrence that we must un-shame its existence, both for the coach and the client. However, it's also something to be careful, responsible, and mindful about.

Things can get deep, intense and messy in the world of trauma resolution. Mixing sex and romance into the pot, when the container didn't originally include it,[57] often blurs and complicates already tricky territory.

---

[57] *Some containers, like sexological bodywork, sexual surrogates or tantric healing, include genital touch, sex and/or romance in the healing dynamic from the beginning. For those containers, an even more thorough ethical contract should be co-created from the onset of the work.*

It's standard practice across therapeutic models to wait six months to three years after a professional healing container has ended to then consider romantic or sexual relationships. This amount of time can help assuage pre-existing power dynamics and give the opportunity for coach and client to meet on even ground.

But what happens if feelings develop and the therapeutic container is incomplete? What happens if one person has feelings and the other doesn't?

Romantic or sexual ruptures in professional settings occur most when there's added shame or absolute thinking that insists it's *wrong* for feelings to develop. The truth is, we're all still humans here. Feelings happen, despite our attempts at self-persuading otherwise. As such, it matters that there's space for conversations to be had in the case that attraction does arise.

I'll also say this: if you sense that you have a crush on a prospective client, prospective student, prospective coach, or prospective teacher, consider naming the crush, and asking that person out on a date, instead of hiring them or letting them hire you. The same applies to the reverse scenario: if you're trying to date someone who you really need to hire or have hire you, can you name that, and course correct?

Questions to consider:

- In the case that one of us develops sexual or romantic feelings for the other, what communication standards feel important for us to have in place?
- What mentors or trusted elders might we seek outside counsel from if need be?
- What non-negotiable lines do we both wish to hold for our container?
- If we decide to end our therapeutic relationship due to romantic or sexual attractions, what process do we want to go through to decide what happens next?

Note: It's likely that thinking through these questions for yourself as the coach can help avoid the situation from happening at all, which is my goal for you in sharing them. If you answer the above questions and get a nervous sense inside, it's likely because you or they already have a crush. Skip the professional container. Ask each other out.

Agreement 7: Coach and client are both open to feedback about how the coaching container is going, and coach specifically solicits feedback and reviews progress throughout the container.

Feedback! It's how we grow. It's how we improve. It's how we know how we're doing. Creating rituals and rhythms around feedback is highly suggested, in both one-on-one containers, classes, and groups. Additionally, making yourself a safe and inviting professional for clients, students, and employees to share their true experience of your work is an important part of the healing process. On the other hand, being closed to feedback or not soliciting it is a huge missed opportunity for you to grow and become your most integrous leader.

Questions to consider:

- What kinds of agreements around feedback do we want to set with one another? (That feedback is always encouraged and welcome, for instance? How we each best receive feedback, emotionally speaking?)
- What's the standard medium and process for giving feedback?
- If something is feeling off or wonky in our working relationship, how would we like to let each other know?
- When things are going really well, how would we like to let each other know?
- How would we like to track progress and how often?
- If there's feedback one of us is nervous to share, what could be supportive?

Agreement 8: In the case of rupture, we will seek repair. We are committed to co-creating a process to make repair more doable.

Let me say something I think needs to be said a whole lot more in the coaching world: ruptures are normal. It's not fun or pretty, but it's true. Good people go through traumatic ruptures. Ethical people make mistakes that others can't forgive. Things fall apart and fall away.

Yes, as coaches, educators, and guides in the sensitive field of trauma resolution, we want to do our best to reduce harm and increase healing. And still. When people come to you to heal their deepest relational difficulties, it's not uncommon that those deep relational difficulties will show up in your interpersonal space. It's also not uncommon that someone's unresolved shit will trigger yours (more on that soon).

So first of all, grace. We must give ourselves grace for being brave enough to say healing is possible, and we will do our best to be part of it. Second of all? Preparation. I regret being ill-prepared for rupture. Not because it's been common in my career. But because when it *has* happened, it's been pretty horrible for everyone involved.

When we co-create a preemptive process around rupture and repair toward the beginning of our healing relationship, in the case that things do go south, you have a plan to fall back on. It's also important to note that through the process of creating potential rupture and repair agreements, you might realize you have different approaches and don't feel safe proceeding together. How wonderful to find that out *before* difficulty arises, not after!

Questions to consider:

- What values feel important to honor in the case of rupture?
- What agreements do we want to make in the case that a rupture does occur?
- What moves could we both make individually to help access our most adult selves in the case of interpersonal difficulty or rupture?
- What outside support could we call on, if need be?
- What dynamics or situations are especially scary, triggering, or activating for us, and what ways do we agree to take care of ourselves in those situations, as well as what requests do we have of one another?
- What type of rupture are you most afraid of experiencing? Why? What feels important for me to know?
- What positive repair experiences have you had? What was present in those situations that made the experience effective or resolving?
- Are there any rupture experiences that you would not be willing to repair? In other words, do you have non-negotiable trust-breakers that feel important to share?

We can't always know what our deal-breakers are before they happen. These questions aren't fool proof, but they can help pave the way for safer and more effective repair possibilities, where there was once only shame, exile, or banishment.

Agreement 9: Coach and client create a process for ending the working relationship in the case that either party no longer feels it's fit to continue with one another.

Whether it's because the work no longer feels like it's effective for the client, a rupture happens, or the coach isn't feeling that the healing relationship is healthy or regenerative, it's important to remember that being in a consensual, wholehearted coaching dynamic is crucial for both parties. Everyone has the right to end things.

That said, if you're the coach and you end the professional relationship early, it can be quite hard on the client. This is why it's recommended to go through a thorough feeler call process with prospective clients and work on growing your sovereignty muscles, ensuring that you only work with people who are deeply aligned.

Questions to consider:

- What are some of your deal breakers—things that, if they happened, you'd feel the need to end our working relationship?
- What would feel important for us to do before deciding to end our working relationship?
- What standards of communication would feel important to you, in the case that our working relationship was coming to a close?
- What kind of completion process would you desire?

Note: if someone has attachment wounds, co-creating a completion process and planning in advance what that will look like and when it will occur is also highly recommended. Even anticipated endings that happen without rupture can be challenging for clients. (For example, a contract has completed, and you don't have space to renew it.) If you know your client struggles with attachment, making arrangements for a ceremonial completion process can be quite supportive.

Agreement 10: Coach and client talk about the client's intersecting identities, and coach seeks continued ongoing cultural competency about said identities.

Your client will only receive healing for the parts of their identities that feel safe in your container. As such, it's important to learn about and understand your client's intersecting identities; first, to determine if you're even a good fit to hold space for them, and second, to serve them holistically.

Questions to consider:

With each of these initial questions, please feel free to share both how you identify, as well as how your identity impacts you as you move through the world.[58]

- What feels important for me to understand about your sexual orientation, perhaps in terms of who you're attracted to or your style of relating (monogamy/non-monogamy)?
- What feels important for me to understand about your gender or gender expression?
- What feels important for me to understand about your race or ethnicity?
- What feels important for me to understand about your class?
- What feels important for me to understand about your religion or spirituality?
- What feels important for me to understand about your abilities or disabilities?
- What feels important for me to understand about your nationality, immigration status, history, or language?
- What feels important for me to understand about your body or health?
- What feels important for me to understand about your age?

---

[58] *These identity questions are developed from the Adaway Group's Inner Circle identity wheel learned via their excellent unlearning program called Whiteness at Work. I highly recommend learning from them at adawaygroup.com.*

Then:

- What feels important to you in terms of how I relate to the parts of your identity that differ from mine?
- What would make you feel most safe, seen and welcomed in this container?
- Are there specific things you've experienced in past containers that felt harmful or hard for you that you'd like for me to not say or do? Please feel free to share them here.

Transference and Countertransference

My vernacular definition of transference is: when a client's projecting their shit onto you because you remind them of an important past relationship, or they have a strong need to heal a previous interpersonal dynamic.

My vernacular definition of countertransference is: when the projections from your client trigger your own shit, and you're less able to serve them in a centered, regulated, unbiased, or compassionate way.

Sound familiar?

Client transference can be both negative and positive. And, in both cases, transference can trigger countertransference inside the coach that muddies the healing container.

Let's take a peek at some examples:

- Your client has a history of abandonment, so they keep implying that you're going to leave them. You happen to have a history of being abandoned as well, so you're paranoid about letting them down. Thus, you over-serve as a way of protecting yourself and your client from the pain of abandonment.
- Your client has a history of being rejected by the "cool girls." In her mind, you *are* a "cool girl" who accepts and celebrates her. She projects a need to be liked by you. You have a history of being clung to by a close family member, and your clients' need to be liked by you triggers avoidant behavior on your behalf, only deepening her pattern of rejection.
- Your client has a crush on you because you give them everything they ever

wanted in terms of attention, care, and curiosity. You notice their crush, and it triggers your own need to be desired and validated. You develop a dynamic wherein their affection for you is feeding you—and you secretly fish for their compliments instead of keeping the focus on helping them identify and receive their needs outside your coaching container.

- Your client has a history of feeling like they never get the right kind of attention. They transfer this pattern onto you with continual complaints that you're not giving them what they need. You're triggered by criticism and have low self-esteem about your professional merit due to your own history of being told by your father that you're stupid. Instead of bringing to your client's awareness that they are transferring their pattern onto you...instead of naming the ways you *are* showing up with care, as well as helping them see and shift their pattern, you over-strive to prove your worth and feel continually anxious inside the dynamic.

- Your client has a history of being unable to access their anger. This activates your own fear of feeling powerless, and as such, you step in *for* them, indulging excessively in your own outrage over *their* situation. With your anger taking up all the space, they don't get a chance to access their own aggression, and it continues their pattern around repressed fire. (On the other hand, a gentle but firm, "that was not okay," on the coach's part would not be excessive indulgence in your own emotions, but rather, affirmative reassurance around their right to feel angry.)

There's nothing *bad* or *wrong* about transference and countertransference happening. They're normal human dynamics. Your own versions of them *will* take place—both as client and as coach. The important part is to address them. Because if left unaddressed, they can get out of hand.

There are two central ways to mitigate transference and countertransference:

1. Knowing the smell of your own shit.
2. Transparency.

Knowing the smell of your own shit:

The more you stay engaged in your own personal development journey and can name, identify, and continue to heal the things that are challenging for you— the more you'll be able to spot when someone's stuff is triggering your own, versus—when their stuff is just *their stuff*.

For example, if you as a practitioner know you've got issues around your parents not approving of you, but you've done a lot of work to cultivate a sense of self-approval, when your client projects onto you that you're not being supportive or nourishing enough about their decisions, you'll stay neutral and compassionate, then name the dynamic instead of getting unconsciously swept into it.

Which brings us to transparency:

Naming the dynamic with grace and neutrality is the best way forward, as often as possible. For example, to continue with the approval dynamic above, you might say:

"It sounds like you've got a strong need for approval. Does that land? If so…perhaps we can get curious about where that came from? I do, in fact, support you, and, it's feeling like no matter how much I name and demonstrate my support, it's not quite enough."

Or, if you're aware that the dynamic is triggering you and creating unhelpful countertransference that you can't self-regulate around, you might say:

"It sounds like you've got a strong need for approval from me. To be honest, working with this dynamic is challenging me right now. It's rubbing up against some of my own stuff and making it hard for me to support you in a regulated way. I wonder if we can both take a pause to journal about how we might be projecting past wounds, challenges or relational dynamics onto each other, then regroup with a more grounded focus on how this pattern can transform for you."

If you're working with someone who's willing to take responsibility for their projections, this kind transparency, mixed with an invitation to pause and self-reflect, often quickly stabilizes shaky, interpersonal ground. Amidst this process, even though you're sharing some transparency about your own experience, it's important to keep the focus on the client rather than going into details about yourself. You've shared about your internal experience not for your own sake, but for the sake of your client and their transformation, which requires a clean relational field between the two of you.

Once you're both more neutral, redirect the focus to what your client is learning or noticing. Often, big breakthroughs can happen from these kinds of stumbling blocks because they're real relational dynamics that have enough similarities to your client's past patterns. If you can find ways to re-regulate from your countertransference, while also staying human in the dynamic, rather than turning into a robot coach, true relational healing can occur for your client, and *bonus points!*—also probably for you.

Integrity, Impeccability and Inevitable Imperfection

I don't have a perfect track record as a coach or a client. I've made mistakes in my practice, as well as in my personal life. I've thought I was qualified to work with certain difficulties, then realized six sessions in that I wasn't, when things were getting deeper and darker than my skills could meet. I've developed romantic feelings across professional lines—both as a client and a practitioner. In the beginning of my career with trauma, I didn't realize how intense things could get, and I overestimated (and over-promised) my professional capacity. I've been hypersocial as a coach, trying to over-give while holding too low of expectations for my clients to rise into their own power. I've learned a lot the hard way, as many of us do. Perfect isn't the point.

It's okay to make mistakes.
It's okay to have regrets.
It's never too late to start over, try again or do better.

Embodying powerful ethics is an ongoing, evolving practice. As I continue to grow and do pieces of work on my own healing, I become more aligned to the Blueprints of healthy intersovereign healing exchanges. I recognize the ways past professional behaviors might have been emerging from more imprinted places in me, and I update my integrity accordingly.

We can all offer ourselves the grace and humility of growing, learning, healing, and improving—even as professionals. And again, as healing professionals, especially working with trauma, it's a sage idea to put ourselves on the long-road of student and client. The more we deepen our learning and the more we receive the same medicine we give, the more wholeness, Blueprint and wellness we bring into the interpersonal field between self and client. With more Blueprint on board, it becomes easier to prevent ruptures and reduce harm, catch unhealthy dynamics before they go too far, or repair when ruptures do occur.

When Ethical Lines are Crossed

Hello, love. *You will mess up.* Accidentally. Half-knowingly. *Oh shit…I did that thing I knew I shouldn't have done!* We all have blind spots. Even as practitioners, we're still human. While shame and hiding are normal responses to messing up, digging a hole, and sticking your head in it only makes things worse.

In ethical dilemmas, I suggest you do three things to avoid a downward spiral:

- Consult a mentor or many mentors. We've all been there. We all want to help.
- Consult your most trusted, sage, confidential friend without revealing the identity of your client.
- Consult Google. Seriously. It's all been done before. Write your question. Someone smart who's been there before will have suggestions.

Mostly, stay close to your tenderness and seek to take radical responsibility. It can be hard to look at the ways our behavior has caused harm, but causing harm is part of being human. We must forgive ourselves for our humanness. Lack of self-forgiveness will lead to a frozen heart. And frozen hearts hurt people way more than remorsing ones do. Self-forgiveness is incredibly brave and responsible. It makes space for things to change.

Chapter 13

Dear human,

It is your right to return.

Return to a sacred cooperation with all of Life.

Return to the sparks of your soul that long to know realization.

Return to the essence of your dreams that yearn to become real.

Return to the animal instincts of your being, the wise survival skills that are waiting to become more agile and active, less repressed, depressed, or agitated.

Return to your communal nature that could never be extinguished, no matter how much systems of oppression tried.

As you begin to return to a sacred cooperation with Life,

All that is violent or forceful, traumatic, or unwell, will show itself to be healed in your powerful presence.

The lies that have been lingering in the back of your psyche.

The conventions that are prisons to the collective thriving of our shared soul.

The structures that disservice wellness.

The systems that oppress flesh.

As you begin to practice sacred cooperation with Life,

Your ability to transform what threatens Life will increase…

Because you will be resourced by the abundant powers and flow of all that wants to regenerate and thrive.

The words you speak,

The spells you cast,

The activism you impart,

The businesses you build,

The communities you gather—

These will all embody the fractal expression of your sacred cooperation with Life.

Whether you work inside or outside conventional structures…

Whether your work is in the family or of the body,

In the community or on the land…

You have a calling.

Your calling is bigger than your job.

Bigger than the role you occupy.

Bigger than any company you might run.

Those things are merely instruments for fulfilling your calling.

No matter who you are, at the deepest level, your individual soul's calling

Is inextricable from our collective soul's calling.

We are all here together,

On this planet in these times,
To return to a sacred cooperation with Life.

When you cooperate with your own Lifeforce
Moving when you have energy and resting when you are tired,
Speaking when you have things to say and listening when you have questions...

When you cooperate with the truth in your clients' hearts
Inviting them to open or close according to their real capacities and instincts...

When you cooperate with your longing to be part of a community of belonging,
To exist as an organism gathered together to live and die and celebrate aliveness...

When you return to your own Indigeneity,
The roots of you that always knew how to turn to the plants and animals, the land
and sky, the song and dance...

You activate the timeless possibility of love and hope and consciousness:
An awakeness to the Bigness of which you are a small, significant, sacred part.

You activate a sense that you might flow with, rather than against,
The river of generosity
That is Life on Earth,
That is Earth in the Universe,
That is Universe in your Mind,
That is Mind in your Body,
That is Body expressing Soul,
That is Soul amidst Eternity.

It is your right to return to all of this,
To all of you,
To all of Life.

May you seize this right with passion.

To be a facilitator of the ReBloom medicine is to facilitate cooperation with Life. In this sense, anyone can take on the roll. You don't have to study with me or come to a workshop. You can throw away all the practices and simply meditate on the question, "How might my life be in service to Life itself?"

As ReBloom facilitators, we are committed to post-traumatic growth, which isn't only about healing past traumas, but also about stepping into aliveness so that we may serve the Source of all that is holy and good. It's about humans helping humans become more available to creativity, love, possibility, courage, and collective care.

This is why it matters how we do business. Our businesses must match our hearts' visions. We can do better than business as usual. The more we cooperate with Life, the more obvious it becomes that sharing and working together is the most regenerative way forward. Sharing resources, sharing our gifts and talents with one another, letting each other in to support us in the places where our skills or confidence lack, relying on one another to grow something more magnificent than we could ever grow alone.

Competing and hoarding, leaving one another to figure everything out by ourselves, presenting as people who have all the answers (when really, we are scrambling to meet our needs for connection as we stand alone on pedestals of false perfection)…these are imprints of capitalism and supremacy, abandonment, and displacement. They are not how we best revive, awaken, and amplify the miraculous powers of Life.

Life is generous. Life is harmonic. Life has natural diversity and sometimes hierarchy, yes, but Life conjoins all the different sounds and tones, rhythms and flows into a symphony of incredible beauty. Life does not distinguish rankings of more or less valuable, better or worse, more or less important. To Life, the ants and the bacteria, the oceans and the mountains, the hummingbirds and the orca whales, the dandelions and the redwoods, are all essential ingredients in the collective body of aliveness.

Life knows itself as one inextricable song that needs every little part to fill out the magnificence of its choir. Why should we act differently?

We, Life's children, could stand to observe and listen a bit more. We, as guides and alchemists, coaches and healers, could stand to lead ourselves and one another back to a remembrance of cooperative mutual care.

If we feel lost, we can start at the beginning, with our Collective Soul Seed. The part of our shared soma that can feel and hunger for our most sensitive human needs. The part of us that knows how to say...

We are here, we are now, we matter.
We are worthy of feeding our needs.
We are designed to grow and thrive.
We need...
We need...
We need...
We are receiving.

We need community. We need mutual aid. We need to share our gifts and receive one another's. We need to know we're not out here fending all alone. We need to pool our resources so we can offer our most potent medicine to the world with greater ease. We need to remember how to collaborate, how to assess our collective assets (intellectual, spiritual, emotional, physical, financial), and see what we can grow together with the glory lying dormant in our garden.

We are receiving the visions and the strategies, the whispers and the guidance. We are receiving the nudges and the invitations, the courage and the faith. We are receiving opportunities to practice and mess up, and learn and grow, and heal together.

The ways of our current systemic programming—the traumatic imprints of capitalism, colonization, white supremacy, patriarchy, classism, racism, dominance, extraction, commodification, separation, and toxic competition—will not be the ways of our future survival, because they are not the ways of Life.

We are crossing through the eye of the needle collectively. It's a narrow passage and one that will strip us down before it allows us to move through. The narrow gate will ask us to heal within us the ways we are loyal to what violates and threatens Life. It will show us those loyalties through the tension of our muscles, the pain in our pleasure centers, and the outbreaks of fear on our skin. It will show us our misalignments under the sheets, in the kitchen, in the pillow talk arguments we can't quite resolve. It will reveal to us all the ways we lack the necessary trust in one another, all the ways we violate others' trust in us. It will illuminate our disregard for our very own hearts and souls. It will take years, decades, lifetimes for us to pass through—to that place where we remember true reverence.

We will die and be reborn endless times trying to remember the heartbeat of Life that is within us, that is eclipsed from us, that is motivating us behind the scenes even when we've forgotten it. Everything that lives, dies. Everything that dies finds itself underground readying to rebloom into something new. There is nothing we can do to undo these truths.

We are here, we are now, we matter. We need rituals for death and rites of passage into the next births of our lives. We need time set aside to go down, down, down underground into the dark, where the beat of love you can't hear when you're too busy fending for yourself can be heard. Because here, in our wider circle of togetherness, we make room for this—this underworld crossing, this unbecoming, this undressing for the sake of reassessing what wants to be worn that can bring forth our more divine medicine.

We are giving and receiving the resources needed to make more narrow passages possible, so we can build something beautiful together on the other side. Each of us having lived, and died, and lived, and died, and lived, and died, again, and again to get there. Each of us carrying different medicines through the needle. Each of us planting unique seeds in our collective garden of possibility.

This is the Whole Holy Point. To regrow the garden together. To help each other get there. To bring back the bees. To revive the sweetness of life, hand-in-hand, song-after-song, long passage-after-long passage home.

Chapter 14

The Next World Coming To Meet Us from the Other Side

"I hope there are orchestras at the end of the world," I told him.

"I'm interested in the orchestras that will play at the beginning of the next," he grinned back, wizardly eyes reminding mine that the story doesn't end here in the necessary catastrophe of adolescent humanity, not if a trillion tiny choices of miraculous maturity rise together in a symphony of amazing grace.

We were sitting in the way back of the Kabbalat Shabbat ceremony at a festival called Beloved in Southern Oregon, imagining a future memory of technicolored harmony—violins dancing tango with the brushstroke of a lover's lips, jaws seductively ajar, butterflies singing.

"In the next passage, art will be the greatest call," he whispered, with an air of hope that somehow caught my imagination on fire.

After the fall, we'll tell myths of how we survived it all, I thought, conjuring up the sight of my great-granddaughter, head back in a rapturous laugh, facing new darknesses, new dead ends, new stories that depended on her.

And my mind drifted back to my questions—the questions I've been carrying like secret seeds, deep in the soil of my soul.

Can I let my vision be hopeful, even now, even amidst all this?

Can I become an embodied prayer—the physical form of Spirit's love—in sacred service to my hopeful vision?

Can I be willing to burn at the stake for it, either way? Whether it's possible or impossible? No matter, who cares, still worth it, I'm in.

I once read a story in *Waking the Tiger* by Peter Levine about a class of kids who were kidnapped and then locked underground in a cellar. They had no food for days, were withering and on the verge of their last, living hours, when one kid tapped a few others, said almost breathlessly, "let's dig our way out."

With metal spoons and their last bits of energy, three kids saved the lives of twenty.

So often, we think, *this is the end*, when really, our story is far from over. We give up, give in, sell out too soon.

While yes, often a non-cognitive immobilization takes hold, and it feels a whole lot harder to rise and shine in the face of disaster, there's a reason why we train in embodied and relational coherence. There's a reason why we do the practices—whether they're the ones laid out in this book, or from any psychosomatic tradition of majesty or mysticism, any practice that connects you to decency, surrender, grace, and courage—both in body and in spirit, personally, and collectively.

Because the truth is, we rarely go extinct. That's the way evolution works. A few overachieving kids figure some shit out and we all end up making it.

If we make it, though, through this next passage, without embodied or relational coherence, then that means we've relied on dysregulation in order to survive. The hyper, the hypo. And what we create from dysregulation seldom grows inspiring new life—it grows old, familiar pain. We ascend from the cellar in a daze, half-asleep, half-awake, forgetful of our great capacity.

This is the way humanity has evolved up until this point. Half-asleep, half-awake, barely embodying our full potential. But we're at a bigger juncture now than ever before.

The old way won't work if we want to make it to where we're going.

They studied those kids who emerged from that cellar. The ones who dug with metal spoons went on to become practical superhumans. CEOs, inventors, philanthropists, doctors. The ones who didn't went on to experience inordinate levels of mental, physical, and emotional pain, trapped in new cellars of personal trauma spells.

It's my wild, mischievous guess that we're not actually amidst the apocalypse. We're gonna live through these times of great collapse, and we're gonna come out of the cellar in one condition or another.

Humans won't look or feel like we did before. This might strike you as scary or sad, but the truth is we can't go back to our supposed immaculate beginnings, our Garden of Eden, before the neglect or exploitation, before the shame or repression, before the tech isolation or unjust colonization. We can't undo those violences of body or mind. We can't make up for the cultures that have been harmed or the entire peoples that have gone through genocide.

Our evolutionary path is clear. We have to grow from *here* to *there*.

We have done things that can't be undone. Things have been done to us that we can never undo. The good news is, that's not the calling now. The calling is to rebloom into something both ancient and all brand-new, familiar and fantastical, maybe even better than before.

Once upon a time, there was a garden. And in this garden there was a cast of characters. Sort of like a family, but more like a village…

Let's write the NEXT story together.

Acknowledgments

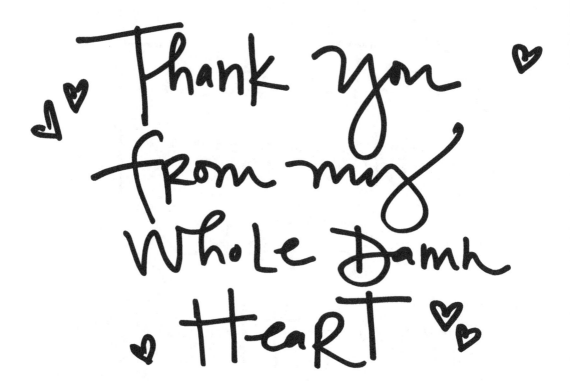

Thank you, from my whole damn heart

ReBloom has been birthed by a village. Dozens of people have been involved in its conception, gestation, labor, and arrival into the world. Hundreds of Kickstarter backers funded its existence. And beyond my immediate human circle, this book was supported by land, ancestors, elders, musicians, baristas, bartenders, and Source itself. Go figure, it couldn't have happened any other way. Not a book like this, so centered on our need for deep togetherness.

An incomplete list of acknowledgments and gratitudes:

To the Kumeyaay earth, Windansea Beach, the rocks, waves, stars, and vast array of succulent wildflowers that rebloomed every spring along the coast—your sunrise mist and sunset skies were my infinite soul food and nourishment. I hope this book blesses you as much as you've blessed it.

To the lil brown house by the sea that held and sheltered me, you were destined for book birthing. I will cherish you always. Thank you to Syd and Gerry, the elders of this home, for letting me live here, tend and be tended to.

To my ancestors who visited me in my moments of doubt, reminding me I am a thing of the stars, indeed I am, indeed we are. I know this now more than ever. Thank you for all the ways you showed up and sang to me.

To my blood lineage of teachers, speakers, preachers, artists, musicians, thinkers, feelers, and business-people. Thank you for all you grew into and passed on. Mom and Dad, Grandma Marylou, Aunt Mary, Great Grandfather Blackburn… I could feel your spirits especially living through mine in these pages. I am so grateful for your radiance and zest.

To the giants whose shoulders I stand upon, without your work, mine would not exist. The elders and masters whose books, recordings, or teachings I've devoured time and again: Joanna Macy, Audre Lorde, David Whyte, Caroline Myss, Bayo Akomolafe, adrienne maree brown, Peter Levine, Michael Meade, Charles Eisenstein, bell hooks, Naomi Wolf, Dan Siegel, Steven Porges, Toko Pa Turner, Bill Plotkin, Clarissa Pinkola Estes, Eve Ensler…you feed me. Your wisdom lives inside these pages. Thank you.

To every client and student who worked with ReBloom while she was still growing and changing, you grew her up just as much as she grew you up. Thank you for trusting the process with me. Thank you for teaching me so much about the human experience. Thank you for tenderizing me with your tears, courage, truth, and dreams. I love you each and am honored to be reblooming together.

Jodi, you are forever my first line of inside support. You helped me listen for the soul of ReBloom's real name, and from there, an entire body of work was unearthed. You realize this book, this method, would not exist without you, yes? At every crowded, confusing crossroad, you brought the kind of compassion, trust, and gentle support that opened the path to clear, fertile possibilities. What else can I say besides the truth? I really couldn't have done it without you.

Brigit Viksnins, thank you for teaching me the nervous system, physiology, and a more robust relationship to the Blueprints of Life—not just through intellect, but embodied transmission and power. Thank you for being a role model of radically healthy rhythms and vital lifeforce. Your presence is a deep-healing balm of wisdom, joy, and wellness. May many more humans have the great privilege of studying with you.

Chela Davison, phew. Over the last five years, you have held me, nurtured me, celebrated me, and stretched me. Thank you for your genius guidance as well as your deep friendship. For rolling up your sleeves and getting into the muddy places with me. For sharing the dream of a more beautiful world. For living the questions together. I cherish you.

Andrew Leonard, you were an impeccable intellectual book guide when the whole thing felt like a lost cause. Smart, encouraging, and always reminding me that the only way to eat an elephant is one bite at a time. This book is a real elephant, I tell ya. Thank you for encouraging patience and depth of process in me. With your help, the archetypes animated in a whole, new way. You brought color to the black and white places. And so much more. Thank you.

Angela Lauria…Priceless. Life-saving. Brilliant. Thank you for chopping and rearranging ReBloom into something digestible and doable. It was the sweetest gift to return to your home and receive your angelic support. Let's keep writing books together!

Bethany Kelly, you doulaed the beginning of this process with enthusiasm, encouragement, and power. Thank you for helping me trust myself and what I had to offer.

Heather Dakota, you doulaed the end of this journey with grace, patience, flexibility, and consistency. I felt so safe in your loving, professional care. Thank you for carrying us out into the world!

Elizabeth DiAlto, you received me with radical excitement on the day I decided to write this book, then gave me unending passionate support until the very day I finished. Thank you for your steadfast love and friendship.

Henry Cordes, your editing was strong and fast, wise and swift. A rare and precious power. Praise. So much gratitude.

Forrest Landry, thank you for breathing cosmic perspective into my being and onto these pages. Yours is the craft of scientific poetry and your sensitive, genius eldership changed me, and this book.

Cândido Gadaga, never had I met a real-life saint until I met you. Thank you for holding me through my dark, middle passage of doubt with total trust in my capacity to complete this book. Unconditional care. Unending regard. Your love forever humbles me.

Thank you to Wendy Oliver for the ongoing transcendental body work that eased my body's tension and helped me integrate this book's bigness.

Deep bow to Chris Dierkes for standing with me at the threshold between worlds, helping my soul root deeper into my body, helping this body of work work on me when I most needed it.

Humble gratitude to Jen Lemen for the decade+ of developmental mentorship. Your lineage is forever in my words, thinking, writing, guiding, ritualing, and loving.

Humongous gratitude to friends and colleagues who peer-reviewed chapters when it felt like pulling teeth to finish: Joann Tucker, Assana Rae Halder, Rachel Sizemore, Tiffany Landry, Bear Hébert, Ann Nguyen, Jodi McLaren, Tada Hozumi.

To my closest friends who were on call with food, hugs, FaceTime SOSes, and co-writing sessions: Elizabeth DiAlto, Dema, Ann, Dave, Kaitlyn…thank you for enduring so many conversations about this book, asking about it, checking in, rooting. Every minute made a difference. I love you. So thankful.

To the Kickstarter backers, who took a chance on me and invested in this book. Who told your friends about it. Who stayed with me even as the book morphed and changed. Who waited patiently for three years…phew, that's some loyalty right there. Thank you from the bottom of my heart. Your support was the foundation that grew this book into being. I am honored beyond belief, and hope you love it. There were 432 of you! Thank you:

Jodi McLaren, Cindy Allen, Tam, Sarah Magdalena, Tanya Street, Amanda, Skaja Wills, Mara, Rasa Ghaffarian, Stephanie Wietrzychowski, Marie Christ, Chelsey Johnson, Anna Holtzman, Leo, John Wolfstone, Lindsey, Jennette LeBlanc, Ashley Chiang, Dori, Tonya Melendez, Amma Li, Katie Bryson, Judy Bankman, Dan Bowen, Tom V, Sarah Bernstein, Elizabeth Matteson, Caitlin, Rachelle, Julie Gittelson, Nancy, Terri Aldred, Leslie Elmore, Jane Bridgman, Deb Ice Thornton, Shannon Jackson Arnold, Julie Brauneis, Natalie Baack, Randy Maddox, Cherie Dugas, Brian Knight, Beverly Maddox, Jennifer Holm, Sunni, Yoji Stephan Sasaki,

Acknowledgments

Lionessa Soleil, Marc Peters, Tigre Pickett, Ann, Tom Harriss, Mindy Tsonas, Jaime Paiser Young, Diana Dentinger, Harmony Larson, Annie Escobar, Skye, Simon, Rachel Roberts, Francesca, Aethyric, Tyson Wilson, Elaine Katherine Watson, Rose DePaolo, moshmaru, starmaru, Amanda Stephens, Jamie Utt, Heather Rinn, Petra Štejfová, Chance Paul Stillman, Mikaela Schey, Christina Jimenez, David Jacob, Jen Knutson, kim, Mallory Wisong, Tim, Annie, Grace, Suzanne, Karen, Sarah Lowenstein, Allison Owen, Shiopei, Mark Viehweg, Beth Stewart, Taylor-Leigh Derchin, José Martins, Kori, Jill Jettie, Dema Al-Kakhan, Elissa Salter, Martin Molch, Meghan Collins, Michelle Bennington, The Selkie Delegation, Leah Harris, David Steel, Lola Medicine Keeper, Eva Casey, PleasureMechanics.com, Jessica Walty, Kit, Shane, Susan S Lee, Amanda Ranae, Josie Jarvis, Nicole Michel, Carly Beaudry, Jennifer M, Anne Marie, Golden, Jessi Kneeland, Lisa Olson, Dan Paul, Laura Czarniecki, Krystal Brandt, Emily, Marion Boulicault, Jennifer Denny, Kim Jacaman, Layla, Marley D, Megan Tognela, Dheana Ramsay, Gabriel Diamond, Shila, Tessa Zeng, Melissa Rivera, Julia Colton, Katie, Amy, Pignatella Cain, Jessica Sapoznick, Afi French, Deborah Schwartz, Candice Vinson, Lacey, Megan Wooding, Kara Baragwanath, Nicci Nunes, Tetyana Davis, Ethan Cohen, Torie, Mikle A. Koons, Joshua Thomas Hart, Zac Hardaker, Nadia Munla, Lisa Nagel, Michael and Liz, Carolin Nobles, Natasha Chisdes, AuVergne Maynard, Ev'Yan W., Joanna, Tom Cruz, Julia Sheldon, Amy Evans, Jessica Libbey, Jims Tricia, Emily Kloc, Bethany Kelly, Ana Saldamando, Samantha Haraszti, Vanessa Lillegren, Hannah Brown, Becky Fromm, Ewen McNeill, James Aplington, Kas, Erin Hughes, Melissa McLean, Chantal, Jenee Hughes, Emily, Honeybee Beer, Alicia Halpern, Catherine Hummel, Tamara McLaughlin, Kit Maloney, Anne Shirley, Max Thomas, Maria Kurylo, La Rae Randall, Kristi Hart, John Bent, Step, Vicki Intara, Jade Wesdorp, Elizabeth, Dena Evans, Mary and John Albright, Christine Lee, Melanie Knight, Mary Ann Mhina, Tara Johnston, Antonia, Sheryl Deakin, Jamie D., Marian McLaughlin, Carl Robinson, Pieter VR, Michael Fallon, Nicole Nir, Donathon Crew, Jennifer Stevens, Tricia Hurtubise, Vanessa, Michael N, Sara Eliason, Megan, Mary Crauderueff, Maya Stein, Nicole, Garrett Book, Kathryn Sullivan, Jessica Kovari, Margaret Johnson, Erica Gibbert, Melinda Scime, Victoria, Alexis, Trina Rose Hofreiter, Maria, Toi Smith, Ashley Shapiro-Shapiro, Jessica,

Joyelle Brandt, Amy, Madeline Adams, Kristina Campbell, Priya, Jackson, Devra, Kara Webber, Lynn Wolfbrandt, The Grey, Kalia Rose Foxen, Jose Bautista, Hermes Winters, Alexane de Montigny, Sonum Dixit, Motti Shulman, Kim Gallup, Mark Sabellico, Mathias Green, Viannah E. Duncan, Yannick Allard, Lyon Pound, Wayne Griffiths, Susan L.K. Gorbet, Ross Williams, Sam, Keyla, STEM Nation, Wendy L. Yost, Ula Zammit, and Matt Haeck. HUMBLED and grateful to you each.

I am forever in love with the Great Mystery that birthed me here on Earth and allowed me the opportunity to live on this precious, glorious, gorgeous, teeming planet.

Finally, to the soul of ReBloom that has its own mission, devotion, and destiny— thank you for trusting me to carry forth your medicine. I am here to help you grow and thrive. Let's do this thing. I love you.

About the Author

Rachael Maddox is a trauma resolution educator, coach, and guide who has helped hundreds of humans move from sexual, complex or developmental trauma into pleasure, power, and trust-filled relationships. Passionate about both personal and collective post-traumatic growth, Rachael is devoted to facilitating the emergence of a more trauma-informed, ethical, and equitable coaching industry.

She is the founder and creator of the ReBloom Coach Training, an advanced 18-month certification program for somatic trauma resolution that takes a soulful, mythical, and liberatory approach. Obsessed with radical economics, Rachael is co-founding a ReBloom Collective of trauma-informed teachers and guides that centers collaboration, wealth-sharing, wealth redistribution, environmental restoration, and racial equity.

Rachael's professional training includes Alchemical Alignment Trauma Resolution & Embodiment of Spirit, The Coaches Training Institute, and The Awakened Leadership Academy. She went to undergrad at the University of Maryland, College Park, where she created her own major called Cooperative Community Studies.

She currently lives, prays, and works on stolen Kumyeey land (so called La Jolla, California).

For fun, Rachael writes songs on her ukulele, swims naked as often as possible, hosts overflowing Shabbat dinners for her closest friends and beloveds, and lays quietly under trees.

Learn more about Rachael and the ReBloom body of work at rebloomtogether. com or rachaelmaddox.com, and @rebloomtogether or @rachaelmaddox on Instagram.

Also by Rachael Maddox

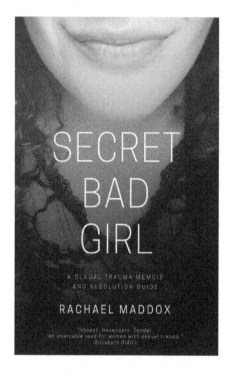

Secret Bad Girl is a deeply healing memoir and trauma resolution guide for women who've suffered secret rapes or sexual abuse and want both stories and instructions for being set free.

Healing happens. Everything changes. This book can be your friend and guide.

The most common testimonial for Secret Bad Girl is, *"It was so good, I picked it up and couldn't put it down!"*

Head to rebloomtogether.com/ secretbadgirl to pick up your copy of this soulful page-turner.